GREEK

LANGUAGE SURVIVAL GUIDE

HarperCollins*Publishers*

HarperCollins Publishers
Westerhill Rd, Bishopbriggs, Glasgow, G64 2QT

www.collins.co.uk

First published 2003

Reprint 10 9 8 7 6 5 4 3 2 1 0

ISBN 0 00 712128 8

A catalogue reference for this book is available from The British Library

Consultant: **Juliet A Quincey**

Photography: Juliet A Quincey
Map: Heather Moore
Additional photography: Athens Metro (pp 27, top; 30, centre left; 31, right); Artville (pp 91, 2; 92, 1; 93, 1; 94, 1; 95, 2; 96, 2; 97, 1; 98, 1; 99, 1; 100, 2); The Anthony Blake Photo Library (pp 92, 1; 93, 1; 94, 2; 95, 1; 97, 2; 100, 1; 101, 2).
Layout: The Printer's Devil, Glasgow

Other titles in the Collins Language Survival Guide series:
French (0 00 710161 9)
Spanish (0 00 710164 3)
Italian (0 00 710163 5)
German (0 00 710162 7)
Portuguese (0 00 712131 8)

These titles are also published in a CD pack containing a CD and Language Survival Guide.

Printed in Italy by Amadeus SpA

CONTENTS

USEFUL WEBSITES

Currency Converters

www.x-rates.com

Foreign Office Advice

www.fco.gov.uk/travel/countryadvice.asp

Passport Office

www.ukpa.gov.uk

Health Advice

www.thetraveldoctor.com

www.doh.gov.uk/traveladvice

Driving Abroad

www.drivingabroad.co.uk/driving_tips_countries/greece/driving_in_greece.htm

Pets

www.defra.gov.uk/animalh/quarantine/qindex.shtml

Weather

www.bbc.co.uk/weather

Facts

www.cia.gov/cia/publications/factbook/geos/gr.html

Internet Cafes

www.cybercafes.com

Transport

www.greekferries.gr

www.ferries.gr

www.dolphins.gr *(hydrofoil service to Greek islands)*

www.osenet.gr/eng.htm *(Hellenic Railways Organisation)*

www.travelinfo.gr/train.htm *(schedules)*

Tourism

www.greektourism.gr *(Greek Naitonal Tourism Organisation)*

www.visiteurope.com/greece

www.travelinfo.gr

www.greektravel.com

www.travelgreece.com

Accommodation

www.greekhotels.gr

www.greecetravel.com/campsites *(camping)*

www.europeanhostels.com/fall/listings/greece *(hostels)*

Food & Wine

www.gourmed.gr

Other

www.xo.gr/en/index.jsp *(Greek Yellow Pages in English)*

INTRODUCTION

As technology sweeps across the world, travellers aren't just faced with the prospect of speaking a foreign language – they also have foreign machines to contend with. Machines for parking, for dispensing cash, for buying tickets and food. Often there is nobody about to ask how they work. *Collins Language Survival Guides* address this problem by showing photographically signs and situations you might come across.

The things that throw you are often the ones that look familiar – such as buses, trains or phones – but which operate slightly differently.

There are usually codes to how things operate and though you might not think you are aware of them, you are probably using them everyday: the colour-coding for roads (blue for motorways, green for major roads, yellow for temporary signs) or when buying milk (generally blue for whole milk, green for semi-skimmed and red for skimmed). It's when these familiar codes don't work in the same way, that you feel slightly at a loss and probably more unsure than you need be. By making a note of how these types of things work and knowing a few keywords, you will feel much more confident.

The unique combination of practical information, photos and phrases found in this book provides the key to hassle-free travel and the colour-coding below shows how information is presented and how to access it as quickly as possible.

General, practical information which will provide useful tips on getting the best out of your trip

keywords

δεξιά
dhekseea
on/to the right
αριστερά
areestera
on/to the left

◀ **keywords**
these are words that are useful to know both when you see them written down or when you hear them spoken

key talk ▶
short, simple phrases that you can change and adapt to suit your own situation

excuse me!
seeghnomee
συγνώμη!

can you help me?
boreete na me voeetheesete
μπορείτε να με βοηθήσετε;

do you know where...?
kserete poo...
ξέρετε πού...;

talking

The **Food Section** allows you to choose more easily from what is on offer both for snacks and at restaurants.

The practical 5000-word English–Greek, Greek–English **Dictionary** means that you will never be stuck for words.

SPEAKING GREEK

In the pronunciation system in this book, Greek sounds are represented by spellings of the nearest possible sounds in English. When you read the pronunciation, sound the letters as if you were reading English (but make sure you also pronounce vowels at the end of a word). The vowels in ***heavy type*** show where the stress falls (in the Greek script it is marked with an accent).

The following notes should help:

	REMARKS	EXAMPLE	PRONOUNCED
gh	*like **r** at back of throat*	γάλα	*gh**a**la*
dh	*like **th** in this*	δάχτυλο	*dh**a**khteelo*
th	*like **th** in thin*	θέατρο	*th**e**atro*
ks	*like **x** in fox*	ξένος	*ks**e**nos*
r	*slightly trilled **r***	ρόδα	*r**o**dha*
kh	*like **ch** in loch*	χάνω	*kh**a**no*
	*like a rough **h** before e or ee*	χέρι	*kh**e**ree*

Here are a few tricky letter combinations:

αι	*met*	***e***	γυναίκα	*gheen**e**ka*
αυ	*café*	***af***	αυτό	*aft**o***
	or *have*	***av***	αύριο	***a**vreeo*
ει	*meet*	***ee***	είκοσι	***ee**kosee*
ευ	*effect*	***ef***	Δευτέρα	*dheft**e**ra*
	or *every*	***ev***	Ευρώπη	*evr**o**pee*
γγ	*hang*	***ng***	Αγγλία	*angl**ee**a*
γκ	*get*	***g***	γκάζι	*g**a**zee*
	hang	***ng***	άγκυρα	***a**ngeera*
ντ	*hand*	***nd***	αντίο	*and**ee**o*
	dog	***d***	ντομάτα	*dom**a**ta*
μπ	*bag*	***b***	μπλούζα	*bl**oo**za*
οι	*meet*	***ee***	πλοίο	*pl**ee**o*
ου	*moon*	***oo***	ούζο	***oo**zo*

The letters **η**, **ι**, **υ**, **οι**, and **ει** have the same sound ***ee*** and **αι** and **ε** have the same sound ***e*** (as in m***e***t).

A vowel combination to look out for is **ευ** as in **ευρώ** (euro). Instead of it being pronounced 'euro', because of the vowel combination in Greek, it is pronounced *evr**o***.

You should also note that the Greek question mark is a semi-colon, i.e. ***;***.

EVERYDAY TALK

There are two forms of address in Greek, formal and informal. Greek people will use the formal until they are on a first-name basis, so for the purposes of this book we will use the formal. The important thing for foreign visitors, though, is that they 'have a go' at Greek. Don't worry too much about formal and informal, or about making mistakes in general – the Greeks will be very happy to hear you try to speak their language!

yes
ne
ναι

no
***o**khee*
όχι

ok/that's fine
*end**a**ksee*
εντάξει

please
*parakal**o***
παρακαλώ

thank you
*efkhareest**o***
ευχαριστώ

thanks very much
*efkhareest**o** pol**ee***
ευχαριστώ πολύ

don't mention it
*parakal**o***
παρακαλώ

that's very kind
*dhen k**a**nee t**ee**pota*
δεν κάνει τίποτα

hello / hi
*y**a** sas / y**a** soo*
γειά σας *(formal)* / γειά σου *(informal)*

hello
*kh**e**rete*
χαίρετε

goodbye
*and**ee**o*
αντίο

good morning
*kaleem**e**ra*
καλημέρα

good afternoon/evening
*kaleesp**e**ra*
καλησπέρα

good night
*kaleen**ee**khta*
καληνύχτα

excuse me! / sorry!
*seeghn**o**mee*
συγνώμη!

I am sorry
*leep**a**me*
λυπάμαι

excuse me
*me seeghkhor**ee**te*
με συγχωρείτε

I don't understand
*dhen katalav**e**no*
δεν καταλαβαίνω

I don't know
*dhen ks**e**ro*
δεν ξέρω

Addressing people

When addressing someone for the first time, or attracting attention, use **Κύριε** *k**ee**ree-e* (Mr), **Κυρία** *keer**ee**a* (Mrs/Ms) or **Δεσποινίς** *dhespeen**ee**s* (Miss). These titles may be used without a name, like French *Monsieur* and *Madame*. It is also quite common to use **Κύριος** *k**ee**reeos* etc with the person's first name.

welcome
*kal**o**s **ee**rthate / kal**o**s or**ee**sate*
καλώς ήρθατε / καλώς ορίσατε

(reply to this)
*kal**o**s sas vr**ee**kame*
καλώς σάς βρήκαμε

how are you?
*pos **ee**ste*
πώς είστε;

fine, thanks
*pol**ee** kal**a** efkhareest**o***
πολύ καλά ευχαριστώ

and you?
*es**ee**s*
εσείς;

*Asking for something in a shop or bar, you would ask for what you want, adding **parakalo**.*

keywords keywords

1	ένα	**e**na
2	δύο	dh**ee**o
3	τρία	tr**ee**a
4	τέσσερα	t**e**sera
5	πέντε	p**e**nde
6	έξι	**e**ksee
7	επτά	eft**a**
8	οκτώ	okht**o**
9	εννέα	en**ee**a
10	δέκα	dh**e**ka

a...
ena... ('ο' words)
ένα...

meea... ('η' words)
μία...

ena... ('το' words)
ένα...

an iced coffee
ena frape
ένα φραπέ

2 iced coffees
dheeo frape
δύο φραπέ

a beer
meea beera
μία μπίρα

2 beers
dheeo beeres
δύο μπίρες

a bottle
ena bookalee
ένα μπουκάλι

2 bottles
dheeo bookaleea
δύο μπουκάλια

a coffee and two beers
enan kafe ke dheeo beeres
έναν καφέ και δύο μπίρες

a tea please
ena tsaee parakalo
ένα τσάι παρακαλώ

the menu please
ton katalogho parakalo
τον κατάλογο παρακαλώ

the bill please
to logharyasmo parakalo
το λογαριασμό παρακαλώ

another/more... ('ο' & 'το' words)
alo ena...
άλλο ένα...

('η' words)
alee meea...
άλλη μία...

another iced coffee
alo ena frape
άλλο ένα φραπέ

another beer
alee meea beera
άλλη μία μπίρα

2 more beers
ales dheeo beeres
άλλες δύο μπίρες

2 more iced coffees
aloos dheeo frape
άλλους δύο φραπέ

To catch someone's attention

The easiest way to catch someone's attention is with **συγνώμη!** *seeghnomee*. Note that the word no in Greek, **όχι** *okhee*, is often accompanied by an upward tilting of the face, or slight raising of the eyebrows and a click of the tongue. You may think that this is a nod for yes, rather than a no!

excuse me!
seeghnomee
συγνώμη!

can you help me?
boreete na me voeetheesete
μπορείτε να με βοηθήσετε;

do you know where...?
kserete poo...
ξέρετε πού...;

By combining key words and phrases you can build up your language and adapt the phrases to suit your own situation.

ekhete **do you have?**	**do you have a map?** *ekhete ena khartee* έχετε ένα χάρτη;	**do you have a room?** *ekhete ena dhomateeo* έχετε ένα δωμάτιο;
poso kanee **how much?**	**how much is the cheese?** *poso kanee to teeree* πόσο κάνει το τυρί;	**how much is the ticket?** *poso kanee to eeseeteereeo* πόσο κάνει το εισιτήριο;
tha eethela... **I'd like ...**	**I'd like a slice of gateau** *tha eethela meea pasta* θα ήθελα μία πάστα	**I'd like an ice cream** *tha eethela ena paghoto* θα ήθελα ένα παγωτό
khreeazome... **I need ...**	**I need a taxi** *khreeazome ena taksee* χρειάζομαι ένα ταξί	**I need a receipt** *khreeazome meea apodheeksee* χρειάζομαι μία απόδειξη
pote **when?**	**when does it open?** *pote aneeghee* πότε ανοίγει;	**when does it close?** *pote kleenee* πότε κλείνει;
	when does it leave? *pote fevyee* πότε φεύγει;	**when does it arrive?** *pote ftanee* πότε φτάνει;
poo eene... **where is...?**	**where is the bank?** *poo eene ee trapeza* πού είναι η τραπέζα;	**where is the hotel?** *poo eene to ksenodhokheeo* πού είναι το ξενοδοχείο;
ekhee... **is there...?**	**is there a market?** *ekhee laeekee aghora* έχει λαϊκή αγορά;	**where is there a market?** *poo ekhee laeekee aghora* πού έχει λαϊκή αγορά;
dhen ekhee... **there is no...**	**there is no bread** *dhen ekhee psomee* δεν έχει ψωμί	**there is no hot water** *dhen ekhee zesto nero* δεν έχει ζεστό νερό
boro na... **can I...?**	**can I smoke?** *boro na kapneeso* μπορώ να καπνίσω;	
	can I hire a car? *boro na neekyaso ena aftokeeneeto* μπορώ να νοικιάσω ένα αυτοκίνητο;	
	where can I buy bread? *poo boro na aghoraso psomee* πού μπορώ να αγοράσω ψωμί;	
eene **is it?**	**is it near?** *eene konda* είναι κοντά;	**is it far?** *eene makreea* είναι μακριά;

These are a selection of small but very useful words to know.

keywords keywords keywords

μεγάλο
meghalo
big

μικρό
meekro
little

λίγο / πολύ
leegho / polee
a little / a lot

αρκετό
arketo
enough

κοντά / μακριά
konda / makreea
near / far

κοντυνότερο
kondeenotero
nearest

πολύ ακριβό
polee akreevo
too expensive

και
ke
and

με / χωρίς
me / khorees
with / without

... μου
... moo
my...

αυτό / εκείνο
afto / ekeeno
this one / that one

αμέσως
amesos
straight away

αργότερα
arghotera
later

a large car
ena meghalo aftokeeneeto
ένα μεγάλο αυτοκίνητο

a small beer
meea meekree beera
μία μικρή μπίρα

a little please
leegho parakalo
λίγο παρακαλώ

a lot please
polee parakalo
πολύ παρακαλώ

that's enough thanks
arketo efkhareesto
αρκετό ευχαριστώ

where is the nearest chemist?
poo eene to kondeenotero farmakeeo
πού είναι το κοντινότερο φαρμακείο;

it is too expensive
eene polee akreevo
είναι πολύ ακριβό

it is too small
eene polee meekro
είναι πολύ μικρό

a tea and an iced coffee
ένα τσάι και ένα φραπέ
ena tsaee ke ena frappé

with milk
me ghala
με γάλα

with ice
me paghakeea
με παγάκια

without sugar
khorees zakharee
χωρίς ζάχαρη

without ice
khorees paghakeea
χωρίς παγάκια

for me
για μένα
ya mena

for her
γι' αυτήν
yafteen

for him
γι' αυτόν
yafton

for us
για μας
ya mas

my passport
to dheeavateereeo moo
το διαβατήριό μου

my key
to kleedhee moo
το κλειδί μου

I'd like this one
tha eethela afto
θα ήθελα αυτό

I'd like that one
tha eethela ekeeno
θα ήθελα εκείνο

I need a taxi straight away
khreeazome taksee amesos
χρειάζομαι ταξί αμέσως

is it safe?
eene asfales
είναι ασφαλές;

I'll phone back later
tha ksanaparo arghotera
θα ξαναπάρω αργότερα

It is always good to be able to say a few words about yourself to break the ice, even if you won't be able to tell your life story.

what's your name?
pos se lene
πώς σε λένε;

my name is...
me lene...
με λένε...

I'm from England
eeme apo teen angleea
είμαι από την Αγγλία

I'm from America
eeme apo teen amereekee
είμαι από την Αμερική

where do you live?
poo menees
πού μένεις;

where do you live? *(plural)*
poo menete
πού μένετε;

I'm single
eeme elefther-os(-ee)
είμαι ελεύθερος(-η)

I'm married
eeme pandremen-os(-ee)
είμαι παντρεμένος(-η)

I'm divorced
eeme khoreesmen-os(-ee)
είμαι χωρισμένος(-η)

I have a boyfriend
ekho aghoree
έχω αγόρι

I have a girlfriend
ekho koreetsee
έχω κορίτσι

I have a partner
ekho seendrofo
έχω σύντροφο

I have ... children
ekho ... pedheea
έχω ... παιδιά

I have no children
dhen ekho pedheea
δεν έχω παιδιά

I'm here on holiday
vreeskome edho ya dheeakopes
βρίσκομαι εδώ για διακοπές

I'm here for work
vreeskome edho ya dhooleea
βρίσκομαι εδώ για δουλειά

where do you live?
poo menees
πού μένεις;

I live in Glasgow
zo stee ghlaskovee
ζω στη Γλασκώβη

you have a beautiful home
ekhete oreo speetee
έχετε ωραίο σπίτι

the meal was delicious
to fagheeto eetan nosteemotato
το φαγητο ήταν νοστιμότατο

this is a gift for you
eene ena dhoro ya sas
είναι ένα δώρο για σας

pleased to meet you
khareeka ya tee ghnoreemeea
χάρηκα για τη γνωριμία

this is my husband
apo dho o seezeeghos moo
από 'δω ο σύζυγος μου

this is my wife
apo dho ee seezeeghos moo
από 'δω η σύζυγος μου

thanks for your hospitality
efkhareesto ya teen feelokseneea
ευχαριστώ για την φιλοξενία

I've enjoyed myself very much
perasa polee oraya
πέρασα πολύ ωραία

what is your address?
pya eene ee dheeeftheensee sas
ποιά είνα η διεύθυνσή σας;

Although problems are not something anyone wants, you might come across the odd difficulty, and it is best to be armed with a few phrases to cope with the situation.

excuse me!
*seeghn**o**mee*
συγνώμη!

can you help me?
*bor**ee**te na me voeeth**ee**sete*
μπορείτε να με βοηθήσετε;

I don't speak Greek
*dhen meel**a**o eleeneek**a***
δεν μιλάω Ελληνικά

do you speak English?
*meel**a**te angleek**a***
μιλάτε Αγγλικά;

I'm lost
e**kho khath**ee
έχω χαθεί

how do I get to...?
*pos bor**o** na p**a**o sto / stee...*
πώς μπορώ να πάω στο / στη...;

I've lost...
***e**khasa...*
έχασα...

my purse
*to portof**o**lee moo*
το πορτοφόλι μου

my passport
*to dheeavat**ee**ree**o** moo*
το διαβατήριό μου

my keys
*ta kleedhy**a** moo*
τα κλειδιά μου

I've left my bag in...
*ks**e**khasa teen ts**a**nda moo...*
ξέχασα την τσάντα μου...

on the bus
*sto leofor**ee**o*
στο λεωφορείο

on the boat
*sto pl**ee**o*
στο πλοίο

I've missed...
***e**khasa...*
έχασα...

my flight
*teen pt**ee**see*
την πτήση

my connection
*teen andap**o**kreesee moo*
την ανταπόκριση μου

I'm late
***e**kho argh**ee**see*
έχω αργήσει

I need to get to...
*pr**e**pee na ft**a**so sto...*
πρέπει να φτάσω στο...

I have no money
*dhen **e**kho khr**ee**mata*
δεν έχω χρήματα

my luggage hasn't arrived
*ee aposkev**e**s moo dhen **e**ftasan*
οι αποσκευές μου δεν έφτασαν

this is my address
*aft**ee** **ee**ne **ee**ne ee dhee**e**ftheensee moo*
αυτή είναι η διεύθυνση μου

I'm sorry
*leep**a**me*
λυπάμαι

I didn't know
*dhen **ee**ksera*
δεν ήξερα

this is broken
e**spase aft**o
έσπασε αυτό

where can I get this repaired?
*poo tha moo to epeeskev**a**soon*
πού θα μου το επισκευάσουν;

someone's stolen my...
*k**a**peeos moo **e**klepse...*
κάποιος μου έκλεψε...

handbag
*teen ts**a**nda*
την τσάντα

traveller's cheques
*tees takseedheeoteek**e**s epeetay**e**s*
τις ταξιδιωτικές επιταγές

leave me alone!
*af**ee**ste me **ee**seekho*
αφήστε με ήσυχο!

go away!
*f**ee**yete*
φύγετε!

Greeks like to receive good service and quality. They will complain when things are not as they ought to be

there is no...
*dhen **e**khee...*
δεν έχει...

there is no toilet paper
*dhen **e**khee khart**ee** tooal**e**tas*
δεν έχει χαρτί τουαλέτας

there is no hot water
*dhen **e**khee zest**o** ner**o***
δεν έχει ζεστό νερό

there is no bread
*dhen **e**khee psom**ee***
δεν έχει ψωμί

it is dirty
***ee**ne vr**o**meeko*
είναι βρώμικο

the bath is dirty
*to b**a**nyo **ee**ne vr**o**meeko*
το μπάνιο είναι βρώμικο

it is broken
*kh**a**lase*
χάλασε

can you repair it?
*bor**ee**te na to epeedheeorth**o**sete*
μπορείτε να το επιδιορθώσετε;

the shower doesn't work
*to doos dhen dhool**e**vee*
το ντους δεν δουλεύει

the light
to fos
το φως

the toilet
*ee tooal**e**ta*
η τουαλέτα

the telephone
*to teel**e**fono*
το τηλέφωνο

the heating
*ee th**e**rmansee*
η θέρμανση

...doesn't work
*...dhen dhool**e**vee*
...δεν δουλεύει

it is too noisy
***e**khee pol**ee** th**o**reevo*
έχει πολύ θόρυβο

I didn't order this
*dhen z**ee**teesa aft**o***
δεν ζήτησα αυτό

I want to complain
*th**e**lo na k**a**no par**a**pona*
θέλω να κάνω παράπονα

I want a refund
*th**e**lo ta left**a** moo p**ee**so*
θέλω τα λεφτά μου πίσω

we've been waiting for a long time
*pereem**e**noome pol**ee** **o**ra*
περιμένουμε πολή ώρα

we're in a hurry
ee**maste veeasteek**ee
είμαστε βιαστικοί

it's very expensive
ee**ne pol**ee** akreev**o
είναι πολύ ακριβό

where is the manager?
*poo **ee**ne o dheeeftheent**ee**s*
πού είναι ο διευθυντής;

there is a mistake
***e**gheene l**a**thos*
έγινε λάθος

EVERYDAY GREECE

The next four pages should give you an idea of the type of things you will come across in Greece.

Είσοδος

▲ **ENTRANCE** ***ee**sodhos*

▲ **EXIT** ***e**ksodhos*

▲ **PULL** ***ee**lthate*

▲ **PUSH** *oth**ee**sate*

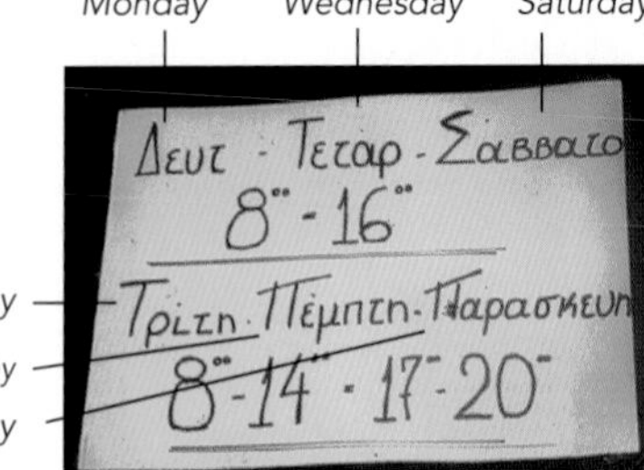

▲ Shops generally open in the morning (8–9 am until 1–2 pm) and again in the evening (approx 5–8 pm). They close in the afternoon and all day Sun. However, in busy tourist areas they usually open all day every day.

◀ The euro symbol. Greece is in the euro zone.

▲ Kiosk (*per**ee**ptero*). These kiosks sell all kinds of things including maps, postcards, stamps, cigarettes, snacks and drinks. They often have a payphone and will give directions.

▲ Tickets on sale for the lottery, which is drawn twice a week.

talking

do you have...?
***e**khete...*
έχετε...;

where can I buy...?
*poo bor**o** na aghor**a**so...*
πού μπορώ να αγοράσω...;

stamps
*ghramat**o**seema*
γραμματόσημα

bread
*psom**ee***
ψωμί

phonecards
*teelek**a**rtes*
τηλεκάρτες

tickets
*eeseet**ee**reea*
εισιτήρια

welcome Greek people may say this (*kalos eelthate*) to you. They like you to feel welcome in their country, and appreciate it if you try to speak the language, however tentatively.

ΔΩΜΑΤΙΑ

ROOMS *dhomateea*
All over Greece you can find rooms to rent, usually with car-parking space. If there are no signs, just ask.

ανοικτο

OPEN *aneekto*

CLOSED *kleesto*

Greece is full of friendly little cafe-bars. Greeks are generally welcoming towards foreigners, although in Athens people are usually less friendly than elsewhere, and can seem rude.

The Greek alphabet can seem daunting. But if you learn it, the language will come alive.

δ Δ = d
η Η = e
λ Λ = l
μ Μ = m
ν Ν = n
ξ Ξ = x
π Π = p
ρ Ρ = r

Capital letters are written differently from lower case letters. These are ones that might fool you.

ΤΑΜΕΙΟ

PAY HERE/CASH DESK *tameeo*

Greek post boxes are yellow and it is usually quite easy to find one. Red boxes are for express post around Athens. Times of collections are sometimes on the box. ΕΛΤΑ is the Greek postal company.

excuse me!
seeghnomee
συγνώμη!

can you show me?
boreete na moo dheeksete
μπορείτε να μου δείξετε;

how does this work?
pos dhoolevee afto
πώς δουλεύει αυτό;

what does this mean?
tee seemenee afto
τι σημαίνει αυτό;

▲ **INFORMATION**
Feel free to ask for all kinds of information, about the local area and Greece in general.

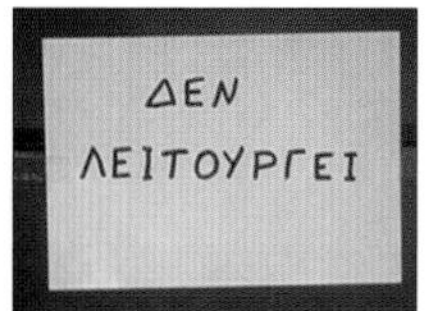

▲ **OUT OF ORDER**

◀ British & US papers are sold in cities and tourist areas in the summer.

▲ **CLOSED** *happy holidays!*

▲ **DANGER** *k**ee**ndheenos*

▼**NO SMOKING**

A service charge is generally included in bills and tipping is a matter of choice. Some Greeks tip, some don't, so there is no obligation. It's entirely up to you. ▶

talking

can I smoke here?
*bor**o** na kapn**ee**so edh**o***
μπορώ να καπνίσω εδώ;

do you mind if I smoke?
*sas peer**a**zee na kapn**ee**so*
σας πειράζει να καπνίσω;

I don't smoke
*dhen kapn**ee**zo*
δεν καπνίζω

please don't smoke
*parakal**o** mee kapn**ee**zete*
παρακαλώ μην καπνίζετε

an ashtray please
e**na tass**a**kee parakal**o
ένα τασάκι παρακαλώ

a non-smoking table please
*ena trap**e**zee ya mee kapneest**e**s parakal**o***
ένα τραπέζι για μή καπνιστές παρακαλώ

*There are a few public toilets in Greece, but not many. There may be a small charge. Otherwise look for toilets in shopping centres, department stores and petrol stations. Bars, snack bars etc will let you use the toilet but of course it's polite to buy a drink first – cans of soda or small bottles of water are cheap! It is wise to carry tissues at all times. A word about Greek plumbing: because of the sewerage system, all (yes, **all**) toilet paper **must** be deposited in the bin beside the toilet, not thrown into the toilet bowl. This applies wherever you are in Greece. It may seem strange, but please abide by this rule, otherwise the drains get blocked and some unfortunate person has the task of removing all the toilet paper from the pipes.*

▲ **GENTS** *andhr**o**n*

ΤΟΥΑΛΕΤΕΣ

▲ **TOILETS** *tooal**e**tes*

▼ **LADIES** *yeenek**o**n*

ζεστό κρύο

▲ **HOT** *zest**o*** **COLD** *kr**ee**o*

Watch out as sometimes you find that someone has swapped the tap colours round and you get hot water from the cold tap!

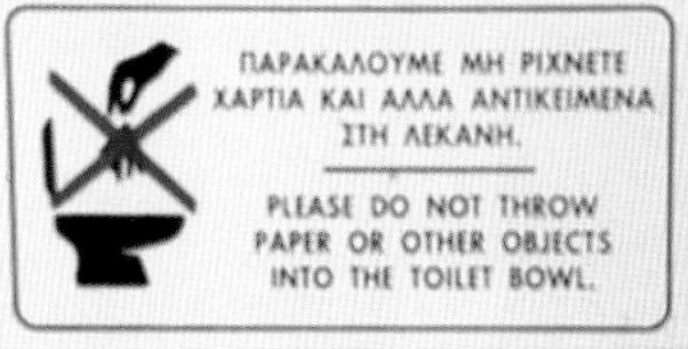

◀ Greek toilets have very narrow plumbing and you must put toilet paper in the wastebins provided, rather than in the toilet.

excuse me! where is the toilet?
*seeghn**o**mee! poo **ee**ne ee tooal**e**ta*
συγνώμη! πού είναι η τουαλέτα;

may I use the toilet?
*bor**o** na p**a**o steen tooal**e**ta*
μπορώ να πάω στην τουαλέτα;

do you have toilets for the disabled?
***e**khete tooal**e**tes ya anap**ee**roos*
έχετε τουαλέτες για αναπήρους;

the toilet doesn't work
*ee tooal**e**ta dhen leetoory**ee***
η τουαλέτα δεν λειτουργεί

do I need a key?
*khree**a**zome kleedh**ee***
χρειάζομαι κλειδί;

talking talking

ASKING THE WAY

*Tourist offices usually have free maps, in addition to brochures and leaflets about local attractions, trips etc. They can also help you with accommodation, transport and general information. You can buy all kinds of different maps at bookshops, newsagents and at traditional Greek kiosks (***pereeptera***).* ***Pereeptera*** *can be seen on many street corners. They sell a multitude of things and often have a pay phone, too.*

▲ Office of tourism *Syntagma Square*

▲ **TOURIST INFORMATION OFFICE**

Local maps are often available free from Tourist Offices. You can also buy them cheaply at newsagent's or kiosks. ▶

excuse me!
*seeghn***o***mee*
συγνώμη!

where is...?
poo ***ee****ne...*
πού είναι...;

where is the hotel?
poo ***ee****ne to ksenodhokh***ee***o*
πού είναι το ξενοδοχείο;

I'm looking for...
*ps***a***khno ya to* (with ο and το words) / *tee* (with η words)...
ψάχνω για το / τη...

I'm looking for the station
*ps***a***khno ya to stathm***o**
ψάχνω για το το σταθμό

is it far?
ee*ne makree***a**
είναι μακριά;

do you know where...?
*ks***e***rete poo* ***ee****ne...*
ξέρετε πού είναι...;

do you know where the tourist office is?
*ks***e***rete poo* ***ee****ne to ghraf***ee***o tooreesm***oo**
ξέρετε πού είναι το γραφείο τουρισμού

how do I get to...?
*pos bor***o** *na p***a***o sto* (with ο and το words) / *stee* (with η words)...
πώς μπορώ να πάω στο / στη...;

where is the nearest...?
poo ***ee****ne to kondeen***o***tero...*
πού είναι το κοντινότερο...;

▲ Brown signs show the way to local places of interest. Plaka is the area beneath the Acropolis which is full of lively bars, shops and restaurants.

◀ *to the Holy Church of Saint Kharalambos*

◀ Sites of historical interest often have English translations.

▲ **ΟΔΟΣ** *dhr**o**mos* road, street
ΑΠΟ *ap**o*** from (8–2)

ΑΡΙΣΤΕΡΑ

▲ **LEFT** *areester**a***

RIGHT *dekhsee**a*** ▼

keywords keywords keywords

δεξιά
*dekhsee**a***
to the right

αριστερά
*areester**a***
to the left

ευθεία
*efth**ee**a*
straight ahead

δρόμος
*dhr**o**mos*
road

πρώτο δρόμο δεξιά
*pr**o**to dhr**o**mo dheksee**a***
first on right

δεύτερο δρόμο αριστερά
*dh**e**ftero dhr**o**mo areester**a***
second on left

πλατεία
*plat**ee**a*
square

φανάρια
*fan**a**reea*
traffic lights

δίπλα στο
*dh**ee**pla sto*
next to

κοντά στο
*kond**a** sto*
near to

*apod**o** / apok**ee***
απο εδώ / από εκεί
this way / that way

πήγαινε / στρίψε
*p**ee**gene / str**ee**ptse*
go / turn

απέναντι
*ap**e**nandee*
opposite

εκκλησία
*ekleese**e**a*
church

BANKS & MONEY

Banking hours are usually 8 am till 2 pm Mon to Thur and 8 am till 1 pm on Fri, but check opening-hours signs just to make sure.You can change cash and travellers' cheques at banks, travel agencies and at some hotels, but it's a good idea to check out the best exchange rate and ask about the commission before deciding where to change your money. It's also very easy to find a 24 hour ATM (cash dispenser). ATMs accept Switch, Maestro, Cirrus and most credit cards.

*price teem**ee***   *euro evr**o***

◀ The price of an item

▲ These are two of the major banks in Greece. The Greek word for bank is **τράπεζα** *tr**a**peza.*

You will find 24-hour cash-points at many banks and in tourist areas, with instructions in English, French, German and Italian. ▼

24-hour indoor cash dispenser; swipe your card to get in ▼

Cashpoint interface is as you would find at home. ▼

Travel agents as well as banks offer exchange services; these are ususally signed in English. ▶

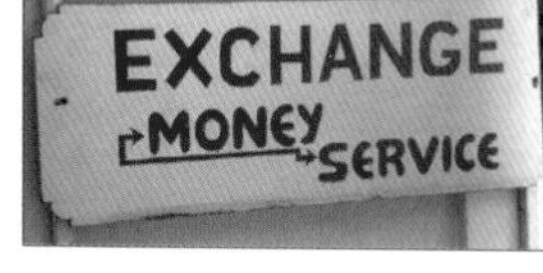

Greece's currency is the euro, ευρώ (*evr**o***), which breaks down into 100 euro cents. Euro notes are the same across Europe. The coins are officially cents, but Greek people call them λεπτά (*lept**a***) The reverse of the coins carry different designs in each European member country.

Notes: 5, 10, 20, 50, 100, 200, 500 ◀

▲ Coins: 2 euro, 1 euro, 50 cent, 20 cent, 10 cent, 5 cent, 2 cent, 1 cent

keywords keywords

ATM
ay tee em
cash dispenser

κωδικός PIN
*kodeek**o**s pin*
PIN number

συνάλλαγμα
*seen**a**laghma*
change

βάλε
*v**a**le*
insert

χαρτονομίσματα
*khartonom**ee**smata*
notes

μετρητά
*metreet**a***
cash

νόμισμα
*n**o**meesma*
coin

πιστωτική κάρτα
*peestoteek**ee** k**a**rta*
credit card

talking talking

where can I change money?
*poo bor**o** na al**a**kso khr**ee**mata*
πού μπορώ να αλλάξω χρήματα;

where is there a bank?
*poo **ee**ne m**ee**a tr**a**peza*
πού είναι μία τράπεζα;

where is there a bureau de change?
*poo **ee**ne **e**na enalakt**ee**reeo seenal**a**ghmatos*
πού είναι ένα εναλλακτήριο συναλλάγματος;

when does the bank open?
*p**o**te an**ee**ghee ee tr**a**peza*
πότε ανοίγει η τράπεζα;

when does the bank close?
*p**o**te kl**ee**nee ee tr**a**peza*
πότε κλείνει η τράπεζα;

where is there a cash dispenser?
*poo **e**khee **e**na ay tee em*
πού έχει ένα ay tee em;

I want to cash these traveller's cheques
*tha **ee**thela na al**a**kso aft**a** ta takseedhyoteek**a** tsek*
θα ήθελα να αλλάξω αυτά τα ταξιδιωτικά τσεκ

WHEN IS...?

Greece is two hours ahead of Great Britain all year round.
Π.μ. *means a.m.* (**πριν μεσημέρι** *preen meseemeree – before midday*).
Μ.μ. *means p.m.* (**μετά μεσημέρι** *meta meseemeree after midday*).

keywords keywords

πρωί
proee
morning

απόγευμα
apoyevma
afternoon

απόψε
apopse
this evening

σήμερα
seemera
today

αύριο
avreeo
tomorrow

χθές
khthes
yesterday

τώρα
tora
now

τότε
tote
then

αργότερα
arghotera
later

THE 24 HOUR CLOCK

at midnight
ta mesaneekhta
τα μεσάνυχτα

stees eekosee tesera
στις είκοσι τέσσερα

stees eekosee treea
στις είκοσι τρία

stees endeka
στις έντεκα

stees eekosee dheeo
στις είκοσι δύο

stees dheka
στις δέκα

stees eekosee ena
στις είκοσι ένα

stees enea
στις εννέα

stees eekosee
στις είκοσι

stees okto
στις οκτώ

stees dhekaenea
στις δεκαεννέα

stees epta
στις επτά

at 25 to ...
stees ... ke treeanta pente
στις ... και τριάντα πέντε

talking

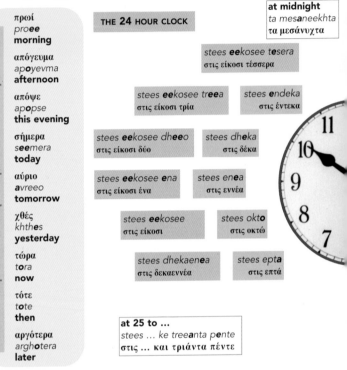

when is the next...	**boat**	**bus**	**train**	**to...?**
pote fevyee to epomeno...	*pleeo*	*leoforeeo*	**τραίνο**	*ya...*
πότε φεύγει το επόμενο...;	**πλοίο**	**λεωφορείο**	*treno*	**για...;**

what time is...?
tee ora serveerete...
τι ώρα σερβίρεται...;

breakfast
to proeeno
το πρωινό

dinner
to vradheeno
το βραδυνό

when does it leave?
pote fevyee
πότε φεύγει;

when does it arrive?
pote ftanee
πότε φτάνει;

when does it open?
pote aneeyee
πότε ανοίγει;

when does it close?
pote kleenee
πότε κλείνει;

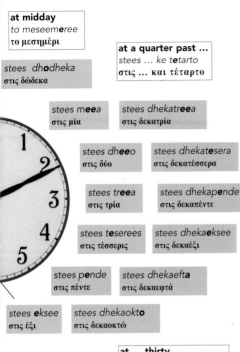

at midday
*to meseem**e**ree*
το μεσημέρι

at a quarter past ...
*stees ... ke t**e**tarto*
στις ... και τέταρτο

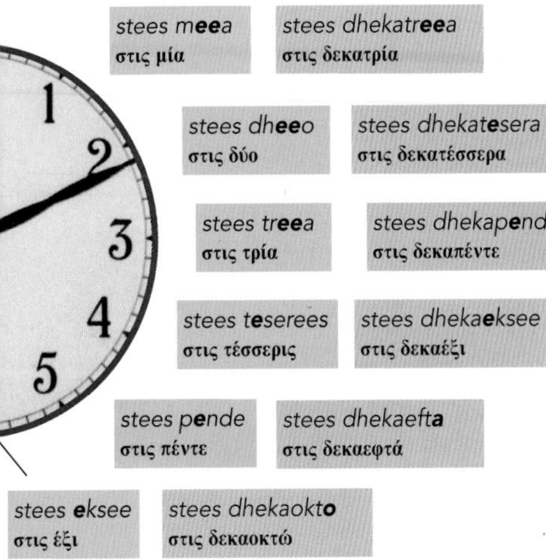

*stees dh**o**dheka*
στις δώδεκα

*stees m**ee**a*
στις μία

*stees dhekatr**ee**a*
στις δεκατρία

*stees dh**ee**o*
στις δύο

*stees dhekat**e**sera*
στις δεκατέσσερα

*stees tr**ee**a*
στις τρία

*stees dhekap**e**nde*
στις δεκαπέντε

*stees teser**ee**s*
στις τέσσερις

*stees dheka**e**ksee*
στις δεκαέξι

*stees p**e**nde*
στις πέντε

*stees dhekaeft**a***
στις δεκαεφτά

*stees **e**ksee*
στις έξι

*stees dhekaokt**o***
στις δεκαοκτώ

at ... thirty
*stees ... ke mees**ee***
στις ... και μισή

keywords keywords

Ιανουάριος
*eeanoo**a**reeos*
January

Φεβρουάριος
*fevroo**a**reeos*
Febuary

Μάρτιος
*m**a**rteeos*
March

Απρίλιος
*apr**ee**leeos*
April

Μάιος
*m**a**eeos*
May

Ιούνιος
*ee**oo**neeos*
June

Ιούλιος
*ee**oo**leeos*
July

Αύγουστος
***a**vghoostos*
August

Σεπτέμβριος
*sept**e**mvreeos*
September

Οκτώβριος
*okt**o**vreeos*
October

Νοέμβριος
*no**e**mvreeos*
November

Δεκέμβριος
*dhek**e**mvreeos*
December

what time is it please?
*tee **o**ra **ee**ne parakal**o***
τι ώρα είναι, παρακαλώ;

it's 9 o'clock
***ee**ne en**e**a ee **o**ra*
είναι εννέα η ώρα

in an hour's time
*se m**ee**a **o**ra*
σε μία ώρα

in a while
*se l**ee**gho*
σε λίγο

two hours ago
*preen ap**o** dh**ee**o **o**res*
πριν από δύο ώρες

what's the date?
*tee eemeromeen**ee**a **e**khoome s**ee**mera*
τι ημερομηνία έχουμε σήμερα;

which month?
*pyos m**ee**nas*
ποιός μήνας;

it's the 5th of August 2003
***ee**ne ee p**e**mtee avgh**oo**stoo dh**ee**o kheelee**a**dhes tr**ee**a*
είναι η 5η Αυγούστου 2003

TIMETABLES

Key words to look out for are **καθημερινές** *(kath***ee***mereen***e***s) meaning weekday (i.e. Mon–Sat) and* **Κυριακές και γιορτές** *(keereey***a***k***e***s ke yort***e***s) meaning Sundays and public holidays. Timetables vary according to whether they are* **θερινές** *(theree***ne***s – summer) or* **χειμερινές** *(kheemeree***ne***s – winter).*

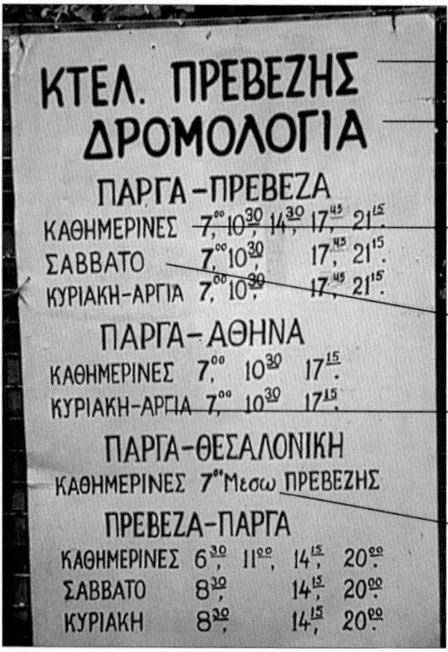

ΚΤΕΛ. ΠΡΕΒΕΖΗΣ
ΔΡΟΜΟΛΟΓΙΑ
ΠΑΡΓΑ-ΠΡΕΒΕΖΑ
ΚΑΘΗΜΕΡΙΝΕΣ 7.00 10.30 14.30 17.45 21.15
ΣΑΒΒΑΤΟ 7.00 10.30 17.45 21.15
ΚΥΡΙΑΚΗ-ΑΡΓΙΑ 7.00 10.30 17.45 21.15
ΠΑΡΓΑ-ΑΘΗΝΑ
ΚΑΘΗΜΕΡΙΝΕΣ 7.00 10.30 17.15
ΚΥΡΙΑΚΗ-ΑΡΓΙΑ 7.00 10.30 17.15
ΠΑΡΓΑ-ΘΕΣΑΛΟΝΙΚΗ
ΚΑΘΗΜΕΡΙΝΕΣ 7.00 Μεσω ΠΡΕΒΕΖΗΣ
ΠΡΕΒΕΖΑ-ΠΑΡΓΑ
ΚΑΘΗΜΕΡΙΝΕΣ 6.30 11.00 14.15 20.00
ΣΑΒΒΑΤΟ 8.30 14.15 20.00
ΚΥΡΙΑΚΗ 8.30 14.15 20.00

ΚΤΕΛ. *(KTEL) Greek national bus/coach service*

ΔΡΟΜΟΛΟΓΙΑ *services dromol***o***gheea*

ΚΑΘΗΜΕΡΙΝΑ *week-days katheemereeene***s**

ΣΑΒΒΑΤΟ *Saturday s***a***vato*

ΚΥRΙΑΚΗ-ΑΡΓΙΑ *Sunday-holiday keereeak***ee***-argh***ee***a*

Μέσω *via m***e***so*

▲ Timetable for long-distance coaches to Preveza, Athens and Thessalonika

09.00 π.μ.

▲ **9 AM**

1 PM ▼

13.00 μ.μ.

ΟΡΧΗΣΤΡΑ ΠΑΡΓΑΣ
Τηλ: 0684 - 31.176 & 0944-28.27.42
ΣΗΜΕΡΑ

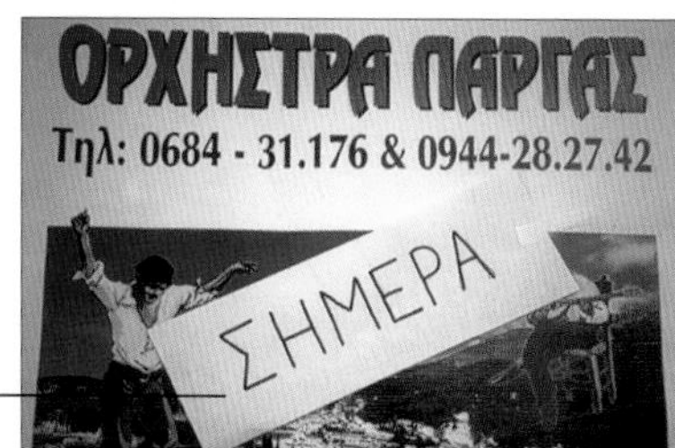

today

talk

have you a timetable?	when does it leave?	when does it arrive?
ekhete to orareeo	*pote fevyee*	*pote ftanee*
έχετε το ωράριο;	πότε φεύγει;	πότε φτάνει;

▲Timetables, especially in tourist areas, will often have English translations alongside the Greek.

◀Bus station timetable board showing local and longer-distance routes.

Δευτέρα *dheft**e**ra* Monday

Τρίτη *tr**ee**tee* Tuesday

Τετάρτη *tet**a**rtee* Wednesday

Πέμπτη *p**e**mptee* Thursday

Παρασκευή *paraskev**ee*** Friday

Σάββατο *s**a**vato* Saturday

Κυριακή *keereeak**ee*** Sunday

▲ In Greek days of the week begin with a capital letter, as do months of the year. Signs are often written in capital letters.

keywords

αναχώρηση
*anakh**o**reesee*
departure

άφιξη
***a**feeksee*
arrival

καθημερινά
*katheemereen**a***
daily

λειτουργεί
*leetoorgh**ee***
operates

εκτός λειτουργίας
*ekt**o**s leetoorgh**ee**as*
no service

έως / από
e**os / ap**o
until / from

διακοπές
*deeakop**e**s*
holidays

καλοκαίρι
*kalok**e**ree*
summer

χειμώνας
*kheem**o**nas*
winter

▲ **ARRIVALS** *af**ee**ksees*

ΑΝΑΧΩΡΗΣΗ

▲ **DEPARTURES** *anakh**o**reesee*

▲ **TIME** *o**ra***

TICKETS

In Athens, tickets for the Metro, bus, trolley-bus and trains must be validated. Keep your ticket till the end of your journey. On the Metro, buy your ticket (at the desk or from a machine) and validate it as you walk past the validating machines. On the buses you will see the validating machines as you get on. Other cities have a similar ticketing system to Athens, although Athens alone has a Metro. In the rural areas, buy a ticket and keep it throughout the journey.

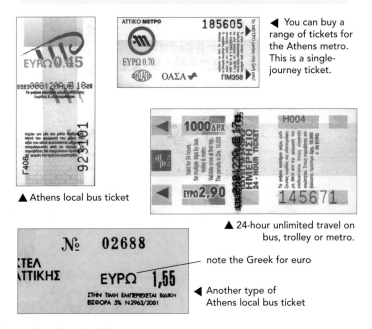

▲ Athens local bus ticket

◀ You can buy a range of tickets for the Athens metro. This is a single-journey ticket.

▲ 24-hour unlimited travel on bus, trolley or metro.

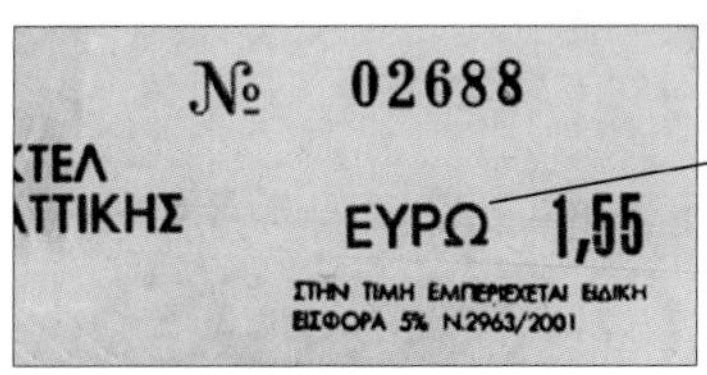

note the Greek for euro

◀ Another type of Athens local bus ticket

Inter-city train ticket

▼ All information is printed in English as well as in Greek.

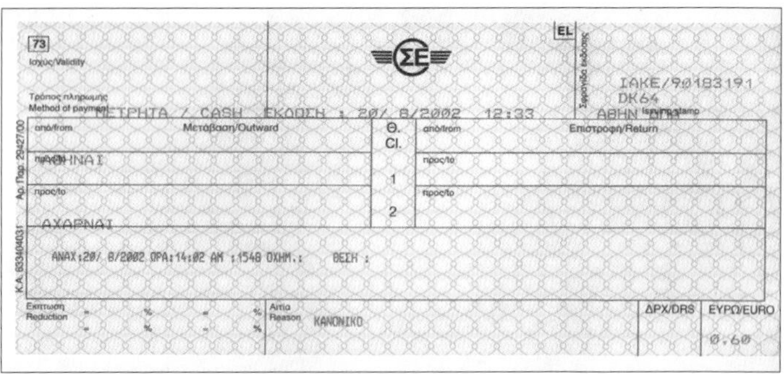

▲ You have to validate any ticket you buy for public transport in a validating machine. These are found at the entrance of buses, train platforms and metro stations, as shown here. Simply insert your ticket in the slot for punching.

▲ Cinema ticket booth

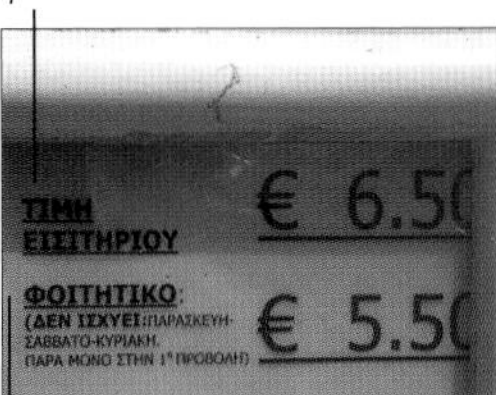

▲ Ticket prices

Most signs will have translations. The word for ticket is *eeseet**ee**reeo* and the plural is *eeseet**ee**reea*

▼

ΚΤΕΛ Ν. ΠΡΕΒΕΖΗΣ Τηλ. (0684) 31218
ΕΙΣΙΤΗΡΙΑ – TICKETS
ΑΘΗΝΑ | ATHENS | ΠΡΕΒΕΖΑ | PREVEZA
ΘΕΣΣ/ΝΙΚΗ | SALONIKA | ΑΡΤΑ | ARTA
ΠΑΤΡΑ | PATRA | ΗΓΟΥΜΕΝΙΤΣΑ | IGUMENITSA

keywords

εισιτήριο
*eeseet**ee**reeo*
ticket

απλό
*apl**o***
single

με επιστροφή
*me epeestro-f**ee***
return

ημερήσιο εισιτήριο
*eemer**ee**seeo eeseet**ee**reeo*
all day ticket

εισιτήριο διαρκείας
*eeseet**ee**reeo deearkh**ee**as*
season ticket

ταξιδιωτικό πάσο
*takseedheeo-teek**o** p**a**so*
travel pass

ολόκληρο
*ol**o**kleero*
adult

παιδικό
*pedeek**o***
child

οικογενειακό
*eekoyeneeak**o***
family

φοιτητικό
*feeteeteek**o***
student

ηλικιωμένων
*eelee-keeom**e**non*
over 60

αναπηρικό
*anapeereek**o***
disabled

PUBLIC TRANSPORT

Buses and trains are reasonably priced and reliable. There are good bus services within cities and regular long-distance coaches catering for people in towns and in country villages. Tickets are bought from a ticket office or on the bus in rural areas. Because Greece is so mountainous, the railway system is more limited. There is a line from Athens to Thessalonika and from Thessalonika across to the Turkish border. There is also a line from Athens to Patras and around the Peloponnese, which is very scenic. You buy tickets at the stations.

◀ **BUS STATION**

A bus-stop in Athens showing where this Averof IKA stop is on the bus-route. ▼

▲ Bus stop with route numbers

Ticket office

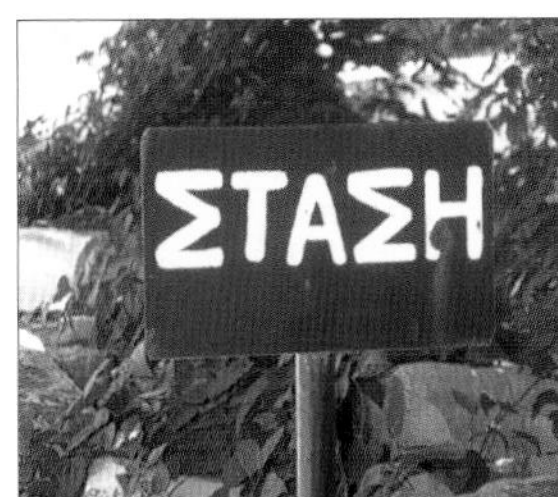

▲ *bus-stop (st**a**see)* ▼

ΣΤΑΣΗ
ΚΤΕΛ

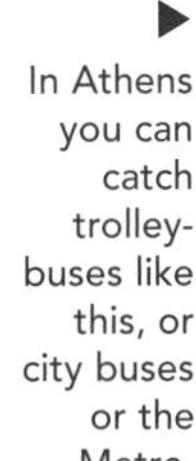

▶ In Athens you can catch trolley-buses like this, or city buses or the Metro.

You can buy bus and trolley-bus tickets here. ▼

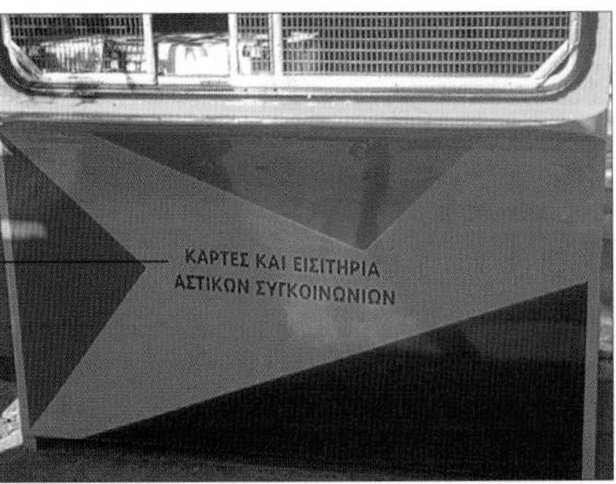

ΚΑΡΤΕΣ = *cards*
ΚΑΙ = *and*
ΕΙΣΙΤΗΡΙΑ = *tickets*

where is the bus station?
*poo **ee**ne o stathm**o**s leofor**ee**on*
πού είναι ο σταθμός λεωφορείων;

where is the bus stop?
*poo **ee**ne ee st**a**see too leofor**ee**oo*
πού είναι η στάση του λεωφορείου

where is the bus to the centre?
*poo **ee**ne to leofor**ee**o ya to k**e**ntro*
πού είναι το λεωφορείο για το κέντρο;

which bus goes to Pireus?
*pyo leofor**ee**o p**a**-ee ston peeray**a***
ποιο λεωφορείο πάει στον Πειραιά;

to the station
*sto stathm**o***
στο σταθμό

to the museum
*sto moos**ee**o*
στο μουσείο

to the Acropolis
*steen akr**o**polee*
στην Ακρόπολη

to Plaka
*steen pl**a**ka*
στην Πλάκα

where is this bus going?
*poo p**a**-ee aft**o** to leofor**ee**o*
πού πάει αυτό το λεωφορείο;

talking talking

The new Metro in Athens is very impressive. It is built in pink and grey marble and contains many exhibits of archaeological discoveries made during construction. Security is high there: there is no smoking, no eating/drinking and most definitely no graffiti. It opens at 5.30 am and closes at midnight. A ticket is valid for one single journey of any length.You can also get a ticket valid for 24 hours (as many trips as you want) The 24 hour ticket is also valid for use on the buses, trolley-buses and trains in the same period of time.

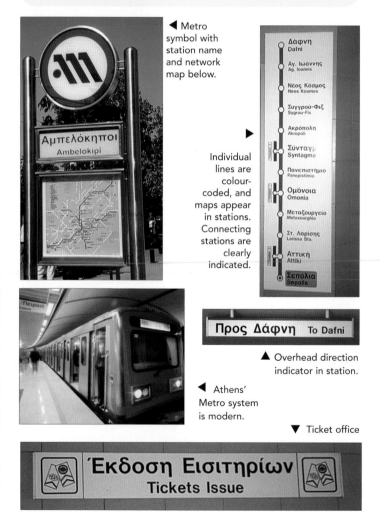

◀ Metro symbol with station name and network map below.

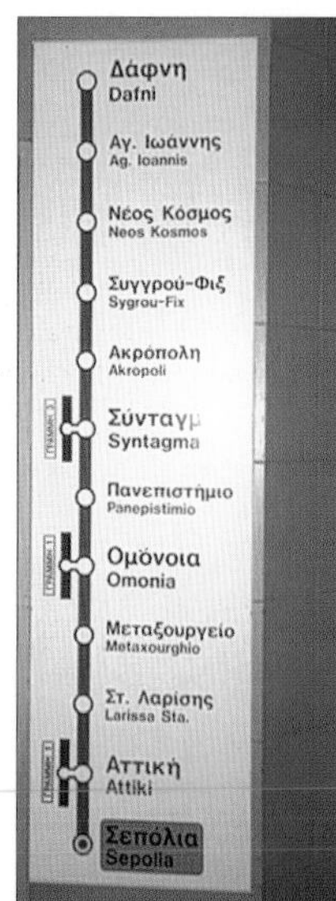

▶ Individual lines are colour-coded, and maps appear in stations. Connecting stations are clearly indicated.

◀ Athens' Metro system is modern.

Προς Δάφνη To Dafni

▲ Overhead direction indicator in station.

▼ Ticket office

Έκδοση Εισιτηρίων
Tickets Issue

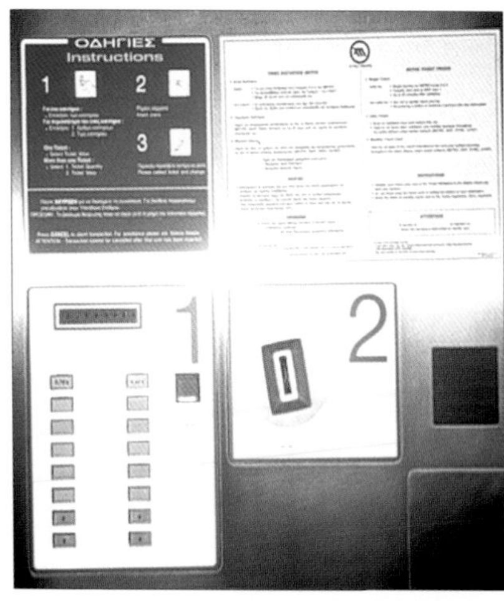

▲ Automatic ticket machines in the Athens Metro are easy to use and are multilingual.

▲ In the Metro you must validate your ticket in one of these machines and then keep it during your journey.

where is the nearest metro station?
*poo **ee**ne o kondeen**o**teros stathm**o**s too metr**o***
πού είναι ο κοντινότερος σταθμός του μετρό;

a ticket / 4 tickets, please
e**na eeseet**ee**reeo / **t**essera eeseet**ee**reea parakal**o
ένα εισιτήριο / τέσσερα εισιτήρια παρακαλώ

have you a map of the metro?
e**khete kh**a**rtee ya to metr**o
έχετε χάρτη για το μετρό;

I want to go to...
*th**e**lo na p**a**o sto / stee...*
θέλω να πάω στο / στη...

can I go by underground?
*bor**o** na p**a**o me to metr**o***
μπορώ να πάω με το μετρό;

do I have to change?
*pr**e**pee nal**a**kso ghram**ee***
πρέπει ν'αλλάξω γραμμή;

where?
poo
πού;

which line do I take?
*pya ghramm**ee** pr**e**pee na p**a**ro*
ποια γραμμή πρέπει να πάρω;

excuse me!
*me seeghkhor**ee**te*
με συγχωρείτε!

I'm getting off
*katev**e**no*
κατεβαίνω

Because Greece is so mountainous the train service is quite limited, but inexpensive. Trains tend to be rather slow and do not go to more remote areas or many places of archaeological interest. The initials of the Greek National Railway are **ΟΣΕ** *and you can visit their website for details of trains and timetables on www.ose.gr. Tickets can be bought at railway stations and travel agents. However, you must remember (as with all other forms of public transport) to validate your ticket at the validating machines in the station before you begin your journey.*

ΕΙΣΙΤΗΡΙΑ ΕΣΩΤΕΡΙΚΟΥ
ΠΛΗΝ ΑΜΑΞ/ΧΙΩΝ INTERCITY

▲ TICKETS WITHIN GREECE EXCEPT INTERCITY TICKETS

ATHENS STATION ▲

WAITING ROOM ▶

a single to...
ena apl**o** eeseet**ee**reeo ya…
ένα απλό εισιτήριο για...

2 singles to...
dh**ee**o apl**a** eeseet**ee**reea ya…
δύο απλά εισιτήρια για...

a return to...
ena eeseet**ee**reeo me epeestrof**ee** ya…
ένα εισιτήριο με επιστροφή για...

2 returns to...
dh**ee**o eeseet**ee**reea me epeestrof**ee** ya…
δύο εισιτήρια με επιστροφή για...

a child's ticket to...
ena pedheek**o** eeseet**ee**reeo ya…
ένα παιδικό εισητήριο για...

he/she is ... years old
eene … khron**o**n
είναι ... χρονών

I want to book 2 seats
th**e**lo na kl**ee**so dh**ee**o th**e**sees
θέλω να κλείσω δύο θέσεις

economy class
tooreesteek**ee** th**e**see
τουριστική θέση

smoking
kapn**ee**zontes
καπνίζοντες

non smoking
mee kapn**ee**zontes
μη καπνίζοντες

is there a supplement to pay?
eep**a**rkhee epeepl**e**on epeev**a**reensee
υπάρχει επιπλέον επιβάρυνση;

Arrivals and departures board in the station. In major stations, information is displayed in both Greek and English, alternating continually. ▼

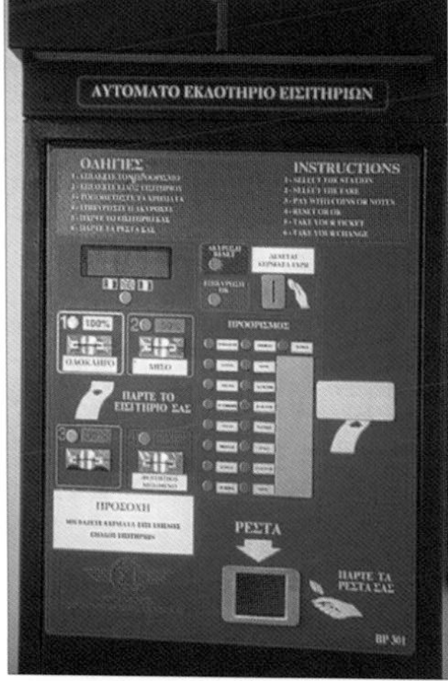

Automatic ticket machine in the railway station. Instructions are available in English as well as Greek. ◀

◀ Overhead departure board on platform

keywords

απλό
aplo
single

μετ επιστροφής
met epeestrofees
return

κράτηση
krateesee
reservation

επιτρέπεται το κάπνισμα
epeetrepete to kapneesma
smoking is allowed

απαγορεύεται το κάπνισμα
apagorevete to kapneesma
non-smoking

γραφείο εισιτηρίων
grafeeo eessee-teereeon
ticket office

γραφείο αποσκευών
grafeeo aposkevon
left luggage

βαγόνι
vagonee
carriage

πλατφόρμα
platforma
platform

talking

is this the train for...?
eene afto to treno ya...
είναι αυτό το τρένο για...;

is this seat free?
eene ee thesee elevtheree
είναι η θέση ελεύθερη;

which platform does it leave from?
apo peea platforma fevyee
από ποια πλατφόρμα φεύγει;

this is my seat
aftee eene ee thesee moo
αυτή είναι η θέση μου

TAXI

Taxis abound in Greece. Each town has its own colour for taxis. Taxis in Athens are yellow. It is easy to flag them down in cities, as the local people do. You can also ask at a kiosk for the phone number of a taxi firm, or ask your hotel to call a taxi for you. Tipping is not all that common in Greece but small tips are always gratefully received.

▲ Taxis are quite cheap, but you should still ask the price beforehand. The grey taxis are for long-distance journeys, i.e. town to town.

All taxis have meters. ▼

▲ You can ring for a taxi, wait at a stand or flag one down in the street.

A taxi stand and phone in a small town. ▼

talking talking

where can I get a taxi?
poo boro na vro taksee
πού μπορώ να βρω ταξί;

to the airport
sto aerodhromeeo
στο αεροδρόμιο

please take me to this address
se afteen teen dheeevtheensee parakalo
σε αυτήν την διεύθυνση, παρακαλώ

how much will it cost?
poso kosteezee
πόσο κοστίζει;

how much is to the centre?
poso kosteezee ya to kentro
πόσο κοστίζει για το κέντρο;

can I have a receipt?
boreete na moo dhosete apodheeksee
μπορείτε να μου δώσετε απόδειξη;

it's too much
eene polee akreeva
είναι πολύ ακριβά

please order me a taxi
parakalo kaleste ena taksee
παρακαλώ καλέστε ένα ταξί

keep the change
krateeste ta resta
κρατήστε τα ρέστα

CAR HIRE

You will find all the major car-hire companies in Greece, plus various local ones. You can also book a car from abroad, before your trip, and the car should be waiting for you at the airport - usually a cheap, easy option. Within Greece, restrictions vary. You HAVE to have held a driving licence for at least one year, but the minimum age differs between companies from 21 to 25. Some companies charge supplements for young drivers. A few local companies will let you rent a car at age 20.

I want to hire a car
thelo na neekyaso ena aftokeeneeto
θέλω να νοικιάσω ένα αυτοκίνητο

for one day
ya meea mera
για μία μέρα

for ... days
ya ... meres
για ... μέρες

I want a...
proteemo ena...
προτιμώ ένα ...

large
meghalo
μεγάλο

small
meekro
μικρό

car
aftokeeneeto
αυτοκίνητο

how much is it...?
πόσο κάνει...;
poso kanee...

per day
τη μέρα
tee mera

per week
τη βδομάδα
tee vdhomadha

how much is the deposit?
πόση είναι η προκαταβολή;
posee eene ee prokatavolee

is there a charge per kilometre?
γίνεται χρέωση ανά χιλιόμετρο;
yeenete khreosee ana kheeleeometro

how much?
πόσο κάνει;
poso kanee

what is included in the insurance?
tee pereelamvanete steen asfaleea
τι περιλαμβάνεται στην ασφάλεια;

I want to take out additional insurance
thelo na paro prosthetee asfaleea
θέλω να πάρω πρόσθετη ασφάλεια

what do I do if I break down?
tee tha kano an meeno apo vlavee
τι θα κάνω αν μείνω από βλάβη;

where are the documents?
poo eene ee adheea keekloforeeas ke ee asfaleea
πού είναι η άδεια κυκλοφορίας και η ασφαλεία;

DRIVING

The minimum age for driving in Greece is 18. Greek people generally drive carefully and the roads are good. Watch out when driving in Athens, though, as it can get quite chaotic. Take care at all times, especially on zebra crossings, as you will occasionally come across impatient drivers and people who overtake dangerously. Cars do not often stop for pedestrians – the zebra crossing is really just an accepted crossing point for pedestrians once the road is clear. There are many excellent new highways in Greece, linking major towns and cities. In Greece's mountainous areas, you will find twisting roads with hairpin bends but there won't usually be a lot of traffic about. Even the remotest roads nowadays have tarmac but you might still find the odd dirt track, linking tiny villages. If you take your own car to Greece, a Green Card may or may not be necessary – ask your Insurance Company to explain this in full. Keep your driving licence, car documents and passport with you at all times. Police often set up speed checks, especially where there is a small village along an otherwise deserted highway – so watch your speed! Seatbelts and motorbike helmets are compulsory and fines are issued. Occasionally you may see three people on one motorbike without a helmet in sight, but don't let this deceive you, fines are hefty for these offences!

Speed restrictions

built up area	50 km/h
(motorcycles)	40 km/h
main roads	90 km/h
(motorcycles)	70 km/h
motorway	120 km/h
(motorcycles)	90 km/h

▲ Speed restrictions vary for cars and motorcycles. It is compulsory to wear seatbelts.

▲ Each county has its own set of designated letters, 'ATE' is Athens. Only letters recognizable throughout Europe are used on numberplates.

caution

roadworks in progress

slow

◀ Greek main roads are all 'E' roads, with a number, similar to our 'A' roads.

caution

in progress

roadworks

speed 10 kph

Toll-free main roads are signed in blue, while you pay a toll on the motorways. ▼

*motorway (aftokeeneet**o**dhromos) signs are green in Greece*

▲ Beaches are well signposted

◀ No motorbikes allowed at night. Note that it is compulsory to wear a crash helmet.

Από *ap**o*** from

Έως ***e**os* till

Π.μ.. = am

Μ.μ. = pm

◀ Signpost indicating Vrahos tunnel

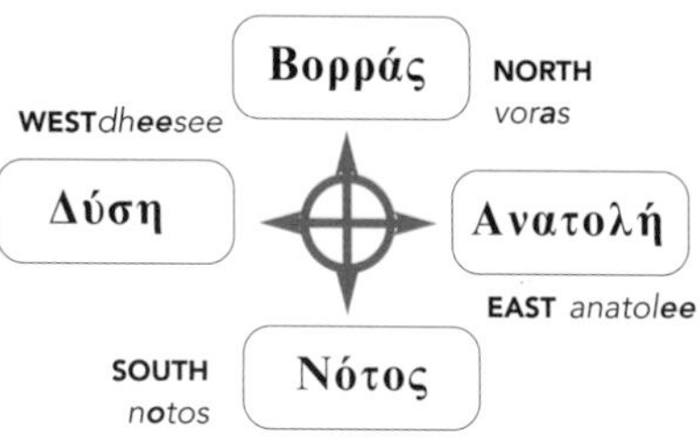

▲ Direction indicators

▲ No overtaking: Uneven surface

Caution: Road narrows : No overtaking ▼

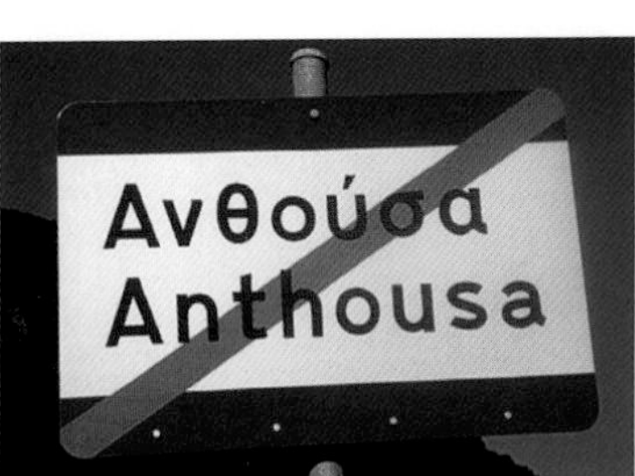

▲ A diagonal red line shows that you are leaving a town or village.

▶ A high-wind sign

Restricted ▶ access times for heavy vehicles

from 10 am to 11 pm

talking

we're going to...
*py**e**noome sto...*
πηγαίνουμε στο...

what is the best route?
*py**a** **ee**ne ee kal**ee**teree dheeadhrom**ee***
ποια είναι η καλύτερη διαδρομή;

how do I get to the motorway?
*pos tha p**a**o steen ethneek**ee***
πως θα πάω στην εθνική;

which junction is it for...?
*se py**a** dheeast**a**vrosee **ee**ne...*
σε ποια διαστάυρωση είναι...;

when is the best time to drive?
*py**a** **ee**ne ee kal**ee**teree **o**ra ya odh**ee**yeesee*
ποια είναι η καλύτερη ώρα για οδήγηση;

is the road good?
***ee**ne kal**o**s o dhr**o**mos*
είναι καλός ο δρόμος;

When driving on the motorway you pay a toll. Toll-stations are well signed and easy to deal with. Rates are quite low and you pay a fixed rate per section, e.g Patras to Corinth. You pay at the start of the motorway and should keep your ticket in case they check it on leaving. Keep your eye on the speed limit and watch out for occasional impatient overtaking.

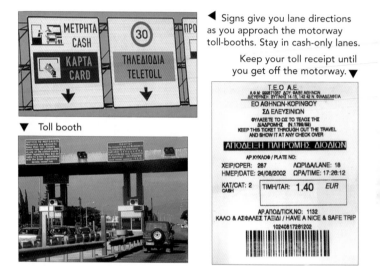

◀ Signs give you lane directions as you approach the motorway toll-booths. Stay in cash-only lanes.

Keep your toll receipt until you get off the motorway. ▼

T.E.O A.E.

ΕΟ ΑΘΗΝΩΝ-ΚΟΡΙΝΘΟΥ
ΣΔ ΕΛΕΥΣΙΝΙΩΝ

ΦΥΛΑΞΕΤΕ ΤΟ ΩΣ ΤΟ ΤΕΛΟΣ ΤΗΣ ΔΙΑΔΡΟΜΗΣ (Ν.1799/88)
KEEP THIS TICKET THROUGH OUT THE TRAVEL AND SHOW IT AT ANY CHECK OVER

ΑΠΟΔΕΙΞΗ ΠΛΗΡΩΜΗΣ ΔΙΟΔΙΩΝ

ΑΡ.ΚΥΚΛΟΦ / PLATE NO:
ΧΕΙΡ/OPER: 287 ΛΩΡΙΔΑ/LANE: 18
ΗΜΕΡ/DATE: 24/08/2002 ΩΡΑ/TIME: 17:26:12
ΚΑΤ/CAT: 2 CASH
ΤΙΜΗ/TAR: 1.40 EUR

ΑΡ.ΑΠΟΔ/TICK.NO: 1132
ΚΑΛΟ & ΑΣΦΑΛΕΣ ΤΑΞΙΔΙ / HAVE A NICE & SAFE TRIP
10240817261202

▼ Toll booth

If you break down

For roadside help, dial 104. The Automobile and Touring Club of Greece provides 24-hour information to foreign tourists on 174.

can you help me?
*bor**ee**te na me voeeth**ee**sete*
μπορείτε να με βοηθήσετε;

my car has broken down
*to aftok**ee**neet**o** moo kh**a**lase*
το αυτοκίνητό μου χάλασε

I'm on my own *(female)*
***ee**me m**o**nee moo*
είμαι μόνη μου

there are children in the car
***e**kho pedy**a** sto aftok**ee**neeto*
έχω παιδιά στο αυτοκίνητο

the car is...
*to aftok**ee**neeto **ee**ne...*
το αυτοκίνητο είναι...

a blue Fiat
***e**na ble Fiat*
ένα μπλε Fiat

registration number...
*o areethm**o**s keekloforee**ea**s...*
ο αριθμός κυκλοφορίας...

You can park by the roadside in small towns. In bigger places there will be various restrictions. A tow-away sign makes the situation fairly obvious, but other signs may be less easy to be sure about. If in doubt, ask before parking, as fines are high. The safest place to park in a big town is a 'parking' where you pay a fixed amount for a fixed length of time. In Athens you can leave your car long-term in a technologically operated 'robot' car-park, where it will be completely safe. Parking meters are very rarely seen.

▲ **NO PARKING** ▼

▼ **PARKING** *50m right*

▲ *Parking*
ΔΕΧΟΜΕΘΑ = *receiving*
ΑΥΤΟΚΙΝΗΤΑ = *cars*
ΔΙΑΝΥΚΤΕΡΕΥΕΙ = *open all night*

Underground parking (private) ▲

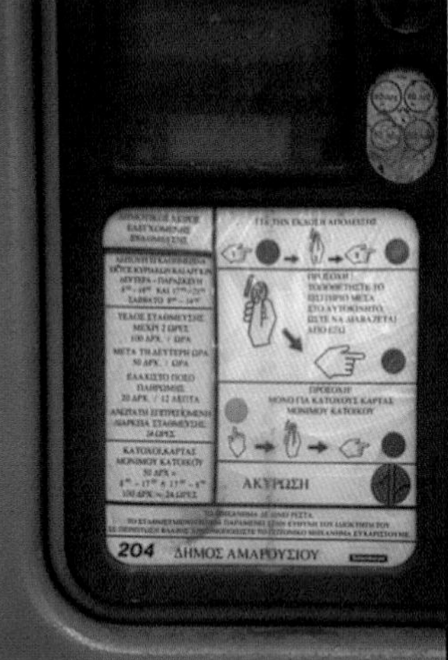

◀ There are not many pay-and-display parking meters in Greece, and you will probably find them only in Athens. Instructions for use are the same as the meters in the UK.

can I park here?
*bor**o** na park**a**ro edh**o***
μπορώ να παρκάρω εδώ;

where is the best place to park?
*poo **ee**ne kal**ee**tera na park**a**ro*
πού είναι καλύτερα να παρκάρω;

how long can I park here?
*ya p**o**see **o**ra bor**o** na park**a**ro edh**o***
για πόση ώρα μπορώ να παρκάρω εδώ;

do I need a parking ticket?
*khree**a**zome k**a**rta st**a**thmefsees*
χρειάζομαι κάρτα στάθμευσης;

is there a car park?
*eep**a**rkhee k**a**pyo p**a**rking*
υπάρχει κάποιο πάρκινγκ;

Petrol is relatively cheap and diesel even less. Opening hours of petrol stations vary, but they are plentiful and many open all day and into the evening. The attendant will fill your tank – there is no self-service. Filling stations also have air, oil, water and sometimes a carwash and vacuum cleaner, and some will mend punctures.

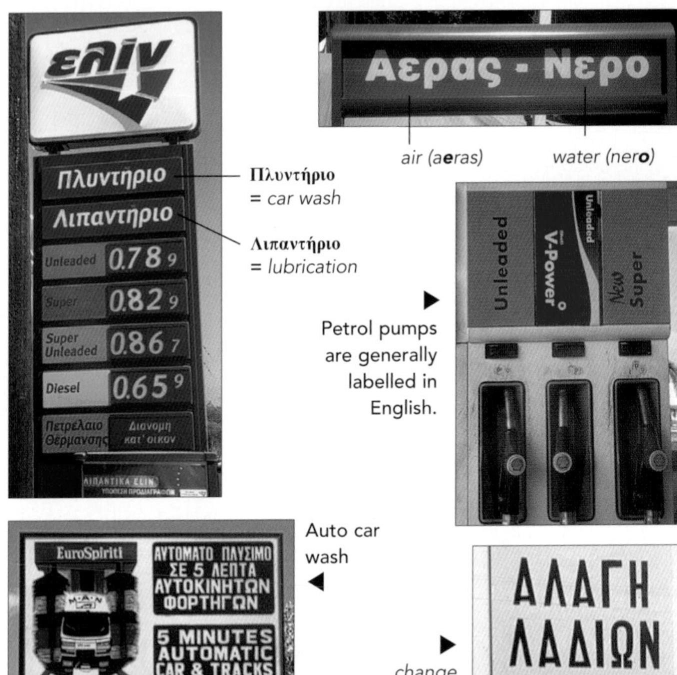

Πλυντήριο = *car wash*

Λιπαντήριο = *lubrication*

*air (a**e**ras)* *water (ner**o**)*

▶ Petrol pumps are generally labelled in English.

Auto car wash ◀

▶ *change of oil free of charge*

talking

is there a petrol station near here?
*eep**a**rkhee venzeen**a**dheeko edh**o** kond**a***
υπάρχει βενζινάδικο εδώ κοντά;

fill it up, please
*yem**ee**ste to parakal**o***
γεμίστε το, παρακαλώ

unleaded
*am**o**leevdhee*
αμόλυβδη

20 euros worth of unleaded petrol
***ee**kosee evr**o** am**o**leevdhee venz**ee**nee*
είκοσι ευρώ αμόλυβδη βενζίνη

You can find all the main dealerships in the major towns. There are also lots of smaller garages and auto-electricians. It's a good idea to ask the price of the repair first, as in any country. If you break down, there are a number of companies you can call, two of which are ELPA (tel 104) and Express Service (tel 154). Check their rates rates before you ask them to come out.

▲ Express Service and ELPA are breakdown services like the AA. Non-members can also phone for help but will pay a supplement.

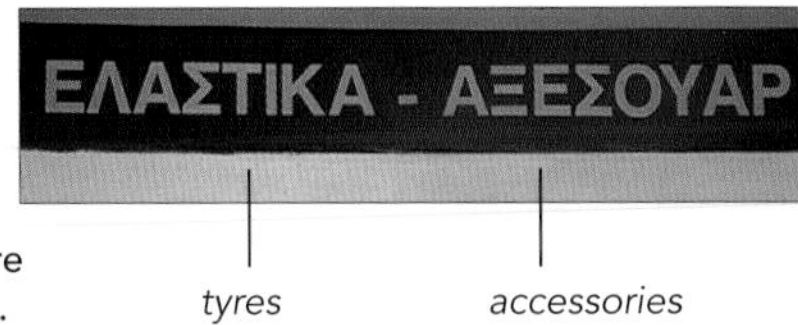

tyres *accessories*

I've broken down
khalase to aftokeeneeto moo
χάλασε το αυτοκίνητό μου

where is the nearest garage? *(for repairs)*
poo eene to pyo kondeeno garaz
πού είναι το πιο κοντινό γκαράζ;

is it serious?
eene sovaro
είναι σοβαρό;

the ... doesn't work properly
o/ee/to ... dhen dhoolevee kala
ο/η/το ... δεν δουλεύει καλά

the ... don't work properly
ee/ta ... dhen dhoolevoon kala
οι/τα ... δεν δουλεύουν καλά

I don't have a spare tyre
dhen ekho rezerva
δεν έχω ρεζέρβα

have you the parts?
ekhete ta andalakteeka
έχετε τα ανταλλακτικά;

could you please help me to change the tyre
boreete na me voeetheesete na alakso lasteekho
μπορείτε να με βοηθήσετε να αλλάξω λάστιχο;

when will it be ready?
pote tha eene eteemo
πότε θα είναι έτοιμο;

how much will it cost?
poso tha kosteesee
πόσο θα κοστίσει;

the car won't start
ee meekhanee dhen ksekeena
η μηχανή δεν ξεκινά

the battery is flat
ee batareea eene adheea
η μπαταρία είναι άδεια

the engine is overheating
afksanete ee thermokraseea tees mekhanees
αυξάνεται η θερμοκρασία της μηχανής

I have a flat tyre
me epyase lasteekho
με έπιασε λαστιχό

can you replace the windscreen?
boreete na ftyaksete to parbreez
μπορείτε να φτιάξετε το παρμπρίζ;

SHOPPING

When you go into a shop, especially a small one, it is polite to say ***kaleemera*** *or* ***ya sas*** *to the shopkeeper (even* ***tee kanete*** *if you're feeling really daring!) before asking /looking for what you want, as Greece is a much more 'personal' part of the world than more northernly countries. Our impersonal approach can sometimes seem rude! Shops generally open in the morning (8–9 am until 1–2 pm) and again in the evening (approx 5–8 pm). They close in the afternoon and all day on Sundays. However, in busy tourist areas they usually open all day every day (including Sunday) during the summer.*

keywords

φούρνος
*f**oo**rnos*
baker's

κρεοπωλείο
*krayopol**ee**o*
butcher's

ιχθυοπωλείο
*eetheeopol**ee**o*
fish shop

παντοπωλείο
*pandopol**ee**o*
grocer's

μανάβικο
*man**a**veeko*
greengrocer's

καπνοπωλείο
*kapnopol**ee**o*
tobacconist's

ζαχαροπλαστείο
*zakharoplast**ee**o*
cake shop

▲ **BAKERY** Bread is baked freshly every day at the baker's shop. For a big loaf, ask for **ένα κιλό** ***e**na keel**o*** (a kilo loaf). For a small loaf ask for **μισόκιλο** *mees**o**keelo* (a half kilo loaf). For a round sandwich bun ask for **ένα ψώμακι** ***e**na psom**a**kee. Many bakers sell sandwiches.* **ΑΡΤΟΣ** is the ancient Greek for bread (used in shop signs only).

butcher's

since 1942

BOOKSHOP ▶

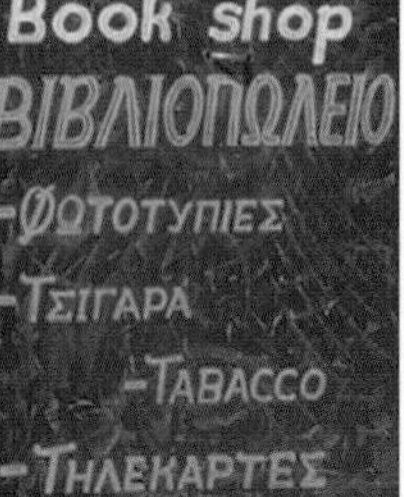

book shop

photocopies

cigarettes

phonecards

optician

contact lenses

In Greece, especially in big towns and cities, you will find well-stocked supermarkets and hypermarkets. There are both national and international chains. Some will open all day, others will open in the morning and evening only, depending on the size of the supermarket, time of year, etc. All kinds of food and drink are available in supermarkets and mini-markets. In most cases, though, fresh bread is best bought at the baker's.

◀ One of the large Greek supermarket chains

Co-operative supermarkets, like this one, tend to be cheaper.▼

◀ Special offers at the supermarket

ΤΙΜΗ *teemee* = *price*

co-op

where can I buy...? *poo boro na aghoraso...* πού μπορώ να αγοράσω...;	**matches** *speerta* σπίρτα	**bread** *psomee* ψωμί	**milk** *ghala* γάλα
do you have...? *ekhete...* έχετε...;	**milk** *ghala* γάλα	**bread rolls** *psomakeea* ψωμάκια	

I'm looking for a present
psakhno ya ena dhoro
ψάχνω για ένα δώρο

how does it cost?
poso kosteezee
πόσο κοστίζει;

is there a market?
ekhee laeekee aghora
έχει λαϊκή αγορά;

I'd like a good wine
tha eethela ena kalo krasee
θα ήθελα ένα καλό κρασί

can I pay with this card?
boro na pleeroso me aftee teen karta
μπορώ να πληρώσω με αυτή την κάρτα;

which day?
pya mera
ποια μέρα;

talking talking

*Quantities are expressed in kilos and grams. One kilo (**keelo**) is roughly equivalent to 2lb; half a kilo (**meeso keelo**) is equivalent to 1lb. If you want roughly a quarter (1/4 lb) of something, ask for 100 grams (**ekato gramareea**). If you want to ask for ham, cheese, salami, etc in slices, ask for **fetes**. 10 slices is **dheka fetes**. Many towns have a weekly market which is great for fresh, local produce. It's best to go good and early. As well as food, markets sell clothes, shoes and all kinds of household items. It's a lot of fun, too!*

◀ Fruit and vegetables are generally sold by the kilo, although larger items, such as melons, are sold individually. Small supermarkets/mini-markets may well have no fish/meat or fruit/vegetables, so you have to get these from the fishmonger/butcher or greengrocer.

◀ Butcher's stall in the market.
ΜΟΣΧΑΡΙ *(moskh**a**ree) beef*
ΚΥΜΑΣ *(keem**a**s) mince*
ΧΟΙΡΙΝΟ *(kheereen**o**) pork*
ΜΠΡΙΖΟΛΑ *(bree**zo**la) chop*

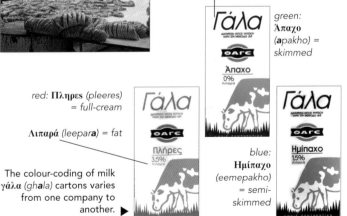

milk

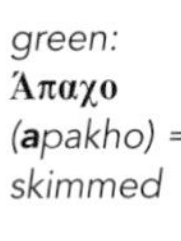

green: **Άπαχο** *(**a**pakho) = skimmed*

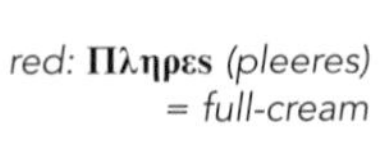

red: **Πληρες** *(pleeres) = full-cream*

Λιπαρά *(leepar**a**) = fat*

The colour-coding of milk **γάλα** *(gh**a**la)* cartons varies from one company to another. ▶

blue: **Ημίπαχο** *(eemepakho) = semi-skimmed*

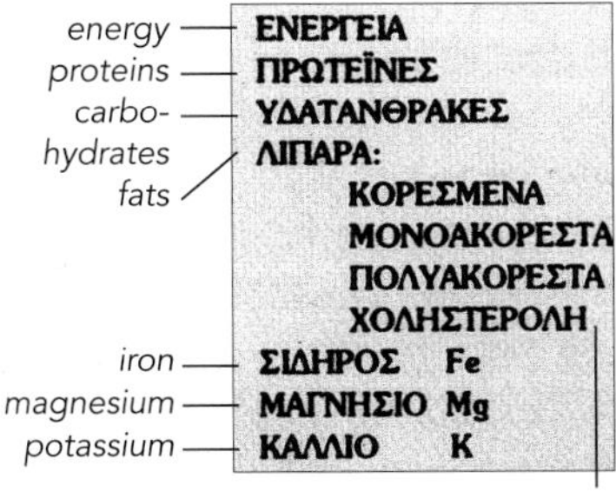

▼ EAT BEFORE

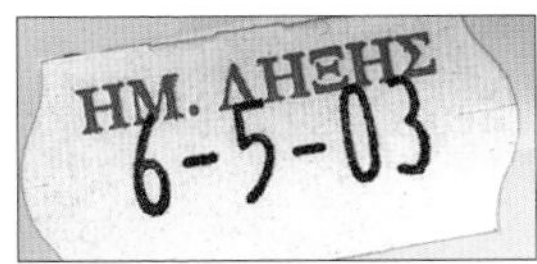

▲ *children's biscuits, with vitamins, iron and calcium*

a piece of cheese
ena komatee teeree
ένα κομμάτι τυρί

a little more
leegho akoma
λίγο ακόμα

a little less
leeghotero
λιγότερο

that's enough, thanks
ftanee efkhareesto
φτάνει ευχαριστώ

a portion of macaroni
meea mereedha pasteetseeo
μία μερίδα παστίτσιο

that's enough, thanks
ftanee efkhareesto
φτάνει ευχαριστώ

10 slices of ham
deka fetes zambon
δέκα φέτας ζαμπόν

a litre of milk
ena leetro ghala
ένα λίτρο γάλα

bottled water
emfeealomeno nero
εμφιαλωμένο νερό

sparkling	**still**
aeryookho	*mee aeryookho*
αεριούχο	μη αεριούχο

a tin of tomatoes
ena kootee domates
ένα κουτί ντομάτες

half a kilo of green beans
meeso kilo fasolakya
μισό κιλό φασολάκια

a kilo of potatoes
ena keelo patates
ένα κιλό πατάτες

two cheese pies
dheeo teeropeetes
δύο τυρόπιτες

ΚΑΡΑΜΕΛΛΕΣ LIHN ΧΩΡΙΣ ΖΑΧΑΡΗ (ΜΕ ΣΟΡΒΙΤΗ)
ΜΕ ΑΡΩΜΑ ΦΡΟΥΤΟΥ

◀ *Sweets –* **χωρίς ζάχαρη** *(khorees zakharee) without sugar*

Everyday Foods

biscuits τα μπισκότα *beesk**o**ta*
bread το ψωμί *psom**ee***
bread roll τα ψωμάκια *psom**a**keea*
butter το βούτυρο *v**oo**teero*
cereal τα δημητριακά *dheemeetreeak**a***
cheese το τυρί *teer**ee***
cheese pie η τυρόπιτα *teer**o**peeta*
chicken το κοτόπουλο *kot**o**poolo*
chips οι πατάτες τηγανητές *pat**a**tes teegh**a**neetes*
chocolate η σοκολάτα *sokol**a**ta*
coffee *(instant)* το Νεσκαφέ *Nescafe®*
cream η κρέμα *kr**e**ma*
crisps τα πατατάκια *patat**a**keea*
eggs τα αβγά *avgh**a***
fish το ψάρι *ps**a**ree*
flour το αλεύρι *al**e**vree*
ham το ζαμπόν *zamb**o**n*
herbal tea το τσάι από βότανα *ts**a**ee ap**o** v**o**tana*
honey το μέλι *m**e**lee*
jam η μαρμελάδα *marmel**a**dha*
lamb το αρνάκι *arn**a**kee*
margarine η μαργαρίνη *marghar**ee**nee*
marmalade η μαρμελάδα πορτοκάλι *marmel**a**dha portok**a**lee*
meat balls οι κεφτέδες *keft**e**dhes*
milk το γάλα *gh**a**la*
mustard η μουστάρδα *moost**a**rdha*
olive oil το λάδι ελιάς *l**a**dhee elee**a**s*
orange juice ο χυμός πορτοκάλι *kheem**o**s portok**a**lee*
pasta τα ζυμαρικά *zeemareek**a***
pepper το πιπέρι *peep**e**ree*
pork το χοιρινό *kheereen**o***
rice το ρύζι *r**ee**zee*
salt το αλάτι *al**a**tee*
spinach pie η σπανακόπιτα *spanak**o**peeta*
sugar η ζάχαρη *z**a**kharee*
tea το τσάι *ts**a**ee*
tomatoes *(tin)* οι ντομάτες κονσέρβα *dom**a**tes kons**e**rva*
tuna ο τόνος *t**o**nos*
vegetable oil το φυτικό λάδι *feeteek**o** l**a**dhee*
vinegar το ξύδι *ks**ee**dhee*
yoghurt το γιαούρτι *ya**oo**rtee*

Fruit

apples τα μήλα *m**ee**la*

apricots το βερύκοκκα *ver**ee**koka*

bananas οι μπανάνες *ban**a**nes*

cherries τα κεράσια *ker**a**seea*

figs τα σύκα *s**ee**ka*

grapefruit το γκρέιπφρουτ *gr**ei**pfroot*

grapes τα σταφύλια *staf**ee**leea*

lemon το λεμόνι *lem**o**nee*

melon το πεπόνι *pep**o**nee*

nectarines τα νεκταρίνια *nektar**ee**neea*

oranges τα πορτοκάλια *portok**a**leea*

peaches τα ροδάκινα *rodh**a**keena*

pears τα αχλάδια *akhl**a**dheea*

pineapple ο ανανάς *o anan**a**s*

plums τα δαμάσκηνα *dham**a**skeena*

strawberries οι φράουλες *fr**a**ooles*

watermelon το καρπούζι *karp**oo**zee*

Vegetables

asparagus τα σπαράγγια *spar**a**ngeea*

aubergine η μελιτζάνα *meleetz**a**na*

basil ο βασιλικός *vaseeleek**o**s*

bean (haricot) το φασόλι *fas**o**lee*

(broad) το κουκί *kook**ee***

cabbage το λάχανο *l**a**khano*

carrots τα καρότα *kar**o**ta*

cauliflower το κουνουπίδι *koonoop**ee**dhee*

celery το σέλινο *s**e**leeno*

chickpeas τα ρεβίθια *rev**ee**theea*

courgettes τα κολοκυθάκια *kolokeeth**a**keea*

cucumber το αγγούρι *ang**oo**ree*

eggplant η μελιτζάνα *meleetz**a**na*

garlic το σκόρδο *sk**o**rdho*

green beans τα φασολάκια *fasol**a**keea*

lettuce το μαρούλι *mar**oo**lee*

mushrooms τα μανιτάρια *maneet**a**reea*

olives οι ελιές *ely**e**s*

onions τα κρεμμύδια *krem**ee**dheea*

parsley ο μαϊντανός *maeendan**o**s*

peas ο αρακάς *arak**a**s*

peppers οι πιπεριές *peeperee-**e**s*

potatoes οι πατάτες *pat**a**tes*

spinach το σπανάκι *span**a**kee*

tomatoes οι ντομάτες *dom**a**tes*

zucchini τα κολοκυθάκια *kolokeeth**a**keea*

In the cities there are many high-quality department stores. One of the most popular of these is the 'Hondos Centre' which has branches throughout Greece.

keywords

πολυκατάστημα
*poleekat**a**steema*
department store

υπόγειο
*eep**o**yo*
basement

ισόγειο
*ees**o**yo*
ground floor

πρώτος όροφος
*pr**o**tos **o**rofos*
1st floor

κατάστημα
*kat**a**steema*
department

ηλεκτρικά είδη
*eelektreek**a** **ee**dee*
electrical goods

κοσμήματα
*kosm**ee**mata*
jewellery

γυναικεία
*yeenek**ee**a*
ladies'

ανδρικά
*andreek**a***
men's

παιδικά
*pedeek**a***
children's

◀ **SHOE SHOP** The word for shoes is παπούτσια (*pap**oo**t-seea*) and for sandals σανδάλια (*sand**a**leea*).

▲ **4TH FLOOR** (*o**rofos*)

Μόνο — (*m**o**no*) only
1.230 €
το άτομο — (*to **a**toma*) per person

SALE ▼

ΕΚΠΤΩΣΕΙΣ
30%

FREE GIFT ▶ (*d**o**po*)

Δώρο!

◀ The rural answer to the department store! In the country areas and smaller villages you will sometimes find vans like this selling clothes, food, linen, chairs and tables, even baby chicks. They have a megaphone to advertise their wares.

talking

where can I find...?
poo na vro...
πού να βρω...;

batteries for this
*batar**ee**es yee aft**o***
μπαταρίες γι' αυτό

toys
*peghn**ee**dhya*
παιγνίδια

shoes
*pap**oo**tsya*
παπούτσια

Women's clothes sizes

UK/Australia	8	10	12	14	16	18	20	22
Europe	36	38	40	42	44	46	48	50
US/Canada	6	8	10	12	14	16	18	20

Men's clothes sizes (suits)

UK/US/Canada	36	38	40	42	44	46
Europe	46	48	50	52	54	56
Australia	92	97	102	107	112	117

Shoes

UK/Australia	2	3	4	5	6	7	8	9	10	11
Europe	35	36	37	38	39	41	42	43	45	46
US/Canada women	4	5	6	7	8	9	10	11	12	-
US/Canada men	3	4	5	6	7	8	9	10	11	12

Children's Shoes

UK/US/Canada	0	1	2	3	4	5	6	7	8	9	10	11
Europe	15	17	18	19	20	22	23	24	26	27	28	29

can I try this on?
*bor**o** na to dhokeem**a**so*
μπορώ να το δοκιμάσω;

it's too big for me
*moo **ee**ne megh**a**lo*
μου είναι μεγάλο

it's too small for me
*moo **ee**ne pol**ee** sten**o***
μου είναι πολύ στενό

it's too expensive
ee**ne pol**ee** akreev**o
είναι πολύ ακριβό

I'll take this one
*tha to p**a**ro*
θα το πάρω

I take a size ...
*for**o** ... n**oo**mero*
φορώ ... νούμερο

where are the changing rooms?
*poo **ee**ne ta dhokeemast**ee**reea*
πού είναι τα δοκιμαστήρια;

have you a smaller one?
***e**khete meekr**o**tero n**oo**mero*
έχετε μικρότερο νούμερο;

have you a larger one?
***e**khete meghal**ee**tero n**oo**mero*
έχετε μεγαλύτερο νούμερο;

do you have this in my size?
***e**khete aft**o** sto n**oo**mer**o** moo*
έχετε αυτό στο νούμερό μου;

can you give me a discount?
*tha moo k**a**nete kal**ee**teree teem**ee***
θα μου κάνετε καλύτερη τιμή;

I like it
*moo ar**e**see*
μου αρέσει

I don't like it
*dhen moo ar**e**see*
δεν μου αρέσει

*Post Offices open in the morning, from 8-9 am until 1-2 pm, according to the location. They do not open in the afternoon or on Saturdays, with the exception of the main Post Office in Syntagma Square in Athens, which opens on Saturdays and Sundays in summer. Stamps can also be bought at kiosks (**pereeptero**) and at shops selling postcards.*

▲ Post Offices may be signposted

▲ Opening hours are sometimes printed in English. Post offices usually open only in the morning.

▶ Red post-boxes are for express mail in the Athens area. Yellow boxes are for general post, and often detail collection times.

talking

where is the post office?
*poo **ee**ne to takheedhrom**ee**o*
πού είναι το ταχυδρομείο;

do you sell stamps?
*ekhete ghrammat**o**seema*
έχετε γραμματόσημα;

where can I buy stamps?
*poo bor**o** na aghor**a**so ghramat**o**seema*
πού μπορώ να αγοράσω γραμματόσημα;

10 stamps
*dh**e**ka ghramat**o**seema*
δέκα γραμματόσημα

for postcards
*ya k**a**rtes*
για κάρτες

urgent mail
*ep**ee**ghon*
επείγον

to Britain
*ya angl**ee**a*
για Αγγλία

to America
*ya amereek**ee***
για Αμερική *amereek**ee***

I want to send this letter registered post
*th**e**lo na st**ee**lo aft**o** to ghr**a**ma seesteem**e**no*
θέλω να στείλω αυτό το γράμμα συστημένο

how much is it to send this parcel?
*p**o**so kost**ee**zee na st**ee**lo aft**o** to pak**e**to*
πόσο κοστίζει να στείλω αυτό το πακέτο;

by air
*aeroporeek**o**s*
αεροπορικώς

Many photographers develop and print in their shops

Pay attention to prohibitions: photography is not allowed in some areas and laws may be strictly enforced.

Photo booths can be found in airports, some railway stations and larger shopping centres.

keywords

φίλμ
feelm
film

μπαταρία
batareea
battery

ματ
mat
mat

γυαλιστερό
waleestero
glossy

εμφάνιση
emfaneesee
developing

φωτογραφίες
fotografeees
photographs

βιντεοκάμερα
videokamera
camcorder

κασσέτες
kasetes
tapes

talking

where can I buy...?
poo boro na aghoraso...
πού μπορώ να αγοράσω...;

film
film
φιλμ

tapes for a camcorder?
kasetes ya videocamera
κασέτες για βιντεοκάμερα;

a colour film
ena enkhromo film
ένα έγχρωμο φιλμ

24
eekoseetesaree
εικοσιτεσσάρι

36
treeantaeksaree
τριανταεξάρι

have you batteries for this camcorder?
ekhete batareees yaftee tee videocamera
έχετε μπαταρίες γι'αυτή τη βιντεοκάμερα;

is it OK to take pictures here?
peerazee an traveekso fotoghrafeees edho
πειράζει αν τραβήξω φωτογραφίες εδώ;

would you take a picture of us, please?
boreete na mas traveeksete meea fotoghrafeea parakalo
μπορείτε να μας τραβήξετε μία φωτογραφία, παρακαλώ;

PHONES

Payphones abound in Greece – just look for the blue sign. The instructions are easy to follow. Cards are easier to use than coins – ask for **teelekarta**. *The cheapest of these cost 3 euros. You can get cards from supermarkets, kiosks, newsagents and Post Offices. To phone direct from a hotel phone will cost you a lot more than if you use a phonecard. Some kiosks have a small payphone on the counter – the card goes in at the side. The telephone offices (OTE) have cardphones too, and it may be possible to have someone call you back on a phone in the OTE office.*

◀ Public phones take coins and cards.

A Greek pay-phone ▶ Pictograms show you how to use the phone. The easiest way to phone is by using a phonecard, available at kiosks, newsagents and some supermarkets.

a phonecard
meea teelekarta
μία τηλεκάρτα

Mr Antonionou, please
ton keereeo antoneeon parakalo
τον κύριο Αντωνίου, παρακαλώ

can I speak to...?
boro na meeleeso ston / steen...
μπορώ να μιλήσω στον / στην...;

do you have phonecards?
ekhete teeleekartes
έχετε τηλεκάρτες

extension ..., please
esotereeko ... parakalo
εσωτερικό ... παρακαλώ

this is Caroline
eemay ee caroline
είμαι η caroline

can I have an outside line
boro na ekho meea eksotereekee ghrammee
μπορώ να έχω μία εξωτερική γραμμή

what is your phone number?
pyos eene o areethmos too teelefonoo soo
ποιός είναι ο αριθμός του τηλεφώνου σου;

my phone number is...
o areethmos too teelefonoo moo eene...
ο αριθμός του τηλεφώνου μου είναι...

▲ Look for this sign if you need a phone-box. OTE is the Greek phone company.

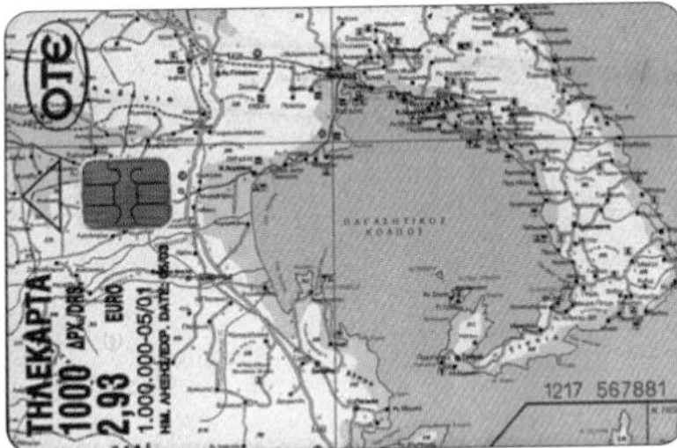

▲ OTE phonecard. The cards are economical and easy to use.

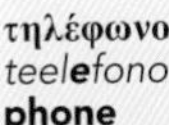

keywords keywords

τηλέφωνο
*teel**e**fono*
phone

τήλεκαρτα
*t**ee**lekarta*
phonecard

κινητό
*keeneet**o***
mobile

κωδικός
*kodeek**o**s*
code

κατάλογος
*kat**a**logos*
phone book

χρυσός οδηγός
*khrees**o**s odeeg**o**s*
yellow pages

πληροφορίες καταλόγου
*pleerofor**ee**es katal**o**goo*
directory enquiries

International dialling codes
UK 00 44
USA & Canada 00 1
Australia 00 61
Greece 00 30

τηλ: ◀ Abbreviation for tel:

YELLOW PAGES ▶

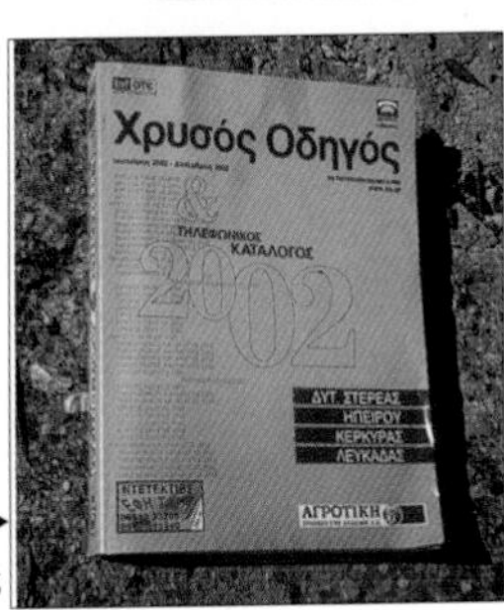

talking

I'll call later
*tha p**a**ro argh**o**tera*
θα πάρω αργότερα

do you have a mobile?
e**khete keeneet**o
έχετε κινητό;

I'll call back tomorrow
*tha ksanap**a**ro **a**vreeo*
θα ξαναπάρω αύριο

what is the number?
*pyo **ee**ne to n**oo**mero*
ποιο είναι το νούμερο;

my mobile number is...
*o areethm**o**s too keeneet**oo** moo teelef**o**noo **ee**ne...*
ο αριθμός του κινητού μου τηλεφώνου είναι...

E-MAIL, INTERNET, FAX

It is usually easy to find an Internet cafe to check your e-mail messages etc. National and local tourist information can be accessed via the Internet. Greek web-sites end in gr. Rates at Internet cafes will vary so ask beforehand about the price.

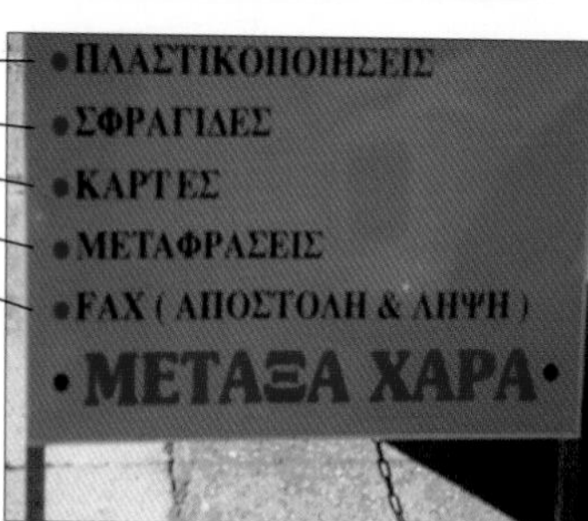

laminating
stamps
cards
translating
fax (sending & receiving)

◀ An internet café

The Greek ▶ for 'at' is **παπάκη** *papakee* (which literally means little duck).

talking talking

I want to send an e-mail
thelo na steelo ena email
θέλω να στείλω ένα e-mail

did you get my e-mail?
peerate to e-mail moo
πήρατε το e-mail μου;

do you have e-mail?
ekhete e-mail
έχετε e-mail;

what is your e-mail address?
tee eene ee e-mail dhee-eftheensee sas
τι είναι η e-mail διεύθυνσή σας;

how do you spell it?
pos grafete
πώς γράφεται;

my e-mail address is...
ee e-mail dhee-eftheensee moo eene..
η e-mail διεύθυνσή μου είναι...

caroline dot zmith@harpercollins dot co dot uk
caroline teleea zmith papakee harpercollins teleea co teleea uk
caroline τελεία zmith παπάκη harpercollins τελεία co τελεία uk

do you have a website?
ekhete website
έχετε website;

can I book by e-mail?
boro na kano krateesee me e-mail
μπορώ να κάνω κράτηση με e-mail;

▲ Internet café interior

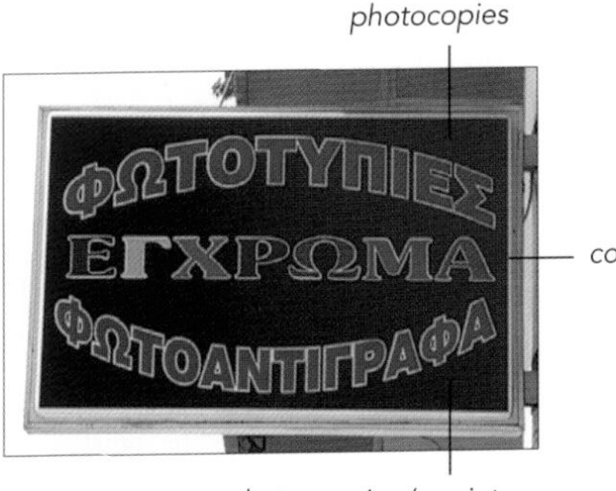

keywords

οθόνη
othonee
screen

πληκτρολόγιο
pleektrologeeo
keyboard

επισύναψη
epeeseenapse e
attachment

κατέβασμα
katevasma
download

ποντίκι
ponteekee
mouse

ιστοσελίδα
eestoseleeda
website

τελεία
teleea
dot

βοήθεια
voeetheea
help

talking

I want to send a fax
thelo na steelo ena fax
θέλω να στείλω ένα φαξ

what's your fax number?
pyo eene to noomero too fax sas
ποιο είναι το νούμερο του φαξ σας;

please resend your fax
parakalo ksanasteelte to fax sas
παρακαλώ ξαναστείλτε το φαξ σας

your fax is constantly engaged
to fax sas eene seenekhos kateeleemeno
το φαξ σας είναι συνεχώς κατειλημένο

where can I send a fax from?
poo boro na steelo ena fax
πού μπορώ να στείλω ένα φαξ;

do you have a fax?
ekhete fax
έχετε φαξ;

did you get my fax?
lavate to fax moo
λάβατε το φαξ μου;

I can't read it
dhen boro na to dheeavaso
δεν μπορώ να το διαβάσω

OUT & ABOUT

Tourist offices will have information on all the local sites and places of interest. Check on the opening times of archaeological sites and museums to avoid disappointment! Try to avoid going in the heat of the day in summer, though.

◀ **TOURIST INFORMATION OFFICE**

▲ **SWIMMING POOL**

▲ Street signs to places of interest are normally brown.

◀ You can rent motor-bikes and scooters in many places. It's great fun and a good way to explore Greece. Be sure to check out the insurance situation carefully and make sure your bike is roadworthy.

◀ Local tourist information offices have free brochures, leaflets and maps.

▲ Signs on the beach will often be in English

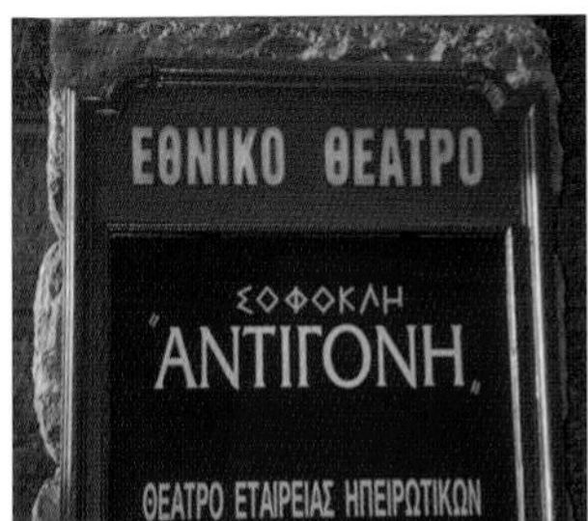

◀ Throughout the summer you see Greek plays and other shows performed in the ancient theatres.

Tickets for museums and visitor attractions often have English translations, as in this ticket for the Acropolis. ▼

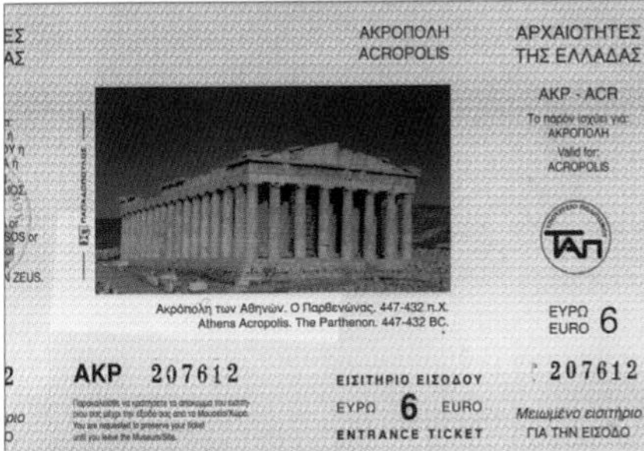

keywords

βόλτα
*v**o**lta*
walk, trek

ορειβασία
*orevas**ee**a*
mountaineering

εκκλησία
*eklees**ee**a*
church

ναός
*na**o**s*
temple

παλάτι
*pal**a**tee*
palace

θέατρο
*th**a**yatro*
theatre

σινεμά
*seenem**a***
cinema

δημαρχείο
*deemarh**ee**o*
town hall

talking

where is the tourist office?
*poo **ee**ne to tooreesteek**o** ghraf**ee**o*
πού είναι το τουριστικό γραφείο;

we want to visit...
*th**e**loome na epeeskeft**oo**me...*
θέλουμε να επισκεφτούμε...

have you any leaflets?
*ekhete odheey**ee**es*
έχετε οδηγίες;

are there any excursions?
*eep**a**rkhoon orghaneesm**e**nes ekdhrom**e**s*
υπάρχουν οργανομένες εκδρομές;

when does it leave?
*p**o**te f**e**vghoon*
πότε φεύγουν;

where does it leave from?
*ap**o** poo f**e**vghoon*
από που φεύγουν;

how much is it to get in?
*p**o**so kost**ee**zee ee seemetokh**ee***
πόσο κοστίζει η συμμετοχή;

is it open to the public?
ee**ne aneekt**o** sto keen**o
είναι ανοικτό στο κοινό;

There is plenty of excellent walking and mountaineering to be done all over Greece, with clearly marked walking trails and refuge huts. The highest and most spectacular mountain is Mount Olympus, but there are many other scenic walks and climbs. Maps are available, showing you the National Parks and other areas where you can walk or drive.

▲ Panathenaikos football ground

◀ ▲ Greek dancing is popular

where can we...?
*poo bor**oo**me na...*
πού μπορούμε να...;

play tennis
*p**e**ksoome t**e**nnis*
παίξουμε τέννις

play golf
*p**e**ksoome golf*
παίξουμε γκολφ

hire bikes
*neeky**a**soome podh**ee**lata*
νοικιάσουμε ποδήλατα

how much is it...?
*p**o**so kost**ee**zee...*
πόσο κοστίζει...;

per hour
*teen **o**ra*
την ώρα

per day
*tee m**e**ra*
τη μέρα

is there a swimming pool?
*eep**a**rkhee pees**ee**na*
υπάρχει πισίνα;

can you recommend a quiet beach?
*ks**e**rete k**a**pya **ee**seekhee paral**ee**a*
ξέρετε κάποια ήσυχη παραλία;

is there a pool?
*ekhee pees**ee**na*
έχει πισίνα;

are there strong currents?
*eep**a**rkhoon dheenat**a** r**e**vmata*
υπάρχουν δυνατά ρεύματα;

is it a nudist beach?
***ee**ne paral**ee**a yeemneest**o**n*
είναι παραλία γυμνιστών;

There are many ferries to the islands and the high-speed 'flying dolphins' (**ιπτάμενο δελφίνι** *teeptameno dhelf**ee**nee*) *provide a fast service. You can visit their website* ***www.dolphins.gr.***

◀ Prices are listed for various ticket types to different destinations.- There are many day-trips available.

You can buy ferry tickets from travel agents or at the quayside. ▼

High-speed boats provide a fast route to the islands. ▼

is there a hydrofoil to...?
*eep**a**rkhee eept**a**meno dhelf**ee**nee ya...*
υπάρχει ιπτάμενο δελφίνι για...;

when is the next boat?
*p**o**te f**e**vyee to ep**o**meno pl**ee**o*
πότε φεύγει το επόμενο πλοίο;

when does the ferry leave?
*p**o**te f**e**vyee to fereeb**o**t*
πότε φεύγει το φεριμπότ;

can we hire a boat?
*bor**oo**me na neeky**a**soome m**ee**a v**a**rka*
μπορούμε να νοικιάσουμε μία βάρκα;

is there a boat to...?
*eep**a**rkhee pl**ee**o ya...*
υπάρχει πλοίο για...;

talking

ACCOMMODATION

In major cities there are hotels classified by the star system. In general you are more likely to find hotels categorized in the Greek way: **α Α** *(alpha) = 1st class;* **β Β** *(veeta) = 2nd class;* **γ Γ** *(gamma) = 3rd class. Most of these will also provide breakfast if you require it. The Tourist Offices will advise you about hotels and other accommodation. You can also stay in rooms, small guest-houses and self-catering apartments.*

▲ Large hotels use the star system, but the traditional Greek categories are **Α, Β, Γ** classes, for accommodation.

◀ **ΞΕΝΟΔΟΧΕΙΟ** *hotel*
ΔΩΜΑΤΙΑ *rooms*
ΔΙΑΜΕΡΙΣΜΑΤΑ *apartments*
ΚΛΙΜΑΤΙΣΜΟΣ *air conditioning*
ΠΙΣΙΝΑ *swimming pool*
ΜΠΑΡ *bar*
ΠΑΡΚΙΝΚ *parking*
100m ΑΠΟ ΤΗΝ ΑΚΤΗ *100m from the beach*

Booking in advance

The tourist office can help booking hotels and rooms.

I want to book a room...
thelo na kleeso ena dhomateeo...
θέλω να κλείσω ένα δωμάτιο...

double
dheekleeno
δίκλινο

single
monokleeno
μονόκλινο

a family room
ena dhomateeo ya eekoyenya
ένα δωμάτιο για οικογένεια

with bathroom
me banyo
με μπάνιο

with shower
me doos
με ντους

with a double bed
me dheeplo krevatee
με διπλό κρεβάτι

twin-bedded
me dheeo krevateea
με δύο κρεβάτια

we'd like to stay ... nights
tha thelame na meenoome ... vradheea
θα θέλαμε να μείνουμε ... βράδυα

from ... till...
apo ... mekhree...
από ... μέχρι...

I booked a room
ekho kanee meea krateesee
έχω κάνει μία κράτηση

my name is...
to onoma moo eene...
το όνομά μου είναι...

HOTEL ΑΘΩΣ

▲ *Hotel Athos*

▲ The word 'Reception' always appears in English in Greek hotels.

Hotels have to post information about their services on bedroom doors. ▼

ΠΙΝΑΚΙΔΑ ΕΝΗΜΕΡΩΣΗΣ ΤΟΥ ΠΕΛΑΤΗ · GUEST INFORMATION

ΕΙΔΟΣ ΚΑΤΑΛΥΜΑΤΟΣ: TYPE OF ACCOMMODATION: ΕΠΙΠΛΩΜΕΝΑ ΔΩΜΑΤΙΑ ROOMS ΕΠΙΠΛΩΜΕΝΑ ΔΙΑΜΕΡΙΣΜΑΤΑ APARTMENTS 3

ΕΠΩΝΥΜΙΑ ΕΠΙΧΕΙΡΗΣΗΣ: NAME OF ESTABLISHMENT: ΤΟΥΣΗΣ ΑΡΙΣΤΟΤΕΛΗΣ ΚΑΤΗΓΟΡΙΑ: CLASS: Γ'

Number of Beds 2

ΤΙΜΗ ΔΩΜΑΤΙΟΥ / ΔΙΑΜΕΡΙΣΜΑΤΟΣ ΓΙΑ ΤΟ ΕΤΟΣ 199 8 ROOM / APARTMENT RATE FOR 199 8

Υψηλή περίοδος 1/7-31/8/98 High Season	Με λουτρό ΔΡΧ. With bath DRS.	15000	Χωρίς λουτρό ΔΡΧ. Without Bath DRS.	
Μέση περίοδος 1/9-31/10/98 Middle Season	Με λουτρό ΔΡΧ. With bath DRS.	12000	Χωρίς λουτρό ΔΡΧ. Without Bath DRS.	
Χαμηλή περίοδος 1/6-30/6/98 Low Season	Με λουτρό ΔΡΧ. With bath DRS.	9000	Χωρίς λουτρό ΔΡΧ. Without Bath DRS.	

Other Facilities (air conditioning) DRS. Use of common kitchen appliance DRS.

In the above room rate are included:

Hot-cold water/soap/toilet paper and if available central heating.

ΠΑΡΑΤΗΡΗΣΕΙΣ · REMARKS

ΗΜΕΡΟΜΗΝΙΑ DATE 21.5.1998

have you a room for tonight?
ekhete ena dhomateeo ya apopse
έχετε ένα δωμάτιο για απόψε;

for ... nights
ya ... neekhtes
για ... νύχτες

a single room
ena monokleeno dhomateeo
ένα μονόκλινο δωμάτιο

a double room
ena dheekleeno dhomateeo
ένα δίκλινο δωμάτιο

a room for three people
ena treekleeno dhomateeo
ένα τρίκλινο δωμάτιο

with bathroom
me banyo
με μπάνιο

with shower
me doos
με ντους

how much is it...?
poso kanee...
πόσο κάνει...;

per night
to vradhee
το βράδυ

per week
tee vdhomadha
τη βδομάδα

I'd like to see the room
tha eethela na dho to dhomateeo
θα ήθελα να δω το δωμάτιο

is there anything cheaper?
ekhete teepota ftheenotero
έχετε τίποτα φθηνότερο;

is breakfast included?
to proeeno eene steen teemee
το πρωινό είναι στην τιμή;

can you suggest somewhere else?
boreete na proteenete kapoo aloo
μπορείτε να προτείνετε κάπου αλλού;

talking talking talking

A 'garsony**e**ra' or a 'st**oo**deeo' is a small apartment. A 'deeam**e**reesma' is a medium-sized apartment. A 'dhom**a**teeo' is a room, usually without a kitchen. You will see signs for all types of accommodation, but if you are in a small place and there is no sign, just ask instead.

▲ Apartments for rent

▼ Pension or guest house

Guest House Olga
For rent : rooms and small apartments

for rent
studio apartments
air-conditioned

◀ Not all areas have facilities for recycling.

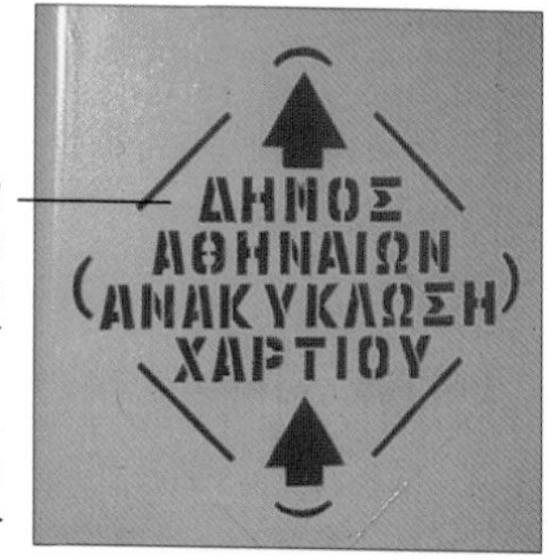

city council of Athens recycling of paper

Paper-recycling bin ▶

▲ Logo of the Hostelling International organisation at the YHA hostel in Athens. The Greek Youth Hostel Asociation is the other hostelling organisation. There are also private hostels with economical rates, especially in cities.

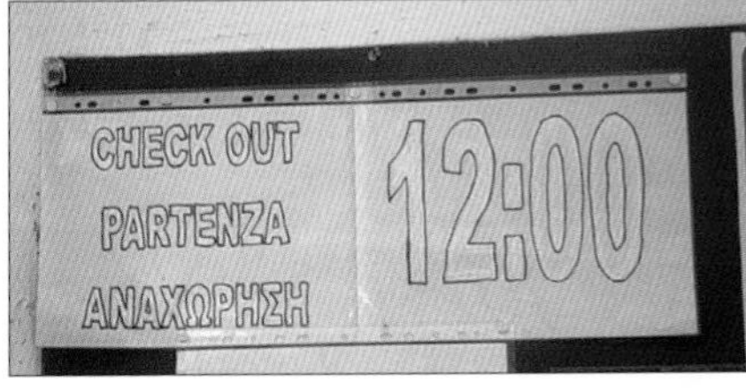

▲ Check out times vary according to where you are staying.

keywords

υγρό πλυσίματος
*eegr**o** pleesee**ee**matos*
washing-up liquid

σκόνη πλυσίματος
*sk**o**nee pleesee**ee**matos*
washing powder

σαπούνι
*sap**oo**nee*
soap

ανοικτήρι
*aneekt**ee**ree*
tin-opener

κεριά
*keree**a***
candles

σπίρτα
*sp**ee**rta*
matches

φυάλη αεριού
*fee**a**lee a-eree**oo***
gas cylinder *(large)*

γκαζάκι
*gaz**a**kee*
camping gas

talking

can we have an extra set of keys?
*bor**oo**me na **e**khoome **e**na **e**xtra set kleedhee**a***
μπορούμε να έχουμε ένα έξτρα σετ κλειδιά;

when does the cleaner come?
*p**o**te **e**rkhete ee kathar**ee**streea*
πότε έρχεται η καθαρίστρια;

is there always hot water?
e**khee p**a**nta zest**o** ner**o
έχει πάντα ζεστό νερό;

who do we contact if there are problems?
*se pee-**on** thape-ftheenth**oo**me an eep**a**rksoon provl**ee**mata*
σε ποιόν θ' απευθυνθούμε αν υπάρξουν προβλήματα;

where is the nearest supermarket?
*poo **ee**ne to kondeen**o**tero supermarket*
πού είναι το κοντινότερο supermarket;

where do we leave rubbish?
*poo pet**a**me ta skoop**ee**dheea*
που πετάμε τα σκουπίδια;

when is the rubbish collected?
*p**o**te **ee**ne ee seelogh**ee** skoopeedhee-**on***
πότε είναι η συλλογή σκουπιδιών;

what are the neighbours called?
*pos l**e**ghonte ee gh**ee**tones*
πώς λέγονται οι γείτονες;

CAMPING

There is no shortage of well-equipped campsites in Greece. Look for the tent/caravan sign, with CAMPING written in English. Prices are reasonable and facilities are good. Most campsites have hot showers (generally heated by solar power).

▲ Road sign for campsite

◀ Campsite sign

▲ In smaller places you can have clothes washed or dry-cleaned at small laundries like this, where they charge per item. In towns there are bigger versions of the same thing. Self-service launderettes do not exist.

we're looking for a campsite
psakhnoome ya thesee kamping
ψάχνουμε για θέση κάμπινγκ

have you a list of campsites?
ekhete leesta me ta kamping
έχετε λίστα με τα κάμπινγκ;

have you any vacancies?
ekhete thesees
έχετε θέσεις;

we'd like to stay for ... nights
theloome na meenoome ... vradya
θέλουμε να μείνουμε ... βράδυα

how much is it per night...?
poso kosteezee tee neekhta...
πόσο κοστίζει τη νύχτα...;

for a tent
ee skeenee
η σκηνή

per person
to atomo
το άτομο

is there a restaurant on the campsite?
eeparkhee esteeatoreeo sto camping
υπάρχει εστιατόριο στό κάμπινγκ;

how far is the beach?
poso makreea eene ee paraleea
πόσο μακριά είναι η παραλία;

can we camp here overnight?
boroome na perasoome edho tee neekhta
μπορούμε να περάσουμε εδώ τη νύχτα;

Typical pricelist for campsite ▶ Tariffs can be listed in English as well as Greek.

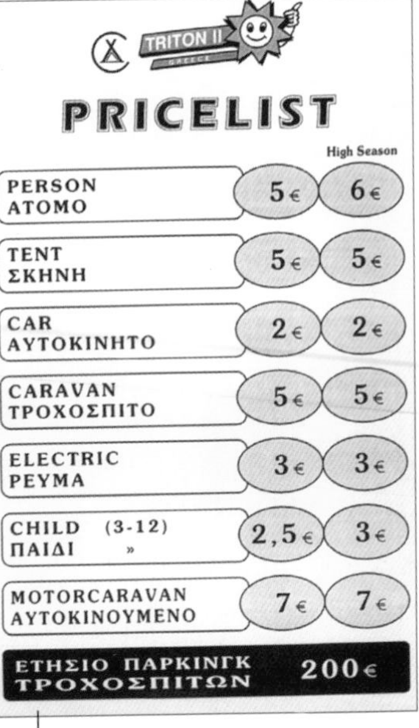

TRITON II

PRICELIST

		High Season
PERSON ΑΤΟΜΟ	5€	6€
TENT ΣΚΗΝΗ	5€	5€
CAR ΑΥΤΟΚΙΝΗΤΟ	2€	2€
CARAVAN ΤΡΟΧΟΣΠΙΤΟ	5€	5€
ELECTRIC ΡΕΥΜΑ	3€	3€
CHILD (3-12) ΠΑΙΔΙ »	2,5€	3€
MOTORCARAVAN ΑΥΤΟΚΙΝΟΥΜΕΝΟ	7€	7€
ΕΤΗΣΙΟ ΠΑΡΚΙΝΓΚ ΤΡΟΧΟΣΠΙΤΩΝ	200€	

annual parking fee for mobile homes

▲ Most sites have at least basic laundry facilities.

On-site laundrette ▼

washing machines ▼

◀ **DRY CLEANERS** are often open only in the morning

where can I do some washing?
*poo bor**o** na pl**ee**no mereek**a** r**oo**kha*
που μπορώ να πλύνω μερικά ρούχα;

do you have a laundry service?
*ekhete eepeeres**ee**a pleendeer**ee**oo*
έχετε υπηρεσία πλυντηρίου;

when will my things be ready?
*p**o**te tha **ee**ne **e**teema ta pr**a**ghmat**a** moo*
πότε θα είναι έτοιμα τα πράγματά μου;

is there a dry-cleaner's near here?
*eep**a**rkhee kathareest**ee**reeo edh**o** kond**a***
υπάρχει καθαριστήριο εδώ κοντά;

can I borrow an iron?
*bor**o** na dhaneest**o** **e**na s**ee**dhero*
μπορώ να δανειστώ ένα σίδερο;

where can I dry clothes?
*poo bor**o** na steghn**o**so r**oo**kha*
πού μπορώ να στεγνώσω ρούχα;

SPECIAL NEEDS

Recent new facilities on the Metro and at the Venizelos Airport are superb. Elsewhere they are gradually improving, but it is still difficult to get around on public transport.

▲ Disabled parking sign

Disabled lift access sign in the metro station ▶

▶ Disabled lift access sign

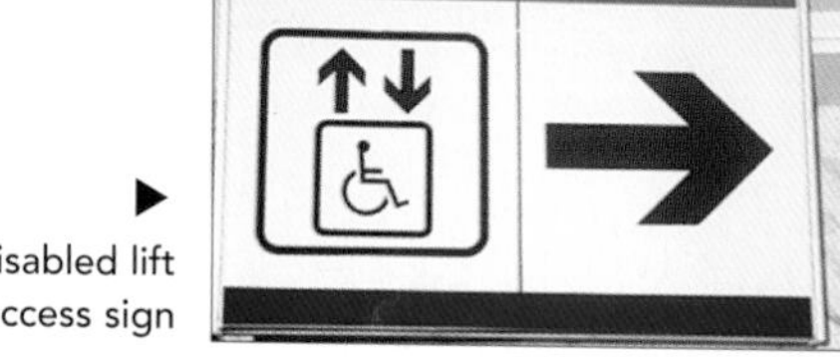

are there any toilets for the disabled?
*eep**a**rkhoon tooal**e**tes ya **a**toma me eedheek**e**s an**a**nges*
υπάρχουν τουαλέτες για άτομα με ειδικές ανάγκες;

do you have any bedrooms on the ground floor?
***e**khete eepnodhom**a**teea sto ees**o**yeeo*
έχετε υπνοδωμάτια στο ισόγειο;

is there a lift?
*eep**a**rkhee asans**e**r*
υπάρχει ασανσέρ;

where is the lift?
*poo **ee**ne to asans**e**r*
πού είναι το ασανσέρ;

how many stairs are there?
*p**o**ses sk**a**les eep**a**rkhoon*
πόσες σκάλες υπάρχουν;

do you have wheelchairs?
***e**khete kar**o**tseea*
έχετε καρότσια;

can you visit ... in a wheelchair?
*bor**ee** kan**ee**s na episkeft**ee** ... me kar**o**tsee*
μπορεί κανείς να επισκεφτεί ... με καρότσι;

where is the wheelchair-accessible entrance?
*poo **ee**ne ee **ee**sodhos me pr**o**svasee ya ta kar**o**tseea*
πού είναι η είσοδος με πρόσβαση για τα καρότσια;

is there a reduction for disabled people?
*y**ee**nete **e**kptosee sta **a**toma me eedheek**e**s an**a**nges*
γίνεται έκπτωση στα άτομα με ειδικές ανάγκες;

WITH KIDS

Greek people make a fuss of children and are welcome wherever you go. Greek children are generally polite and well-behaved. Greeks tend to eat altogether as a family, so you don't usually find special menus designed for children, except in the national/international fast-food eateries such as MacDonalds, Pizza Hut, Goody's etc. In the summer (schools close from mid-June to mid-September) children stay up late with their parents and most families have a 'siesta' in the afternoon.

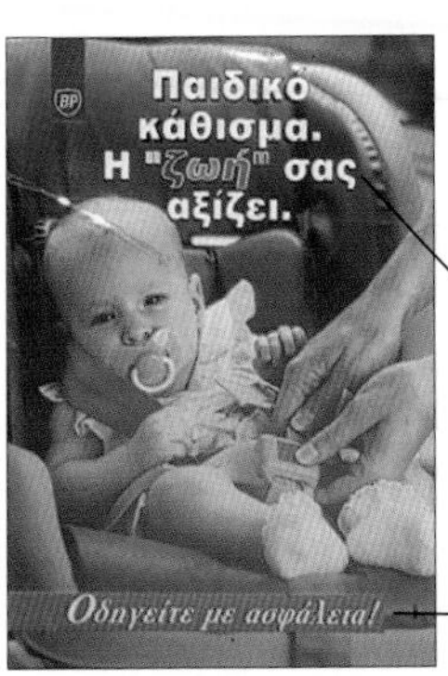

◀ Children should be securely strapped in the car.

your child deserves it

drive safely!

keywords

παιδί
pedee
child

παιδικό κάθισμα
pedeeko katheesma
high-chair

κούνια
koonya
cot

παιδική χαρά
pedeekee hara
play park

πάνες
panes
nappies

talking talking

a child's ticket
ena pedheeko eeseeteereeo
ένα παιδικό εισητήριο

he/she is ... years old
eene ... khronon
είναι ... χρονών

is there a reduction for children?
eeparkhee eedheekee teemee ya pedya
υπάρχει ειδική τιμή για παιδιά;

is there a children's menu?
eeparkhee pedheeko menoo
υπάρχει παιδικό μενού;

have you...?
ekhete...
έχετε...;

a high chair
meea pedheekee karekla
μία παιδική καρέκλα

a child's bed
ena pedheeko krevatee
ένα παιδικό κρεββάτι;

is it safe for children?
eene asfales ya ta pedhya
είναι ασφαλές για τα παιδιά;

what is there for children to do?
tee boroon na kanoon ta pedhya
τι μπορούν να κάνουν τα παιδιά;

where is there a play park?
poo eene ee pedheekee khara
πού είναι η παιδική χαρά;

HEALTH

Make sure you take your stamped E111 form with you (available from post offices). This will be a safeguard against any medical problems or emergencies. There will be a health-centre nearby and there are many private doctors, too. Specialists are also easy to find. For minor ailments, ask the pharmacist for advice.

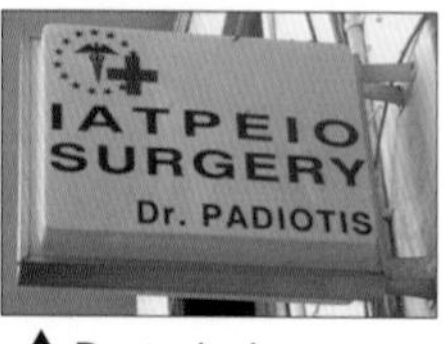

▲ Doctor's sign
You can often see a doctor right away, or at least on the same day.

pharmacy

(name of phrmacist)

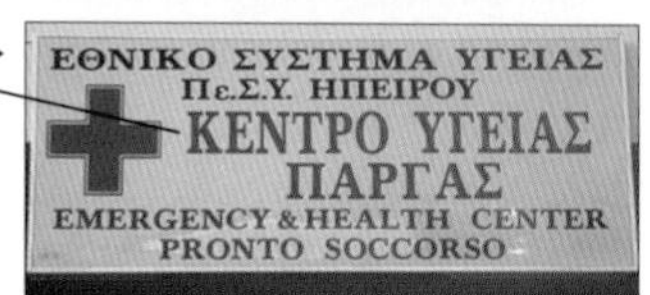

Parga Health Centre

Chemists work on a rota basis, so there is always one open. ▼

day

days of the week

where is there a chemist?
*poo **ee**ne **e**na farmak**ee**o*
πού είναι ένα φαρμακείο;

I don't feel well
*dhen esth**a**nome kal**a***
δεν αισθάνομαι καλά

have you something for...?
***e**khete t**ee**pote ya...*
έχετε τίποτε για...;

sunburn
*ta eng**a**vmata*
τα εγκαύματα

mosquito bites
*tseeb**ee**mata koonoopee**o**n*
τσιμπήματα κουνουπιών

diarrhoea
*tee dhee**a**reea*
τη διάρροια

sunstroke
*teen eel**ee**asee*
την ηλίαση

a headache
*ton pon**o**dhonto*
τον πονόδοντο

I have a rash
***e**kho **e**na eks**a**ntheema*
Έχω ένα εξάνθημα

is it safe to give children?
ee**ne asfal**e**s ya ta pedhy**a
είναι ασφαλές για τα παιδιά;

visiting times ▼

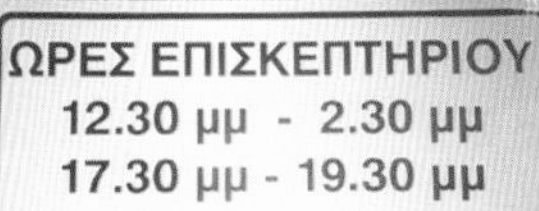

ΩΡΕΣ ΕΠΙΣΚΕΠΤΗΡΙΟΥ
12.30 μμ - 2.30 μμ
17.30 μμ - 19.30 μμ

▶ The dental system is reliable and efficient.

I feel ill
dhen esthanome kala
δεν αισθάνομαι καλά

I need a doctor
khreeazome yatro
χρειάζομαι γιατρό

my son is ill
o yos moo eene arostos
ο γιος μου είναι άρρωστος

my daughter is ill
ee koree moo eene arostee
η κόρη μου είναι άρρωστη

I'm on this medication
perno afta ta farmaka
παίρνω αυτά τα φάρμακα

I have high blood pressure
ekho eepertasee
έχω υπέρταση

I'm diabetic *(m/f)*
eeme dheeaveeteekos/ee
είμαι διαβητικός/ή

I'm pregnant
eeme engeeos
είμαι έγγυος

I'm on the pill
perno anteeseeleepteeka
παίρνω αντισυλληπτικά

I'm allergic to penicillin
ekho aleryeea steen peneekeeleenee
έχω αλλεργία στην πενικιλλίνη

I'm breastfeeding
theelazo to moro moo
θηλάζω το μωρό μου

is it safe to take?
eene asfales kata teen ghalookheea
είναι ασφαλές κατά την γαλουχία;

I need a dentist
khreeazome odhondyatro
χρειάζομαι οδοντιατρό

I have toothache
ekho ponodhondo
έχω πονόδοντο

the filling has come out
moo efeeye to sfrayeesma
μου έφυγε το σφράγισμα

I have an abscess in the tooth
ekho ena aposteema sto dondee
έχω ένα απόστημα στο δόντι

it hurts
me ponaee
με πονάει

can you repair my dentures?
boreete na moo epeedheeorthosete teen odhondosteekheea
μπορείτε να μου επιδιορθώσετε την οδοντοστοιχία;

do I have to pay now?
prepee na pleeroso tora
πρέπει να πληρώσω τώρα;

If you require hospital treatment, take your E111 form and your passport with you. A proportion of the cost will be covered, depending on the type of hospital and the treatment.

GENERAL HOSPITAL (OF PREVEZA) ▲

ΑΠΑΓΟΡΕΥΕΤΑΙ
ΤΟ ΚΑΠΝΙΣΜΑ

SMOKING ▲ PROHIBITED

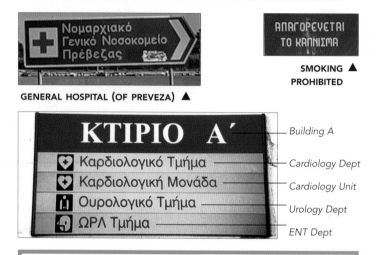

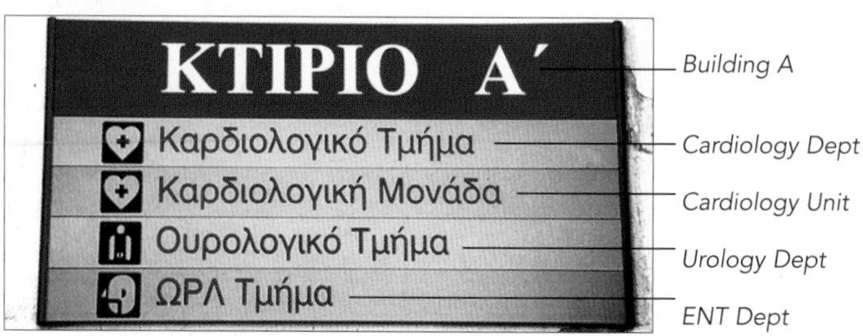

If you need to go to hospital

will he/she have to go to hospital?
*pr**e**pee na bee sto nosokom**ee**o*
πρέπει να μπει στο νοσοκομείο;

where is the hospital?
*poo **ee**ne to nosokom**ee**o*
πού είναι το νοσοκομείο;

to the hospital, please
*sto nosokom**ee**o parakal**o***
στο νοσοκομείο παρακαλώ

I need to go to casualty
*pr**e**pee na p**a**o sta ep**ee**ghonda pereestateek**a***
πρέπει να πάω στα επείγοντα περιστατικά

when are visiting hours?
*p**o**te **e**khee epeeskept**ee**reeo*
πότε έχει επισκεπτήριο;

which ward?
*pya kleeneek**ee***
ποια κλινική;

can you tell me what is the matter?
*bor**ee**te na moo p**ee**te tee seemv**e**nee*
μπορείτε να μου πείτε τί συμβαίνει;

is it serious?
ee**ne sovar**o
είναι σοβαρό;

I need a receipt for the insurance
*khree**a**zome ap**o**dheeksee ya teen asfaleesteek**ee** moo eter**ee**a*
χρειάζομαι απόδειξη για την ασφαλιστική μου εταιρεία

EMERGENCY

If you experience a theft or other crime, you must go to the police (asteenomeea) and make a report. You will need the report for any related insurance claim. Emergency phone numbers: Police – 100, Medical emergency – 166, Fire Brigade – 199

An ▶ ambulance. Vehicles connected with the council or government have orange number-plates.

There are often bush-fires in Greece in summer, so the fire-brigade has to be on the alert. ▲

help!
voeetheea
βοήθεια

can you help me?
boreete na me voeetheesete
μπορείτε να με βοηθήσετε;

there's been an accident
ekhee yeenee ateekheema
έχει γίνει ατύχημα

someone is injured
eeparkhoon travmateees
υπάρχουν τραυματίες

please call...
parakalo kaleste...
παρακαλώ καλέστε...

the police
teen asteenomeea
την αστυνομία

an ambulance
ena asthenoforo
ένα ασθενοφόρο

he was going too fast
etrekhe me meghalee takheeteeta
έτρεχε με μεγάλη ταχύτητα

where's the police station?
poo eene to asteenomeeko tmeema
πού είναι το αστυνομικό τμήμα;

I've been raped
me veeasan
με βίασαν

I want to report a theft
thelo na dheeloso meea klopee
θέλω να δηλώσω μία κλοπή

I've been robbed
ekho pesee theema klopees
έχω πέσει θύμα κλοπής

my car's been broken into
paraveeasan to aftokeeneeto moo
παραβίασαν το αυτοκίνητό μου

I've been attacked
ekho pesee theema efodhoo klepton
έχω πέσει θύμα εφόδου κλεπτών

I need a report for my insurance
khreeazome khartee pereeghrafees seemvandon ya teen asfaleea moo
χρειάζομαι χαρτί περιγραφής συμβάντων για την ασφάλεια μου

how much is the fine?
poso eene to prosteemo
πόσο είναι το προστιμό;

where do I pay it?
poo boro na to pleeroso
πού μπορώ να το πληρώσω;

FOOD AND DRINK

GREEK FOOD

Greek food is not only tasty but healthy, interesting, and reasonably priced. Greece's long and diverse history, along with its varied geography, is reflected in the wide range of dishes on offer. Unlike the UK, regional traditions are very much alive. The unifying theme is simplicity: unfussy, nutritious food with the emphasis on seasonality and fresh local produce.

Fish is of course well represented, as you would expect from a maritime nation. Other mainstays are lamb, goat and pork, cheese (including feta and halloumi), yoghurt, olive oil and salads, with lemon to pep up savoury dishes and honey to sweeten the desserts. Typical vegetables include aubergine/eggplant, courgettes/zucchini, cucumbers, tomatoes, peppers and vine leaves. This is the classic Mediterranean diet, credited with so many medical benefits, including lowering your risk of cancer and heart disease. Wine, whether red, white or rosé, is abundant, often with the famous resinous flavours traditionally associated with Greece. Greeks tend to drink a little and often; being visibly drunk is considered shameful.

*It is often just as cheap to eat out as to cook for yourself, and there is no shortage of places to eat. Restaurants are informal, friendly places, where children are welcome. In the less grand places you can often see the food being prepared, and even go into the kitchen to see what's in the pot (**tapsee**), so you can choose by pointing at what you want. Ideal for those who are not confident of their Greek culinary vocabulary!*

▲ Fried squid (*kalam**a**reea*), stuffed tomatoes (*dom**a**tes yemeest**e**s*), green beans (*fasol**a**keea*) and yogurt and garlic dip (*tsats**ee**kee*).

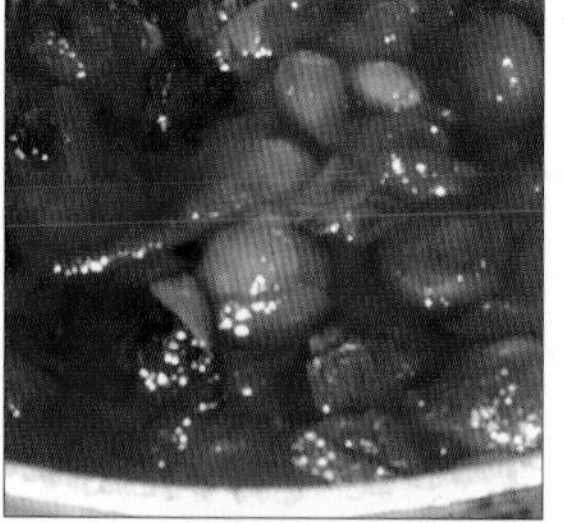

◀ *steef**a**dho* Beef in a rich sauce with onions, tomatoes, wine, peppercorns and spices.

▶ Kebabs are great for a cheap, tasty meal. You will often spot the big doner kebabs from afar, and the little 'souvlakis' (pieces of meat on small skewers) lined up on the charcoal grill.

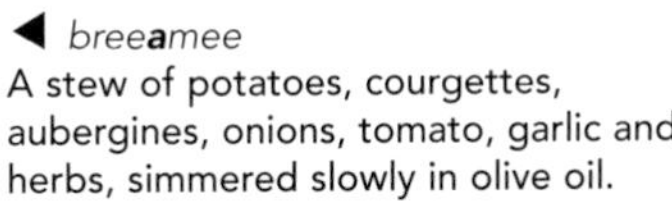

◀ *bree**a**mee*
A stew of potatoes, courgettes, aubergines, onions, tomato, garlic and herbs, simmered slowly in olive oil.

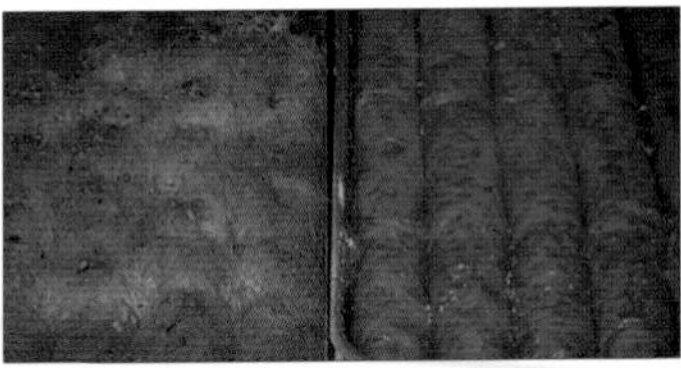

*baklav**a*** and *kata**ee**fee* ▶
Cakes made with nuts and honey

Moussaka, made with mince, aubergines and ▼ béchamel sauce

▲ Stuffed tomatoes (*tom**a**tes yemeest**e**s*), oven-baked. The filling is usually rice, garlic, tomato and herbs, sometimes with mince. There are also stuffed peppers (*peeperee**e**s*) courgettes (*kolookeeth**a**keea*) and aubergines (*meleetz**a**nes*).

where can we have a snack?
*poo bor**oo**me na f**a**me k**a**tee pr**o**kheera*
πού μπορούμε να φάμε κάτι πρόχειρα;

is there a good local restaurant?
*eep**a**rkhee **e**na kal**o** topeek**o** esteeat**o**reeo*
υπάρχει ένα καλό τοπικό εστιατόριο;

not too expensive
o**khee pol**ee** akreev**o
όχι πολύ ακριβό

are there any vegetarian restaurants here?
*eep**a**rkhoon kath**o**loo esteeat**o**reea ya khortof**a**ghoos edh**o***
υπάρχουν καθόλου εστιατόρια για χορτοφάγους εδώ;

can you recommend a local dish?
*bor**ee**te na moo seest**ee**sete **e**na topeek**o** fayeet**o***
μπορείτε να μου συστήσετε ένα τοπικό φαγητό;

what is this?
*tee **ee**ne aft**o***
τι είναι αυτό;

I'll have this
*tha p**a**ro aft**o***
θα πάρω αυτό

excuse me!
*me seengkhor**ee**te*
με συγγχωρείτε!

*Snacking is easy and convenient, with food available on every street corner: cheese, spinach or sausage pies (**teeropeetee**, **spanakopeetee**, **lookaneekopeetee**), toasted sandwiches (**sandveets**), pitta bread (**peeta**), bread rolls (**kooloorakeeya**) and so on, or for the sweet-toothed, **lookoomee** (Turkish delight) and such honey-based treats as **baklava** and **kataeefee**.*

keywords

κρέας
krayas
meat

ψάρι
psaree
fish

λαχανικά
lahaneeka
vegetables

φρούτα
froota
fruit

κέικ
cake
cakes

γλυκά
gleeka
cakes

all with the most pure ingredients

POP-CORN
ΓΛΥΚΟ ΠΟΠ ΚΟΡΝ ΜΕ ΚΑΡΑΜΕΛΑ
SWEET POP CORN WITH CARAMEL
1,20€
ΠΟΠ ΚΟΡΝ ΜΕ ΑΛΑΤΙ
POP CORN WITH SALT
1 €

▲ Pop-corn stands are popular.

talking

I'd like a white cofee
tha eethela ena kafe me ghala
θα ήθελα ένα καφέ με γάλα

a decaffeinated coffee
ena dekafeeene
ένα ντεκαφεϊνέ

a tea...
ena tsaee...
ένα τσάι...

with milk
me ghala
με γάλα

with lemon
me lemonee
με λεμόνι

without sugar
khorees zakharee
χωρις ζάχαρη

an orange juice please
ena kheemo portokalee parakalo
έναο χυμός πορτοκάλι παρακαλώ

an iced coffee
ena frape
ένα φραπέ

for me
ya mena
για μένα

for her
yafteen
γι' αυτήν

for him
yafton
γι' αυτόν

for us
ya mas
για μας

with ice please
me paghakeea parakalo
με παγάκια παρακαλώ

I'm very thirsty
dheepsao polee
διψάω πολύ

a bottle of mineral water
ena bookalee emfeealomeno nero
ένα μπουκάλι εμφιαλωμένο νερό

sparkling
aereeookho
αεριούχο

still
aplo
απλό

Snack and take-away van ◀

Take-away ▶

Quick and easy sit-down or take-away place for a snack (doner kebab with slices of pork or chicken), wrapped up in a pitta bread with tomatoes, onions, chips and plain yogurt.

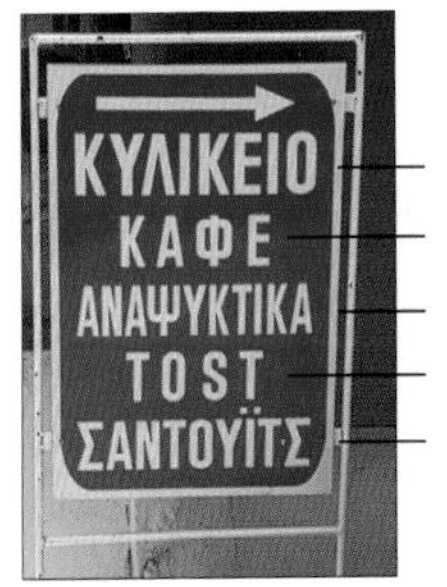

buffet
coffee
soft drinks
cheese & ham toasties
sandwiches

keywords

σοκολάτα
*sokol**a**ta*
chocolate

παγωτό
*paghot**o***
ice cream

πάστες
*p**a**stes*
slices of gateau

λεμόνι
*lem**o**nee*
lemon

ροδάκινο
*rodh**a**keeno*
peach

φράουλα
*fr**a**oola*
strawberry

τυρόπιτα
*teer**o**peeta*
cheese pie

πατάτες
*pat**a**tes*
chips

φραπέ
*frap**e***
iced coffee

talking

I'd like a toasted sandwich
*tha **ee**thela **e**na tost*
θα ήθελα ένα τοστ

what sandwiches do you have?
*tee s**a**ndwich **e**khete*
τι σάντουϊτς έχετε;

a cheese pie
*m**ee**a teer**o**peeta*
μία τυρόπιτα

I'd like an ice cream
*tha **ee**thela **e**na paghot**o***
θα ήθελα ένα παγωτό

with chips
*me pat**a**tes*
με πατάτες

with cheese
*me teer**ee***
με τυρί

with ham
*me zamb**o**n*
με ζαμπόν

what cakes do you have?
*tee ghleek**a** **e**khete*
τι γλυκά έχετε;

what flavours do you have?
*tee gh**e**fsees **e**khete*
τι γεύσεις έχετε;

Particularly convenient for the visitor is the Greek tradition of ordering a selection of different dishes: ***mezedhes****. This is a wonderful way of discovering Greek food without committing yourself to one dish.*

◀ You are never far from a taverna

traditional cuisine
everything chargrilled
views over the Ionian Sea

▼ Seaside taverna

talking talking

I'd like to book a table
tha ***ee****thela na krat****ee****so* ***e****na trap****e****zee*
θα ήθελα να κρατήσω ένα τραπέζι

for tonight
ya ***a****popse*
για απόψε

for tomorrow night
ya ***a****vreeo to vr****a****dhee*
για αύριο το βράδυ

I booked a table
e*kleesa* ***e****na trap****e****zee*
έκλεισα ένα τραπέζι

in a non-smoking area
*stoos mee kapn****ee****zontes*
στους μη καπνίζοντες

for ... people
ya ... ***a****toma*
για ... άτομα

at 8 o'clock
*ya tees okt****o*** *to vr****a****dhee*
για τις οκτώ το βράδυ

for 5th August
*ya tees 5 avgh****oo****stoo*
για τις 5 Αυγούστου

in the name of...
sto ***o****noma...*
στο όνομα...

◀ Grill/Bar

Specialities:
ΚΟΚΟΡΕΤΣΙ *spit-roasted liver and spleen, wrapped in intestines*

ΤΥΡΟΣΟΥΦΛΕ *cheese soufflé*

Some restaurants have Greek dancing, as shown by the illustration. ▼

charcoal/grill house — ΨΗΣΤΑΡΙΑ
restaurant — ΕΣΤΙΑΤΟΡΙΟ
café-bar — ΚΑΦΕ ΜΠΑΡ

a table for two
ena trapezee ya deeo
ένα τραπέζι για δύο

the menu, please
ton katalogho parakalo
τον κατάλογο παρακαλώ

what is the dish of the day?
pyo eene to peeato tees eemeras
ποιο είναι το πιάτο της ημέρας;

can we choose from the display?
boroome na dhoome tee ekhete
μπορούμε να δούμε τι έχετε;

what is this?
tee eene afto
τι είναι αυτό;

I'll have this
tha paro afto
θα πάρω αυτό

do you have any vegetarian dishes?
ekhete fayeeta ya khortofaghoos
έχετε φαγητά για χορτοφάγους;

please bring...
parakalo ferte...
παρακαλώ, φέρτε...

some more bread
kee alo psomee
κι άλλο ψωμί

some more water
kee alo nero
κι άλλο νερό

another bottle
alo ena bookalee
άλλο ένα μπουκάλι

the bill
to loghareeasmo
το λογαριασμό

*Breakfast for many Greeks is simply coffee, perhaps with a bowl of yoghurt and honey. If you prefer something substantial to start the day, fresh bread (**psomee**) with cheese (**teeree**), olives (**elyes**) or jam (**marmeladha**) is a common choice. You can buy it yourself from the bakery (**foorno**), which will also sell* **teeropeetee** *(cheese pies).*

▲ Menu of the day ▼

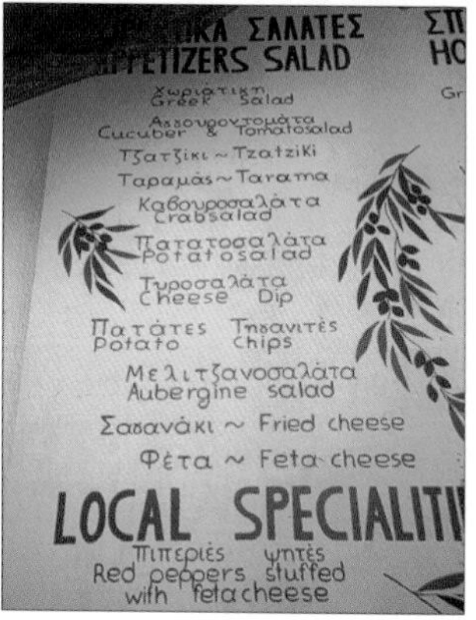

▲ Many restaurants have bilingual menus, like this one.

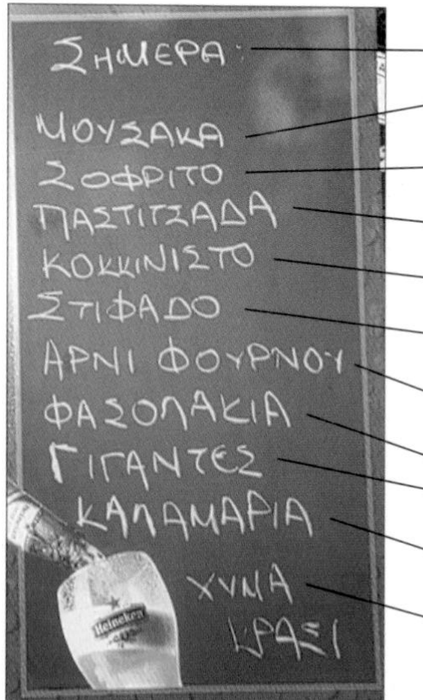

ΣΗΜΕΡΑ today

ΜΟΥΣΑΚΑΣ Moussaka with mince, aubergines and béchamel sauce

ΣΟΦΡΙΤΟ *sofr**ee**to* tender beef in a creamy garlic sauce.

ΠΑΣΤΙΤΣΑΔΑ *pasteets**a**da* beef and pasta in tomato sauce

ΚΟΚΚΙΝΙΣΤΟ *kokeeneest**o** braised beef in red wine sauce*

ΣΤΙΦΑΔΟ *steef**a**do* braised beef in onion and peppercorn sauce

ΑΡΝΙ ΦΟΥΡΝΟΥ *arn**ee** f**oo**rnoo* lamb cooked slowly in the oven

ΦΑΣΟΛΑΚΙΑ *fasol**a**keea* green beans

ΓΙΓΑΝΤΕΣ *g**ee**gantes* large butter beans

ΚΑΛΑΜΑΡΙΑ *kalam**a**reea rings of squid (calamari) in batter*

ΧΥΜΑ ΚΡΑΣΙ *heem**a** kras**ee** draft wine from the barrel*

Lunch is taken between 1 and 3pm, and is usually a cooked meal, though fairly light: typically one main dish, with salad or chips, followed by a simple dessert such as fruit or yoghurt. The evening meal, which is the main one of the day, might be any time from about six until very late. It's accompanied by side-dishes and bread. Classic Greek dishes include moussaka (layers of aubergine, meat and béchamel sauce); **soovlakeea** *(pieces of pork grilled on a skewer like a shish kebab);* **klefteeko** *(lamb or goat in filo pastry); and* **kleftedhes** *(herbed meat patties). These might be accompanied by Greek salad (***khoreeateekee salata***), including chunks of tomato, cucumber, onions and feta cheese;* **tzatzeekee** *(yoghurt, cucumber, garlic and mint); or* **taramosalata** *(a purée of fish roes).*

ΟΡΕΚΤΙΚΑ

APPETISERS

ΛΑΔΕΡΑ

COOKED IN OIL

ΚΥΡΙΑ ΦΑΓΗΤΑ

MAIN DISHES

ΣΑΛΑΤΕΣ

SALADS

ΖΥΜΑΡΙΚΑ

PASTA

ΤΗΣ ΩΡΑΣ

DISHES OF THE DAY

usually fresh meat or fish, barbecued to order

ΤΥΡΙΑ

CHEESE

ΚΙΜΑΔΕΣ

MINCEMEAT

FISH

▲ Typical headings you will come across on restaurant menus.

Whole pigs roasting on spits. You buy the roast pork by the kilo. ▶

Beer, though not native to Greece, is popular. The major international lager brands are widely available, usually brewed in Greece under licence.
*Greek coffee (**eleeneekos kafes**), is small, strong and sweet, like that of Turkey and the Arab countries. Instead of being filtered, it's ground very fine and brewed in a pot with the sugar included, rather than added afterwards. If you prefer yours without sugar, you will need to ask for a 'plain' coffee (**sketo kafe**). Sweet is **gleeko**, and medium is **metreeo**. If you want it white, specify **me ghala** (with milk). The usual alternative to Greek coffee is instant, known by the name Nescafe regardless of brand, which can be served cold as a **frape**. Coffee is often served with a glass of water as a preliminary thirst-quencher, a welcome addition in a hot country. It is not common practice to finish a meal with coffee: in fact some restaurants do not serve it.*
*Tea (**tsaee**) is not quite so popular, but easily available. It will tend to be in the form of a teabag to dip in a glass of (fairly) hot water, which may be a disappointment to a British tea-drinker!*

Bars, café-bars and bistros ▶ all serve beer and wine.

keywords keywords

ΟΥΖΕΡΙ
oozeree
ouzeria

μεζέδες
mezedes
snacks to go with ouzo

ΚΑΦΕ
café
café-bar

ΚΟΝΙΑΚ
konyak
brandy

ΜΠΥΡΑ ΕΛΛΑΣ
beera hellas
'Hellas' beer

ΜΠΥΡΑ ΚΟΡΩΝΑ
beera corona
'Corona' beer

International and Greek beers are available. Retsina is also popular, and is sold chilled.

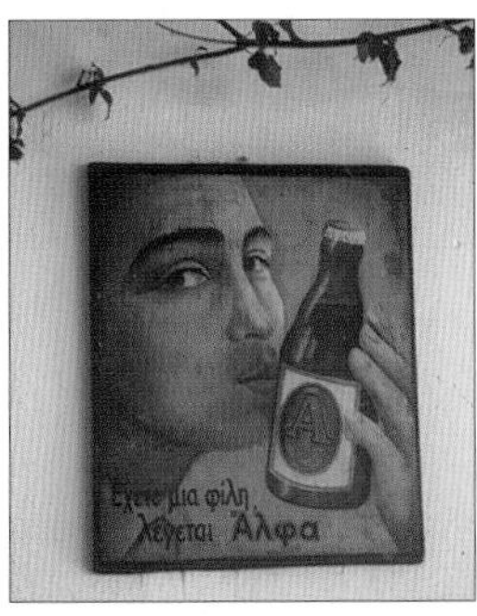

keywords

red
κόκκινο
*k**o**keeno*

white
άσπρο
***a**spro*

rosé
ροζέ
*roz**e***

dry
ξηρό
*xeer**o***

sweet
γλυκό
*gleek**o***

bottle
μπουκάλι
*book**a**lee*

glass
ποτήρι
*pot**ee**ree*

litre
λίτρο
***ee**tro* → *l**ee**tro*

half litre
μισό λίτρο
*mees**o** l**ee**tro*

house wine
σπιτικό κρασί
*speeteek**o** kras**ee***

carafe
καράφα
*kar**a**fa*

from the barrel
από το βαρέλι
*ap**o** to var**e**lee*

talking

a beer please
*m**ee**a b**ee**ra parakal**o***
μία μπύρα παρακαλώ

a glass of wine please
e**na pot**ee**ree kras**ee** parakal**o
ένα ποτήρι κρασί παρακαλώ

a small beer
*m**ee**a mekr**ee** b**ee**ra*
μία μικρή μπίρα

a large beer
*m**ee**a megh**a**lee b**ee**ra*
μία μεγάλη μπίρα

Wine in Greece is plentiful and cheap. It tends to be served by the glass, carafe or jug, straight from the barrel. Rosé is popular, more so than in Britain. You may be sceptical about the famous retsina (white wine flavoured with pine resin) but it Is very refreshing, and can be diluted with soda to quench your thirst. Those looking for fine wines may be disappointed, at least in more basic or traditional establishments. However, new wine-making techniques are finding their way into Greece, and a good restaurant will often have a selection of bottled vintages. Brand names to look out for include Boutari and Kourtaki (also available in Britain) and in a more expensive category, Strofili· and Seméli.

*Perhaps the best-known Greek spirits are ouzo (**oozo**, flavoured with aniseed, a little like French pastis) and Metaxa (Greek brandy). Ouzo is usually served with ice, and diluted to taste by the drinker, which makes the clear spirit turn cloudy. It can be found in ordinary bars or specialist ouzerias. Like retsina, ouzo is not to everyone's taste, but it can be very refreshing. Other famous Greek spirits include raki, from Crete, and* **tseepooro***, an eau-de-vie distilled from the skins, stems, and pips of crushed grapes.*

There are many types of the aniseed-flavoured spirit, ouzo. Metaxa brandy has three categories – 3-, 5- and 7-star.

talking

enjoy your meal!
*kal**ee** **o**reksee*
καλή όρεξη!

would you like a drink?
*tha th**e**late **e**na pot**o***
Θα θέλατε ένα ποτό;

cheers! your health!
*steen eey**a** sas*
στην υγειά σας!

it's my round!
***ee**ne ee seer**a** moo*
είναι η σειρά μου!

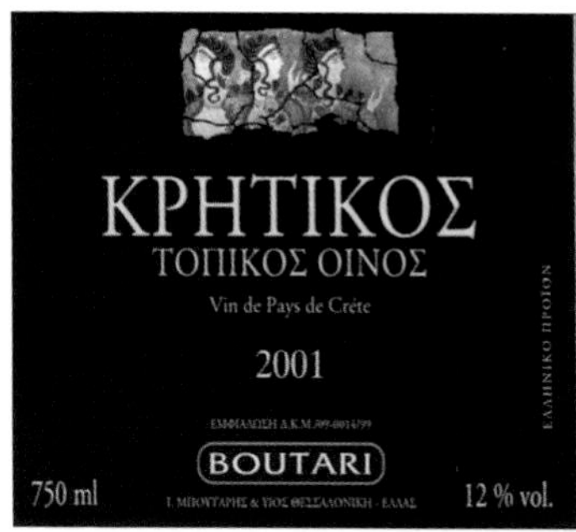

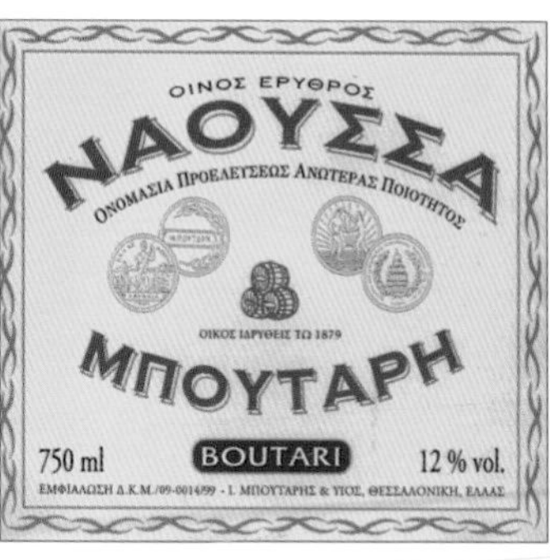

the wine list, please
*ton kat**a**logho krasy**o**n parakal**o***
τον κατάλογο κρασιών, παρακαλώ

a carafe of wine
*m**ee**a kar**a**fa kras**ee***
μία καράφα κρασί

a glass of wine
e**na pot**ee**ree kras**ee
ένα ποτήρι κρασί

a bottle of wine
e**na bouk**a**lee kras**ee
ένα μπουκάλι κρασί

red
*k**o**keeno*
κόκκινο

white
*lefk**o***
λευκό

a bottle...
***e**na bouk**a**lee...*
ένα μπουκάλι...

a carafe...
*m**ee**a kar**a**fa...*
μία καράφα...

of wine
*kras**ee***
κρασί

of dry wine
*kseer**o** kras**ee***
ξηρό κρασί

of sweet wine
*ghleek**o** kras**ee***
γλυκό κρασί

of a local wine
*topeek**o** kras**ee***
τοπικό κρασί

FLAVOURS OF GREECE

Παστιτσάδα (pasteets**a**dha) braised beef in spicy red sauce with pasta
Σοφρίτο (sofr**ee**to) beef casseroled in a creamy sauce with onions, garlic and herbs

Πίτα (p**ee**ta) various pies; you may buy a large one to share, for a main course.
Γίδα βραστή (y**ee**dha vr**a**stee) goat-meat soup, eaten with the juice of fresh lemon
Κυνήγι (keen**ee**ghee) game
Φασολάδα (fasol**a**da) a thick soup with haricot beans and vegetables, served with lemon
Ψάρια φρέσκα (ps**a**reea fr**e**ska) fresh fish
Γραβιέρα (gravee**er**a) gruyère-like cheese
Μπουγάτσα (boog**a**tsa) vanilla custard pie with cinnamon and icing-sugar
Μπακλαβάς (bakl**a**vas) filo pastries with honey, nuts and syrup
Χαλβάς (h**a**lvas) soft, gelatinous cake, garnished with almonds
WINES
Ζίτσα (z**ee**tsa); **Αβέρωφ** (av**e**rof)

Στην σούβλα (steen s**oo**vla) on the spit
Γουρουνόπουλο (gooroonop**oo**lo) suckling pig roasted slowly with herbs
Χυλοπίτες με κοτόπουλο κρασάτο (kheelop**ee**tes me kot**o**poolo kras**a**to) Pie containing chicken marinated in wine
Τουρλού (toorl**oo**) ratatouille with aubergines, courgettes, potatoes, onions and sometimes cheese
Σπανακόπιτα (spanak**o**peeta) spinach pie
Ελιές Καλαμάτας (elee**e**s kalam**a**tas) Kalamata olives
Μηλόπιτα (meel**o**peeta) apple pie with cinnamon
Δίπλες (dh**ee**ples) pastries with honey and walnuts
Μελιτζανάκι γλυκό (meleetzan**a**kee gleek**o**) sweet crystallized aubergine in syrup
Σύκα μαυροδάφνη (s**ee**ka mavrodh**a**fnee) figs in wine syrup
Σταφιδόπιτα (stafeedh**o**peeta) raisin pie
WINES
Νεμέας (nem**e**as); **Αχαία Κλάους** (akh**a**ya kl**a**oos); **Καμπάς** (kamp**a**s)

Πηλιορίτικο μπουμπάρι (peeleeor**ee**teeko boob**a**ree) spicy sausage
Μακαρονόπιτα (makar**o**nopeeta) macaroni pie
Χαλβάς (halv**a**s) fudge-like sweet made from sesame seeds and honey
Μεζέδες (mez**e**dhes) traditional snacks
Εξοχικό (exokheek**o**) vegetable and cheese-stuffed beef or pork

Χοιρινό κρήτικο (heereen**o** kr**ee**teeko) pork chops baked with vegetables in a spicy sauce
Σοφρίτο (sofr**ee**to) beef braised in a creamy garlic sauce with herbs and spices
Σαλιγκάρια (saleengg**a**reea) snails, prepared in different dishes
Ψάρια φρέσκα (ps**a**reea fr**e**ska) fresh fish and shellfish of all kinds

Κοντοσούβλι *(kontosoovlee)*
lamb, pork or beef, spit-roasted with herbs and spices
μέλι θυμαρίσιο *(melee theemareesio) thyme-flavoured honey*
Ούζο *(oozo) aniseed-flavour spirit*
Τσίπουρο *(tseepooro) spirit*
WINES
Τσάνταλη *(tsantalee);* **Μπουτάρη** *(bootaree);* **Κουρτάκη** *(koortakee);* **Καμπάς** *(kampas);* **Χατζημιχάλη** *(khadzeemeehalee)*

Σουτζουκάκια *(sootzookakya)*
meat balls in tomato sauce
Τας κεμπάμπ *(tash kebab) lamb, goat, pork or beef in spicy sauce*
Ντολμάδες *(dolmadhes) spicy, rice-stuffed vine-leaves*
Τυροκαυτερή *(teerokafteree)*
feta cheese and red pepper dip
Τυρί Μετσόβου *(teeree metsovoo)*
smoked cheese from Metsovo
Τουρσί *(toorsee)*
vegetables pickled in vinegar
Μπακλαβάς *(baklavas) and* **καταίφι** *(kataeefee) pastries of filo, with honey, nuts and syrup*
WINES
Μακεδονικός *(makedhoneekos);* **Τσάνταλη** *(tsantalee);* **Μπουτάρη** *(bootaree);* **Αγιορείτικο** *(ayoreeteeko (made by monks on Mt Athos)*

Aegean Islands
Αρνάκι ψητό *(arnakee pseeto)*
grilled lamb cutlets
Παστίτσιο *(pasteetsyo)*
pie made of spiced macaroni and mince (similar to moussaka)
Κακαβιά *(kakaveea) fish soup*
Χταπόδι κρασάτο *(khtapodhee krasato)*
octopus in wine sauce
Μυδοπίλαφο *(meedopeelafo)*
mussels and seafood cooked with rice
Στρείδια *(streedheea) oysters*
Κάβουρας *(kavooras) crab*
Καλαμάρια *(kalamareea) squid*
Γλυκά κουταλιού *(gleeka kootalyoo)*
fruit preserved and crystallized in syrup
Σύκα στο φούρνο με μαυποδάφνη *(seeka sto foorno me mavrodhafnee)*
figs cooked in Mavrodafni red-wine sauce with spices; from Chios and Lesvos islands
WINES
Σάμος *(samos);* **Σαντορίνη** *(santoreenee);* **Πάρος** *(paros)*

Γραβιέρα *(graveeera)*
graviera cheese
Μανούρι *(manooree)*
soft cheese, similar to feta
Σύκα *(seeka) figs*
Καρπούζι *(karpoozee) watermelon*
Ρακί *(rakee) raki, traditional spirit*
WINES
Κοκκινέλι *(kokeenelee) (red only);*
Κρητικός *(kreeteekos)*

There are times when you cannot eat some things. It is as well warning the waiter before making your choice.

I'm vegetarian
__ee__me khortof__a__ghos
είμαι χορτοφάγος

do you have any vegetarian dishes?
__e__khete k__a__tee ya khortof__a__ghoos
έχετε κάτι για χορτοφάγους;

I don't eat meat
dhen tr__oo__ kr__e__as
δεν τρώω κρέας

I don't eat pork
dhen tr__oo__ kheereen__o__
δεν τρώω χοιρινό

I don't eat fish / shellfish
dhen tr__oo__ ps__a__ree / __o__straka
δεν τρώω ψάρι / όστρακα

which dishes have no meat / fish?
peea fayeet__a__ dhen __e__khoon kr__e__as / ps__a__ree
ποια φαγητά δεν έχουν κρέας / ψάρι;

I have an allergy to peanuts
__e__kho aler__yee__a sta feest__ee__keea
έχω αλλεργία στα φυστίκια

what do you recommend?
tee prot__ee__nete
τι προτείνετε;

what is this made with?
me tee __ee__ne fleeaghm__e__no aft__o__
με τι είναι φτιαγμένο αυτό;

I'm on a diet
k__a__no dh__ee__eta
κάνω δίαιτα

is it raw?
__ee__ne om__o__
είναι ωμό;

I don't drink alcohol
dhen p__ee__no alko__o__l
δεν πίνω αλκοόλ

enjoy your meal!
kal__ee__ __o__reksee
καλή όρεξη

τηγανιτό
teeganeet__o__
fried

βραστό
vrast__o__
boiled

ψητό
pseet__o__
roast

γεμιστό
yemeest__o__
stuffed

στο φούρνο
sto f__oo__rno
baked in the oven

στη σούβλα
stee s__oo__vla
on the spit

λαδερά
lader__a__
braised in olive oil

στη σχάρα
steeskh__a__ra
on the grill

στα κάρβουνα
sta k__a__rvoona
barbecued on charcoal

μαγειρευτά
mayeereft__a__
ready cooked (in casserole pots)

της ώρας
tees __o__ras
while you wait

καπνιστό
kapneest__o__
smoked

μαγειρεμένο
mayeerem__e__no
cooked

ωμό
om__o__
raw

MENU READER

α A

αγγούρι *ang***oo***ree* cucumber

αγκινάρες *angeen***a***res* artichokes

αγκινάρες άλα πολίτα *angeen***a***res* **a***la pol***ee***ta* artichokes with lemon juice and olive oil

αγριογούρουνο *agreeog***oo***roono* wild boar

αεριούχο *aereee***oo***kho* fizzy, sparkling

αθερίνα *ather***ee***na* whitebait, usually fried

αλάτι *al***a***tee* salt

αλεύρι *al***e***vree* flour

αλευρόπιτα *alevr***o***peeta* pie made with cheese, milk and eggs

αμύγδαλα *am***ee***gdala* almonds

άνηθος **a***neethos* dill

αρακάδες *arak***a***dhes* peas

αρνάκι ψητό *arn***a***kee pseet***o** lamb chop grilled with herbs

αρνί *arn***ee** lamb

αρνί γκιοβετσι *arn***ee** *gyoov***e***tsee* roast lamb with small pasta

αρνί λεμονάτο *arn***ee** *lemon***a***to* lamb braised in sauce with herbs and lemon juice

αρνί με βότανα *arn***ee** *me v***o***tana* lamb stewed with vegetables and herbs

αρνίσιο *arn***ee***seeo* lamb chops

αρνί ψητό *arn***ee** *pseet***o** roast lamb

αστακός *astak***o***s* lobster (often served with lemon juice and olive oil)

άσπρο **a***spro* white

άσπρο κρασί **a***spro kras***ee** white wine

αυγά *avgh***a** eggs

αυγολέμονο *avghol***e***mono* egg and lemon soup

αυγοτάραχο *avghot***a***rakho* mullet roe (smoked)

αφελία *afel***ee***a* pork in red wine with seasonings (Cyprus)

αχινοί *akheen***ee** sea urchin roes

αχλάδι *akhl***a***dhee* pear

αχλάδι στο φούρνο *akhl***a***dhee sto f***oo***rno* baked pear with syrup sauce

αχνιστό *akhneest***o** steamed

β B

βασιλικός *vaseeleek***o***s* basil

βερίκοκο *ver***ee***koko* apricot

βισινό κασέρι *veeseen***o** *kas***e***ree* sheep's cheese served with cherry preserve

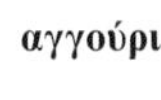

αγγούρι

βερίκοκο

βλίτα *vl**ee**ta* wild greens (like spinach, eaten with olive oil and lemon)
βότκα *v**o**tka* vodka
βοδινό *vodheen**o*** beef
βουτήματα *voot**ee**mata* biscuits to dip in coffee
βούτυρο *v**oo**teero* butter
βραδινό *vradeen**o*** evening meal
βραστό *vrast**o*** boiled

γ Γ

γάλα *gh**a**la* milk
γαλακτομπούρικο *ghalaktob**oo**reeko* custard tart
γαλακτοπωλείο *galaktopol**ee**o* café/patisserie
γαρίδες *ghar**ee**dhes* shrimps; prawns
γαρίδες γιουβέτσι *ghar**ee**dhes yoov**e**tsee* prawns in tomato sauce with feta
γαρύφαλλο *gar**ee**falo* clove (spice)
γαύρος *g**a**vros* sardine-type fish (if salted: anchovy)
γίδα βραστή *y**ee**da vrast**ee*** goat soup
γεμιστά *yemeest**a*** stuffed vegetables
γιαούρτι *ya**oo**rtee* yoghurt
γιαούρτι με μέλι *ya**oo**rtee me m**e**lee* yoghurt with honey
γιαχνί *yakhn**ee*** cooked in tomato sauce and olive oil
γίγαντες *y**ee**ghantes* large butter beans
γιουβαρλάκια *yoovarl**a**kya* meatballs in lemon sauce
γκαζόζα *ghaz**o**za* fizzy drink
γλυκά *ghlyk**a*** dessert
γλυκά κουταλιού *ghlyk**a** kootaly**oo*** dessert
γλώσσα *ghl**o**sa* sole
γόπες *gh**o**pes* bogue, a type of fish
γραβιέρα *ghravy**e**ra* cheese resembling gruyère
γύρος *y**ee**ros* doner kebab

δεντρολίβανο

δ Δ

δάφνη *d**a**fnee* bay leaf
δάκτυλα *dh**a**kteela* almond cakes
δαμάσκηνα *dham**a**skeena* prunes with cream in wine sauce
δείπνο *dh**ee**pno* dinner
δεντρολίβανο *dendrol**ee**vano* rosemary
δίπλες *dh**ee**ples* pastry with honey and walnuts

ε Ε

ελάχιστα ψημένο *el**a**kheesta pseem**e**no* rare (meat)

ελιές

ελαιόλαδο *ele**o**ladho* olive oil

ελιές *ely**e**s* olives

ελιές τσακιστές *ely**e**s tsakeest**e**s* cracked green olives with coriander seeds and garlic (Cyprus)

ελιοτή *elyot**ee*** olive bread

εξοχικό *exokheek**o*** stuffed pork or beef with vegetables and cheese

εστιατόριο *esteeat**o**reeo* restaurant

ζ Ζ

ζαμπόν *zam**bo**n* ham

ζαχαροπλαστείο *zakharoplast**ee**o* cake shop

ζάχαρη *z**a**kharee* sugar

ζελατίνα *zelat**ee**na* brawn

ζεστή σοκολάτα *zest**ee** sokol**a**ta* hot chocolate

ζεστό *zest**o*** hot, warm

θ Θ

Θαλασσινά *thalaseen**a*** seafood

Θυμάρι *theem**a**ree* thyme

ι Ι

Ιμάμ μπαϊλντί *eem**a**m baeeld**ee*** stuffed aubergines (eggplants)

κακαβιά fish soup

κ Κ

κάβα *k**a**va* wine shop

κάβουρας *k**a**vooras* boiled crab

καγιανάς με παστό κρέας *kayan**a**s me past**o** kr**e**yas* salted pork with cheese, tomatoes and eggs

κακαβιά *kakavee**a*** fish soup

κακάο *kak**a**oo* hot chocolate

καλαμάκια *kalam**a**kya* small skewers

καλαμάρια *kalam**a**reea* squid

καλαμάρια τηγανιτά *kalam**a**reea teeghaneet**a*** fried squid

καλαμπόκι

καλαμπόκι *kalamb**o**kee* corn on the cob

καλαμποκόπιτα *kalambok**o**peeta* corn bread

καλοψημένο *kalopseem**e**no* well done (meat)

κανέλα *kan**e**lla* cinnamon

κάπαρι *k**a**paree* pickled capers

καπνιστό *kapneest**o*** smoked

καραβίδα *karav**ee**dha* crayfish

καράφα *kar**a**fa* carafe

καρέκλα *kar**e**kla* chair

καρότο *kar**o**to* carrot

καρπούζι *karp**oo**zee* watermelon

καρύδι *kar**ee**dhee* walnut

καρυδόπιτα *kareedh**o**peeta* walnut cake

καρύδα *kar**ee**dha* coconut

καρυδόπιτα walnut cake

κασέρι *kaseree* sheep's milk cheese, often served fried

κάστανα *kastana* chestnuts

καταΐφι *kataeefee* small pastry drenched in syrup

κατάλογος *kataloghos* menu

κατάλογος κρασιών *kataloghos krasyon* wine list

καταψυγμένο *katapseegmeno* frozen

κατσίκι *katseekee* roast kid

καφενείο *kafeneeo* café

καφές *kafes* coffee (Greek-style)
- **καφέδες** *kafedes* coffees (plural)
- **καφές γλυκύς** *kafes ghleekees* very sweet coffee
- **καφές με γάλα** *kafes me ghala* milky coffee
- **καφές μέτριος** *kafes metreeos* medium-sweet coffee
- **καφές σκέτος** *kafes sketos* coffee without sugar
- **καφές φραπέ** *kafes frappe* iced coffee

κεράσια

κεράσια *keraseea* cherries

κεφαλότυρι *kefaloteeree* type of cheese, often served fried in olive oil

φασολάκια green beans

κεφτέδες *keftedhes* meat balls

κιδώνι *keedhonee* quince

κιδώνι στο φούρνο *keedhonee sto foorno* baked quince

κιμάς *keemas* mince

κλεφτικό *klefteeko* casserole with meat, potatoes and vegetables

κοκορέτσι *kokoretsee* stewed offal or liver, a special Easter dish

κοκτέιλ *kokteyl* cocktail

κολατσιό *kolatsyo* brunch, elevenses

κολοκότες *kolokotes* pastries with pumpkins and raisins

κολοκυθάκια *kolokeethakeea* courgettes, zucchini

κολοκυθόπιτα *kolokeethopeeta* courgette/zucchini pie

κουνουπίδι

κολοκυθόπιτα γλυκιά *kolokeeth**o**peeta gleeky**a*** sweet courgette/zucchini pie

κονιάκ *kon**yak*** brandy, cognac

κοντοσούβλι *kontos**oo**vlee* spicy pieces of lamb, pork or beef, spit-roasted

κοτόπουλο *kot**o**poolo* chicken

κοτόπουλο ριγανάτο *kot**o**poolo reeghan**a**to* grilled basted chicken with herbs

κοτόπουλο καπαμά *kot**o**poolo kapam**a*** chicken casseroled with red peppers, onions, cinnamon and raisins

κουκκιά *kooky**a*** broad beans

κουλούρια *kool**oo**reea* bread rings

κουνέλλι *koon**e**lee* rabbit

κουνουπίδι *koonoop**ee**dhee* cauliflower

κουπέπια stuffed vine leaves

κουπέπια *koop**e**peea* stuffed vine leaves (Cyprus)

κουπές *koop**e**s* meat pasties

κουραμπιέδες *koorambу**e**dhes* small almond cakes eaten at Christmas

κρασί *kras**ee*** wine

κρέας *kr**e**as* meat

κρέμα *kr**e**ma* cream

κρεμμύδια *krem**ee**dheea* onions

κρητικη σαλάτα *kreeteek**ee** sal**a**ta* watercress salad

κρύο *kr**ee**o* cold

κυδώνια *keedh**o**neea* type of clams

κυνήγι *keen**ee**yee* game

κυρίο πιάτο *keer**ee**o py**a**to* main course

λεμόνι

λ Λ

λαβράκι *lavr**a**kee* baked sea-bass

λαγός *lag**o**s* hare

λαδερά *ladher**a*** vegetable casserole

λάδι ***la**dhee* oil

λαδότυρο *lad**o**teero* soft cheese with olive oil

λαχανά *lakhan**a*** vegetables

λαχανικά *lakhaneek**a*** vegetables (menu heading)

λαχανό *lakhan**o*** cabbage

λεμονάδα *lemon**a**dha* lemon drink

λεμόνι *lemonee* lemon

λευκό *lefko* white (used for wine as well as **άσπρο**)

λίγο *leego* a little, a bit

λουκάνικα *lookaneeka* type of highly seasoned sausage

λουκουμάδες *lookoomadhes* small fried dough balls in syrup

λουκούμι *lookoomee* Turkish delight

λουκούμια *lookoomeea* shortbread served at weddings

λούντζα *loondza* loin of pork, marinated and smoked

μ M

μαγειρίτσα *mayeereetsa* soup made of lamb offal, special Easter dish

μαϊντανός *maeedanos* parsley

μακαρόνια *makaronya* spaghetti

μακαρόνια με κιμά *makaronya me keema* spaghetti bolognese

μαρίδες *mareedhes* small fish like sprats, served fried

μαριζόλες *mareezoles* meat cooked in olive oil and lemon juice

μαρούλι *maroolee* lettuce

μαρτίνι *marteenee* martini

μαύρο κρασί *mavro krasee* red wine (although you'll hear *kokeeno krasee* more often)

μανιτάρια *maneedareea* mushrooms

μανιτάρια

μελιτζάνα

μαύρο *mavro* red wine

μαυρομάτικα *mavromateeka* black-eyed peas

μεγάλο *megalo* large, big

μεζές *mezes* mezedhes, selection of starters (served free of charge with ouzo or retsina)

μεζέδες *mezedhes* mezedhes, selection of starters

μεζεδοπωλείο *mezedhopoleeo* mezés shop

μέλι *melee* honey

μελιτζάνα *meleetzana* aubergine

μελιτζάνες ιμάμ *meleetzanes eemam* aubergines stuffed with tomato and onion

μελιτζανοσαλάτα *meleetzanosalata* aubergine mousse (dip)

μελιτζανάκι γλυκό *meleetzanakee gleeko* crystalized sweet in syrup, made from aubergine/eggplant

μεσημεριανό *meseemereeano* lunch

μεταλλικό νερό *metaleeko nero* mineral water

μεταξά *metaxa* Metaxa (Greek brandy-type spirit)

μέτρια ψημένο *metreea pseemeno* medium (meat)

μη αεριούχο *mee aereeookho* still, not fizzy

μήλα *meela* apples

μηλόπιτα *meelopeeta* apple pie

μήλα

μίλκο *m**ee**lko* milky chocolate drink

μιλκσέικ *meelks**ei**k* milkshake

μικρό *meekr**o*** small, little

μοσχάρι *moskh**a**ree* veal

μοσχάρι *moskh**a**ree* beef

μοσχάρι κοκινιστό *moskh**a**ree kokeeneest**o*** beef in wine sauce with tomatoes and onions

μουσακάς *moosak**a**s* moussaka, layered aubergine, meat and potato, with white sauce

μπακαλιάρος *bakalee**a**ros* cod

μπακαλιάρος παστός *bakalee**a**ros past**o**s* salt cod

μουσακάς moussaka

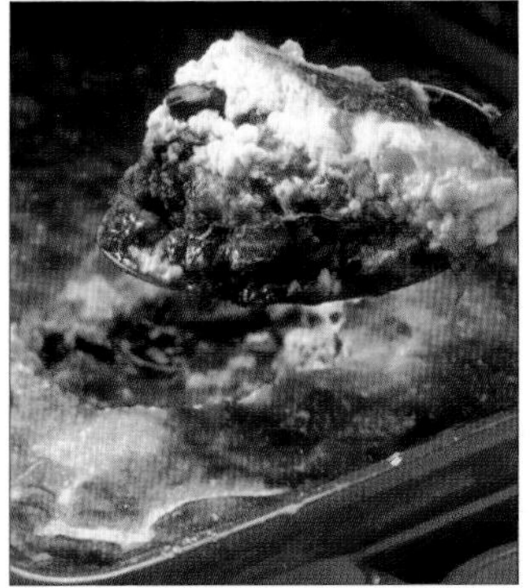

μπακλαβάς *baklav**a**s* filo-pastry with nuts soaked in syrup

μπάμιες *b**a**meeyes* okra (vegetable)

μπαράκι *bar**a**kee* bar

μπαρμπούνι *barb**oo**nee* red mullet

μπέικον *b**a**ykon* bacon

μπίρα, μπύρα *b**ee**ra* beer (lager-type)

μπιφτέκια *beeft**e**kya* meat rissole/burger

μπουγάτσα *boug**a**tsa* cheese or custard pastry sprinkled with sugar and cinnamon

μπουκάλι *book**a**lee* bottle

μπακλαβάς *baklav**a**s*

μπουρέκι *boor**e**kee* cheese potato and courgette pie

μπουρέκια *boor**e**keea* puff pastry filled with meat and cheese (Cyprus)

μπουρδέτο *boord**e**to* fish or meat in a thick sauce of onions, tomatoes and red peppers

μπριάμ *bree**a**m* ratatouille

μπριζόλα *breez**o**la* steak (beef/pork)

μπριζόλα αρνίσια *breez**o**la arn**ee**seea* lamb chop

μπριζόλα μοσχαρίσια *breez**o**la moskhar**ee**seea* veal chop

μύδια *m**ee**dheea* mussels

ν Ν

νες, νεσκαφέ *nes, nescafe* instant coffee (of any brand)

νερό *nero* water

ντολμάδες *dolmadhes* vine leaves, rolled up and stuffed with mincemeat and rice

ντομάτες *domates* tomatoes

ντομάτες γεμιστές *domates yemeestes* tomatoes stuffed with rice and herbs, and sometimes with mince

ξ Ξ

ξιφίας *kseefeeas* swordfish

ξύδι *kseedhee* vinegar

ο Ο

οβελιστήριο

οβελιστήριο *oveleesteereeo* shop selling souvlakia and doner kebabs

οινοπωλείο *eenopoleeo* wine shop

ομελέτα *omeletta* omelette

ορεκτικά *orekteeka* first course/starter

ουζερί *oozeree* small bar selling ouzo and other drinks, maybe with mezedhes (**μεζέδες**)

ούζο *oozo* ouzo (traditional aniseed-flavoured spirit)

ουίσκι *weeskee* whisky

οχταπόδια *okhtapodheea* octopus (see also **χταπόδι**)

οχταπόδι κρασάτο *okhtapodhee krasato* octopus in red wine sauce

π Π

παγάκια *pagakya* ice-cubes

παγωτό *paghoto* ice-cream

παϊδάκια *paeedhakeea* grilled lamb chops

παντζάρια *pandzareea* beetroot with seasonings

παξιμάδια *pakseemadheea* crispy bread (baked twice)

παξιμαδοκούλουρα *paxeemadhokoolooa* tomato and cheese bread

παπουτσάκια *papootsakeea* stuffed aubergines

πασατέμπο *pasatempo* pumpkin seeds

πάστα *pasta* cake, pastry

παστό *pasto* salted

παστιτσάδα *pasteetsada* beef with tomatoes, onions, red wine, herbs, spices and pasta

παστίτσιο *pasteetseeo* baked pasta dish with a middle layer of meat and white sauce

πατσάς *patsas* tripe soup

πατάτες *patates* potatoes

πατάτες τηγανιτές *patates teeghaneetes* chips, fries

πεπόνι *peponee* melon

πεπόνι

ραδίκια
ρίγανη

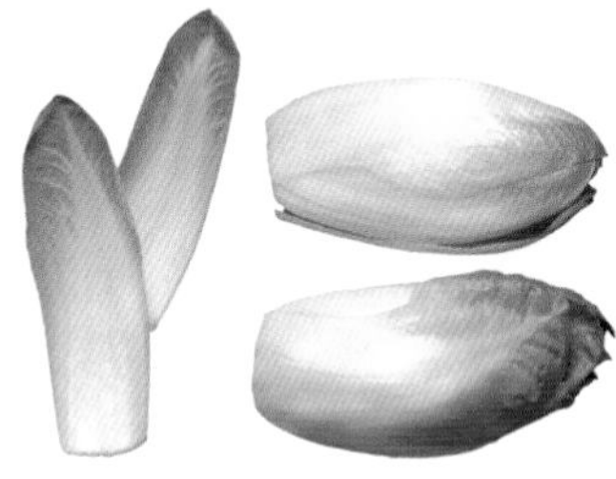

πέστροφα *p**e**strofa* trout

πηλιορίτικο μπουμπάρι *peeleeor**ee**teeko boob**a**ree* spicy sausage

πιάτο της ημέρας *py**a**to tees eem**e**ras* dish of the day

πιλάφι *peel**a**fee* pilau rice

πιπέρι *peep**e**ree* pepper

πιπεριές *peeperу**e**s* peppers

πιπεριές γεμιστές *peeperу**e**s yemeest**e**s* stuffed peppers with rice and meat

πίττα *p**ee**ta* pitta (flat envelope of unleavened bread)

πίττες *p**ee**tes* pies – they have different fillings, such as meat, vegetables or cheese

πλακί *plak**ee*** fish in tomato sauce

πορτοκαλάδα *portokal**a**dha* orange drink

πορτοκάλια *portok**a**lya* oranges

πουργούρι *poorgh**oo**ree* cracked wheat (Cyprus)

πουργούρι πιλάφι *poorgh**oo**ree peel**a**fee* salad made of cracked wheat (Cyprus)

πράσα με σησάμι *pr**a**sa me sees**a**mee* leeks baked and sprinkled with sesame seeds

πρωινό *proeen**o*** breakfast

ρ Ρ

ραβιόλι *ravee**o**lee* pastry stuffed with cheese (Cyprus)

ραδίκια *rad**hee**keea* chicory

ρακή, ρακί *rak**ee*** raki, strong spirit a bit like schnapps

ρεβίθια *rev**ee**theea* chickpeas

ρέγγα *r**e**nga* herring

ρέγγα καπνιστή *r**e**nga kapneest**ee*** smoked herring, kipper

ρετσίνα *rets**ee**na* retsína, traditional resinated white wine

ρίγανη *r**ee**ganee* oregano

ρίγανη *r**ee**ghanee* chicory

ροδάκινο *rod**a**keeno* peach

ροζέ κρασί *roz**e** kras**ee*** rosé wine

ρολο με κιμά *rol**o** me keem**a*** meatloaf

ρύζι *r**ee**zee* rice

ρυζόγαλο *reez**o**ghalo* rice pudding

ρώσσικη σαλάτα *r**o**seekee sal**a**ta* Russian salad (pieces of egg, potatoes, gherkins, peas and carrots in mayonnaise)

σ ς Σ

σαγανάκι *saghan**a**kee* mezedhes dish of fried cheese

σαλάτα *sal**a**ta* salad

σαλάτες *sal**a**tes* salads (on menu)

σαρδέλλες

σαλατικά *salateeka* salads (menu heading)

σαλάχι *salakhee* ray

σαλιγκάρια *saleengareea* snails

σαλιγκάρια γιαχνί *saleengareea yakhnee* snails in tomato sauce

σάντουιτς *sandweets* sandwich (sometimes a filled roll, sometimes a toasted sandwich with your own chosen combination of fillings)

σαραγλί *sarangglee* pastry with walnuts, sesame seeds and syrup; sometimes chocolate too

σαρδέλλες *sardhelles* sardines

σέλινο *seleeno* celery

σεφταλιά *seftalya* minced pork pasty

σικαλέσιο ψωμί *seekaleseeo psomee* rye bread

σικώτι *seekotee* liver

σκορδαλιά *skordhalya* garlic and potato mash

σκορδαλιά με ψάρι τηγανιτό *skordhalya me psaree teeghaneeto* fried fish served with garlic and potato mash

σκόρδο *skordho* garlic

σκόρδο

σόδα *soda* soda

σουβλάκι *soovlakee* meat kebab

σουβλατζίδικο *soovlatseedeeko* shop selling souvlakia, doner kebabs, etc

σπανακόπιτα spinach pie

σούπα *soopa* soup

σουπιά *soopya* cuttlefish

σουτζουκάκια *sootzookakeea* highly seasoned meat balls

σοφρίτο *sofreeto* meat stew, highly seasoned (Corfu)

σπανάκι *spanakee* spinach

σπανακόπιτα *spanakopeeta* spinach pie

σπαράγγι *sparangee* asparagus

σπαράγγια και αγγινάρές *sparangeea ke angeenares* mezedhes of artichokes and asparagus in lemon juice

σπαράγγια σαλάτα *sparangeea salata* asparagus salad

σταφύλια *stafeeleea* grapes

στη σουβλά *stee soovla* spit-roasted

σπαράγγι

φασολάδα bean soup

στιφάδο *steefadho* braised meat in onion and tomato sauce

στο φούρνο *sto foorno* baked in the oven

στρείδια *streedheea* oysters

σύκα *seeka* figs

σύκα στο φούρνο με μαυροδάφνη *seeka sto foorno me mavrodafnee* figs cooked in red wine sauce with spices

σχάρας *skharas* grilled

τ Τ

ταραμοσαλάτα *taramosalata* mousse of cod roe

τζατζίκι *tzatzeekee*

ταχίνι *takheenee* sesame seed paste

τζατζίκι *tzatzeekee* cucumber, garlic and yoghurt dip

τόννος ψητός *tonos pseetos* grilled tuna with vegetables

τραπανός *trapanos* soup made of cracked wheat and yoghurt (Cyprus)

τσάι *tsaee* tea

τσιπούρα *tseepoora* type of sea bream

τσουρέκι *tsoorekee* festive bread

τυρί *teeree* cheese

τυροκαυτερή *teerokafteree* spicy dip made of cheese and peppers

τυρόπιτα *teeropeeta* cheese pie

τυροσαλάτα *teerosalata* starter made of cheese and herbs

φέτα *feta*

φ Φ

φάβα *fava* yellow split peas or lentils, served in a purée with olive oil and capers

φαγγρί *fangree* sea bream

φακές *fakes* lentils

φασολάδα *fasoladha* very popular dish made with large white beans and herbs

φασολάκια *fasolakeea* green beans

φασόλια *fas**o**leea* haricot bean casserole

φέτα *f**e**ta* feta cheese, used in salads and other dishes

φλαούνες *fla**oo**nes* Easter cheese cake (Cyprus)

φράουλες *fr**a**ooles* strawberries

φρέσκα φρούτα *fr**e**ska fr**oo**ta* fresh fruit

φρούτα *fr**oo**ta* fruit

φυστίκια *feest**ee**kya* peanuts

φυστίκια Αιγίνης *feest**ee**kya ey**ee**nees* pistacchios

χ Χ

χαλβάς *khalv**a**s* sesame seed sweet

χαλούμι *khal**oo**mee* ewe's- or goat's-milk cheese, often grilled

χέλι καπνιστό *kh**e**lee kapneest**o*** smoked eel

χοιρινό *kheereen**o*** pork

χοιρινό κρητικό *kheereen**o** kreeteek**o*** baked pork chops (Crete)

χοιρομέρι *kheerom**e**ree* marinated, smoked ham

χόρτα *kh**o**rta* wild greens

χορτοφάγος *khortof**a**ghos* vegetarian

χούμους *kh**oo**moos* dip made with puréed chickpeas

χταπόδι *khtap**o**dhee* octopus, often grilled

χωριάτικη σαλάτα *khoree**a**teekee sal**a**ta* salad, Greek style, with tomatoes, feta cheese, cucumber and onions

ψ Ψ

ψάρι *ps**a**ree* fish

ψάρια καπνιστά *ps**a**reea kapneest**a*** smoked fish

ψάρια πλακί *ps**a**reea plak**ee*** baked whole fish with vegetables and tomatoes

ψαρόσουπα *psar**o**soopa* seafood soup

ψαροταβέρνα *psarotav**e**rna* fish taverna

ψησταρία *pseestar**ee**a* grill house

ψητό *pseet**o*** roast

ψωμάκι *psom**a**kee* bread roll

ψωμί *psom**ee*** bread

ψωμι ολικής αλέσεως *psom**ee** oleek**ee**s al**e**seos* wholemeal bread

ψάρι fish

ψωμί

PHONETIC MENU READER

A

aereeookho fizzy, sparkling

afeleea pork in red wine with seasonings (Cyprus)

agreeogooroono wild boar

akheenee sea urchin roes

akhladhee pear

akhladhee sto foorno baked pear with syrup sauce

akhneesto steamed

alatee salt

alevree flour

alevropeeta pie made with cheese, milk and eggs

ameegdala almonds

aneethos dill

angeenares artichokes

angeenares ala poleeta artichokes with lemon juice and olive oil

angooree cucumber

arakadhes peas

arnakee pseeto lamb chop grilled with herbs

arnee lamb

arnee gyoovetsee roast lamb with small pasta

arnee lemonato lamb braised in sauce with herbs and lemon juice

arnee me votana lamb stewed with vegetables and herbs

arneeseeo lamb chops

arnee pseeto roast lamb

aspro white

aspro krasee white wine

astakos lobster (often served with lemon juice and olive oil)

athereena whitebait, usually fried

avgha eggs

avgholemono egg and lemon soup

avghotarakho mullet roe (smoked)

avrakee baked sea-bass

B

bakaleearos cod

bakaleearos pastos salt cod

baklavas filo-pastry with nuts soaked in syrup

bameeyes okra (vegetable)

barakee bar

barboonee red mullet

baykon bacon

beeftekya meat rissole/burger

beera beer (lager-type)

bookalee bottle

boordeto fish or meat in a thick sauce of onions, tomatoes and red peppers

boorekee cheese potato and courgette pie

boorekeea puff pastry filled with meat and cheese (Cyprus)

bougatsa cheese or custard pastry sprinkled with sugar and cinnamon

breeam ratatouille

breezola steak (beef/pork)

breezola arneeseea lamb chop

breezola moskhareeseea veal chop

D

dafnee bay leaf

dhakteela almond cakes

dhamaskeena prunes with cream in wine sauce

dheepno dinner

dendroleevano rosemary

dheeples pastry with honey and walnuts

dolmadhes vine leaves, rolled up and stuffed with mincemeat and rice

domates tomatoes
domates yemeestes tomatoes stuffed with rice and herbs, and sometimes with mince

E

eemam baeeldee stuffed aubergines (eggplants)

eenopoleeo wine shop

elakheesta pseemeno rare (meat)

eleoladho olive oil

elyes olives

elyes tsakeestes cracked green olives with coriander seeds and garlic (Cyprus)

elyotee olive bread

esteeatoreeo restaurant

exokheeko stuffed pork or beef with vegetables and cheese

F

fakes lentils

fangree sea bream

fasoladha very popular dish made with large white beans and herbs

fasolakeea green beans

fasoleea haricot bean casserole

fava yellow split peas or lentils, served in a purée with olive oil and capers

feesteekya peanuts

feesteekya eyeenees pistacchios

feta feta cheese, used in salads and other dishes

flaoones Easter cheese cake (Cyprus)

fraooles strawberries

freska froota fresh fruit

froota fruit

G

gareefalo clove (spice)

gavros sardine-type fish (if salted: anchovy)

ghala milk

ghalaktobooreko custard tart

galaktopoleeo café/patisserie

ghareedhes shrimps; prawns
ghareedhes yoovetsee prawns in tomato sauce with feta

ghazoza fizzy drink

ghlosa sole

ghlyka dessert

ghlyka kootalyoo dessert

ghopes bogue, a type of fish

ghravyera cheese resembling gruyère

K

kafeneeo café

kafedes coffees (plural)

kafes coffee (Greek-style)

kafes frappé iced coffee

kafes ghleekees very sweet coffee

kafes me ghala milky coffee

kafes metreeos medium-sweet coffee

kafes sketos coffee without sugar

*kakaveea*fish soup

ka-kow hot chocolate

kalamakya small skewers

kalamareea squid

kalamareea teeghaneeta fried squid

kalambokee corn on the cob

*kalambok***o***peeta* corn bread
*kalopseem***e***no* well done (meat)
*kan***e***lla* cinnamon
*k***a***paree* pickled capers
*kapneest***o** smoked
*kar***a***fa* carafe
*karav***ee***dha* crayfish
*kar***ee***dhee* walnut
*kareedh***o***peeta* walnut cake
*kar***ee***dha* coconut
*kar***e***kla* chair
*kar***o***to* carrot
*karp***oo***zee* watermelon
*kas***e***ree* sheep's milk cheese, often served fried
*k***a***stana* chestnuts
*kata***ee***fee* small pastry drenched in syrup
*kat***a***loghos* menu
*kat***a***loghos krasy***o***n* wine list
*katapseegm***e***no* frozen
*kats***ee***kee* roast kid
*k***a***vawine shop
*k***a***vooras* boiled crab
*kayan***a***s me past***o** *kr***e***yas* salted pork with cheese, tomatoes and eggs
*keedh***o***nee* quince
*keedh***o***neea* type of clams
*keedh***o***nee sto f***oo***rno* baked quince
*keem***a***s* mince
*keen***ee***yee* game
*keer***ee***o py***a***to* main course
*kefal***o***teeree* type of cheese, often served fried in olive oil
*keft***e***dhes* meat balls
*ker***a***seea* cherries
*khalv***a***s* sesame seed sweet, halva
*khal***oo***mee* ewe's or goat's milk cheese, often grilled
*kheereen***o** pork
*kheereen***o** *kreeteek***o** baked pork chops (Crete)
*kheerom***e***ree* marinated, smoked ham
*kh***e***lee kapneest***o** smoked eel
*kh***oo***moos* dip made with puréed chickpeas
*kh***o***rta* wild greens
*khoree***a***teekee sal***a***ta* salad, Greek style, with tomatoes, feta cheese, cucumber and onions
*khortof***a***ghos* vegetarian
*kl***e***fteeko* casserole with meat, potatoes and vegetables
*kokor***e***tsee* stewed offal or liver, a special Easter dish
*kokt***e***eel* cocktail
*kolats***yo** brunch, elevenses
*kolokeeth***a***keea* courgettes, zucchini
*kolokeeth***o***peeta* courgette/zucchini pie
*kolokeeth***o***peeta gleeky***a** sweet courgette/zucchini pie
*kolok***o***tes* pastries with pumpkins and raisins
*kontos***oo***vlee* spicy pieces of lamb, pork or beef, spit-roasted
*kony***a***k* brandy, cognac
*kooky***a** broad beans
*kool***oo***reea* bread rings
*koon***e***lee* rabbit
*koonoop***ee***dhee* cauliflower
*koop***e***peea* stuffed vine leaves (Cyprus)
*koop***e***s* meat pasties
*koorambye***e***dhes* small almond cakes eaten at Christmas
*kot***o***poolo* chicken
*kot***o***poolo reeghan***a***to* grilled basted chicken with herbs
*kot***o***poolo kapam***a** chicken casseroled with red peppers, onions, cinnamon and raisins

krasee wine
kreas meat
kreeo cold
kreeteekee salata watercress salad
krema cream
kremeedheea onions
kseedhee vinegar
kseefeeas swordfish
khtapodhee octopus, often grilled

L

ladhee oil
ladhera vegetable casserole
ladoteero soft cheese with olive oil
lagos hare
lakhana vegetables
lakhaneeka vegetables (menu heading)
lakhano cabbage
leego a little, a bit
lemonadha lemon drink
lemonee lemon
lefko white
lookaneeka type of highly seasoned sausage
lookoomadhes small fried dough balls in syrup
lookoomee Turkish delight
lookoomeea shortbread served at weddings
loondza loin of pork, marinated and smoked

M

maeedanos parsley
makaronya spaghetti
makaronya me keema spaghetti bolognese
maneedareea mushrooms
mareedhes small fish like sprats, served fried
mareezoles meat cooked in olive oil and lemon juice
maroolee lettuce
marteenee martini
mavro red wine
mavro krasee red wine (although you'll hear *kokeeno krasee* more often)
mavromateeka black-eyed peas
mayeereetsa soup made of lamb offal, special Easter dish
mee aereeookho still, not fizzy
meedheea mussels
meekro small, little
meela apples
meelopeeta apple pie
meelko milky chocolate drink
megalo large, big
melee honey
meleetzana aubergine
meleetzanakee gleeko crystalized sweet in syrup, made from aubergine (eggplant)
meleetzanes eemam aubergines stuffed with tomato and onion
meleetzanosalata aubergine mousse (dip)
meseemereeano lunch
metaleeko nero mineral water
metaxa Metaxa (Greek brandy-type spirit)
metreea pseemeno medium (meat)
mezedhes mezedhes, selection of starters
mezedhopoleeo mezés shop
mezes mezedhes, selection of starters (served free of charge with ouzo or retsina)
moskharee veal
moskharee beef
moskharee kokeeneesto beef in wine sauce with tomatoes and onions
moosakas moussaka, layered aubergine, meat and potato, with white sauce

N

nes, nescafé instant coffee (of any brand)

*ner**o*** water

O

*okhtap**o**dheea* octopus

*okhtap**o**dhee kras**a**to* octopus in red wine sauce

*omel**e**tta* omelette

*oozer**ee*** small bar selling ouzo and other drinks, maybe with mezedhes

***oo**zo* ouzo (traditional aniseed-flavoured spirit)

*orekteek**a*** first course/starter

*oveleest**ee**reeo* shop selling souvlakia and doner kebabs

P

*pag**a**kya* ice-cubes

*paghot**o*** ice-cream

*paeedh**a**keea* grilled lamb chops

*pakseem**a**dheea* crispy bread (baked twice)

*pandz**a**reea* beetroot with seasonings

*papoots**a**keea* stuffed aubergines

*pasat**e**mpo* pumpkin seeds

*p**a**sta* cake, pastry

*past**o*** salted

*pasteets**a**da* beef with tomatoes, onions, red wine, herbs, spices and pasta

*past**ee**tseeo* baked pasta dish with a middle layer of meat and white sauce

*pats**a**s* tripe soup

*pat**a**tes* potatoes

*pat**a**tes teeghaneet**e**s* chips, fries

*paxeemadhok**oo**looa* tomato and cheese bread

*peel**a**fee* pilau rice

*peeleeor**ee**teeko boob**a**ree* spicy sausage

*peep**e**ree* pepper

*peepery**e**s* peppers

*peepery**e**s yemeest**e**s* stuffed peppers with rice and meat

*p**ee**ta* pitta (flat envelope of unleavened bread)

*p**ee**tes* meaning pies, but they have different fillings, such as meat, vegetables or cheese

*pep**o**nee* melon

*p**e**strofa* trout

*plak**ee*** fish in tomato sauce

*poorgh**oo**ree* cracked wheat (Cyprus)

*poorgh**oo**ree peel**a**fee* salad made of cracked wheat (Cyprus)

*portokal**a**dha* orange drink

*portok**a**lya* oranges

*pr**a**sa me sees**a**mee* leeks baked and sprinkled with sesame seeds

*proeen**o*** breakfast

*ps**a**ree* fish

*ps**a**reea kapneest**a*** smoked fish

*ps**a**reea plak**ee*** baked whole fish with vegetables and tomatoes

*psar**o**soopa* seafood soup

*psarotav**e**rna* fish taverna

*pseestar**ee**a* grill house

*pseet**o*** roast

*psom**a**kee* bread roll

*psom**ee*** bread

*psom**ee** oleek**ee**s al**e**seos* wholemeal bread

Q

*py**a**to tees eem**e**ras* dish of the day

R

*radh**ee**keea* chicory

*rak**ee*** raki, strong spirit a bit like schnapps

raveeolee pastry stuffed with cheese (Cyprus)

reeghanee oregano or chicory

renga herring

renga kapneestee smoked herring, kipper

retseena retsina, traditional resinated white wine

reveetheea chickpeas

rolo me keema meatoaf

rodakeeno peach

roze krasee rosé wine

reezee rice

reezoghalo rice pudding

roseekee salata Russian salad (pieces of egg, potatoes, gherkins, peas and carrots in mayonnaise)

S

saghanakee mezedhes dish of fried cheese

salata salad

salakhee ray

salateeka salads (menu heading)

salates salads (on menu)

saleengareea snails

saleengareea yakhnee snails in tomato sauce

sandweets sandwich (sometimes a filled roll, sometimes a toasted sandwich with your own chosen combination of fillings)

saranglee pastry with walnuts, sesame seeds and syrup; sometimes chocolate too

sardhelles sardines

seeka figs

seekaleseeo psomee rye bread

seeka sto foorno me mavrodafnee figs cooked in red wine sauce with spices

seekotee liver

seftalya minced pork pasty

seleeno celery

skharas grilled

skordhalya garlic and potato mash

skordhalya me psaree teeghaneeto fried fish served with garlic and potato mash

skordho garlic

soda soda

sofreeto meat stew, highly seasoned (Corfu)

soopa soup

soopya cuttlefish

soovlakee meat kebab

soovlatseedeeko shop selling souvlakia, doner kebabs, etc

sootzookakeea highly seasoned meat balls

spanakee spinach

spanakopeeta spinach pie

sparangee asparagus

sparangeea ke angeenares mezedhes of artichokes and asparagus in lemon juice

sparangeea salata asparagus salad

stafeeleea grapes

steefadho braised meat in onion and tomato sauce

stee soovla spit-roasted

sto foorno baked in the oven

streedheea oysters

T

takheenee sesame seed paste

taramosalata mousse of cod roe

teeree cheese

teerokafteree spicy dip made of cheese and peppers

teeropeeta cheese pie

teerosalata starter made of cheese and herbs

*thalaseen**a*** seafood

*theem**a**ree* thyme

*t**o**nos pseet**o**s* grilled tuna with vegetables

*trapan**o**s* soup made of cracked wheat and yoghurt (Cyprus)

*ts**a**ee* tea

*tseep**oo**ra* type of sea bream

*tsoor**e**kee* festive bread

*tzatz**ee**kee* cucumber, garlic and yoghurt dip

V

*vaseeleek**o**s* basil

*veeseen**o** kas**e**ree* sheep's cheese served with cherry preserve

*ver**ee**koko* apricot

*vl**ee**ta* wild greens (like spinach, eaten with olive oil and lemon)

*vodheen**o*** beef

*voot**ee**mata* biscuits to dip in coffee

*v**oo**teero* butter

*v**o**tka* vodka

*vradeen**o*** evening meal

*vrast**o*** boiled

W

***wee**skee* whisky

Y

*yakhn**ee*** cooked in tomato sauce and olive oil

*ya**oo**rtee* yoghurt

*ya**oo**rtee me m**e**lee* yoghurt with honey

*y**ee**da vrast**ee*** goat soup

*y**ee**ghantes* large butter beans

*y**ee**ros* doner kebab

*yemeest**a*** stuffed vegetables

*yoovarl**a**kya* meatballs in lemon sauce

Z

*z**a**kharee* sugar

*zakharoplast**ee**o* cake shop

*zelat**ee**na* brawn

*zamb**o**n* ham

*zest**ee** sokol**a**ta* hot chocolate

*zest**o*** hot, warm

DICTIONARY

english-greek

greek-english

A

a ένας / μία / ένα *enas (masculine* ο *words) / meea (feminine* η *words) / ena (neuter* το *words)*

able: ***to be able to*** μπορώ να κάνω *boro na kano*

abortion η άμβλωση *ee amvlosee*

about: ***a book about Athens*** ένα βιβλίο για την Αθήνα *ena veevleeo ya teen Atheena*
at about ten o'clock περίπου στις δέκα *pereepoo stees dheka*

above πάνω από *pano apo*

abscess το απόστημα *to aposteema*

accident το ατύχημα *to ateekheema*

A & E Τα Επείγοντα Περιστατικά *ta epeeghonta peristatika*

accommodation η στέγη *ee steyee*

to accompany συνοδεύω *seenodhevo*

account ο λογαριασμός *o logharyasmos*
account number ο αριθμός λογαριασμού *o areethmos logharyasmoo*

ache ο πόνος *o ponos*
it aches πονάει *ponaee*

Acropolis η Ακρόπολη *ee Akropolee*

activities οι δραστηριότητες *ee dhrasteereeoteetes*

adaptor ο μετατροπέας *o metatropeas*

address η διεύθυνση *ee dheeeftheensee*
what is your address? ποια είναι η διεύθυνσή σας; *peea eene ee dheeeftheensee sas*

address book η ατζέντα *ee atzenda*

adhesive tape η συγκολλητική ταινία *ee seengoleeteekee teneea*

admission charge η είσοδος *ee eesodhos*

adult ο ενήλικος *o eneeleekos*

advance: ***in advance*** προκαταβολικώς *prokatavoleekos*

Aegean Sea τοΑιγαίο(πέλαγος) *to eyeo (pelaghos)*

after μετά *meta*

afternoon το απόγευμα *to apoyevma*

aftershave το αφτερσέιβ *to aftersheiv*

afterwards αργότερα *arghotera*

again πάλι *palee*

ago: ***a week ago*** πριν μια βδομάδα *preen meea vdhomadha*

AIDS ΕΙΤΖ *e-eetz*

airbag ο αερόσακος *o aerosakos*

air conditioning ο κλιματισμός *o kleemateesmos*

air freshener το αποσμητικό χώρου *to aposmeeteeko khoroo*

airline η αεροπορική εταιρία *ee aeroporeekee etereea*

airmail αεροπορικώς *aeroporeekos*

air mattress το στρώμα για τη θάλασσα *to stroma ya tee thalasa*

airplane το αεροπλάνο *to aeroplano*

airport το αεροδρόμιο *to aerodhromeeo*

airport bus το λεωφορείο για το αεροδρόμειο *to leoforeeo ya to aerodhromeeo*

air ticket τοαεροπορικόεισιτήριο *to aeroporeeko eeseeteereeo*

aisle *(in aircraft)* ο διάδρομος *o dheeadhromos*

alarm *(emergency)* ο συναγερμός *o seenayermos*

alarm clock το ξυπνητήρι *to kseepneeteeree*

alcohol το οινόπνευμα *to eenopnevma*

alcohol-free χωρίς οινόπνευμα *khorees eenopnevma*

alcoholic οινοπνευματώδης *eenopnevmatodhees*

all όλος *olos*
all the milk όλο το γάλα *olo to ghala*
all the time όλον τον καιρό *olon ton kero*

allergic to αλλεργικός σε *aleryeekos se*

alley το δρομάκι *to dhromakee*

allowance: ***duty-free allowance*** η επιτρεπόμενη ποσότητα *ee epeetrepomenee posoteeta*

all right *(agreed)* **εντάξει** *endaksee*

almond **το αμύγδαλο** *to ameeghdhalo*

already **ήδη** *eedhee*, **κιόλας** *keeolas*

also **επίσης** *epeesees*

aluminium foil **το αλουμινόχαρτο** *to aloomeenokharto*

always **πάντα** *panda*

am: ***I am*** **είμαι** *eeme*

amber *(traffic light)* **το πορτοκαλί** *to portokalee*

ambulance **το ασθενοφόρο** *to asthenoforo*

America **η Αμερική** *ee amereekee*

American **ο Αμερικανός / η Αμερικανίδα** *o amereekanos / ee amereekaneedha*

amphitheatre **το αμφιθέατρο** *to amfeetheatro*

anaesthetic **το αναισθητικό** *to anestheeteeko*

anchor **η άγκυρα** *ee angeera*

anchovy **η αντζούγια** *ee andzooya*

and **και** *ke*

angina **η στηθάγχη** *ee steethangkhee*

angry **θυμωμένος** *theemomenos*

to announce **ανακοινώνω** *anakeenono*

announcement **η ανακοίνωση** *ee anakeenosee*

another **άλλος** *alos*
another beer **άλλη μία μπίρα** *alee meea beera*

answer **η απάντηση** *ee apandeesee*

to answer **απαντώ** *apando*

answerphone **ο αυτόματος τηλεφωνητής** *o aftomatos teelefoneetees*

antacid **το αντιοξινό** *to andeeozeeno*

antibiotics **τα αντιβιοτικά** *ta andeeveeoteeka*

antihistamine **το αντιισταμινικό** *to andeestameeneeko*

anti-inflammatory **το αντιφλεγμονώδες** *to anteefleghmonodhes*

antiques **οι αντίκες** *ee anteekes*

antiseptic **το αντισηπτικό** *to andeeseepteeko*

any **καθόλου** *katholoo*
I haven't any money **δεν έχω καθόλου χρήματα** *dhen ekho katholoo khreemata*

anyone **οποιονδήποτε** *opeeondheepote*

anything **οτιδήποτε** *oteedheepote*

anywhere **οπουδήποτε** *opoodheepote*

apartment **το διαμέρισμα** *to dheeamereesma*

apartment block **η πολυκατοικία** *ee poleekateekeea*

aperitif **το απεριτίφ** *to apereeteef*

apple **το μήλο** *to meelo*

appendicitis **η σκωληκοειδίτιδα** *ee skoleekoeedheeteedha*

application form **η αίτηση** *ee eteesee*

appointment **το ραντεβού** *to randevoo*
I have an appointment **έχω ένα ραντεβού** *ekho ena randevoo*

approximately **περίπου** *pereepoo*

apricot **το βερίκοκο** *to vereekoko*

April **ο Απρίλιος** *o apreeleeos*

archaeology **η αρχαιολογία** *ee arkheoloyeea*

architect **ο αρχιτέκτωνας** *o archeetektonas*

architecture **η αρχιτεκτονική** *ee arkheetektoneekee*

are: ***they are*** **είναι** *eene*
we are **είμαστε** *eemaste*
you are **είσαι** *eese (sing)* // **είστε** *eeste (plural)*

arm **το μπράτσο** *to bratso*

armbands *(for swimming)* **τα μπρατσάκια** *ta bratsakeea*

around **γύρω** *yeero*

to arrest **συλλαμβάνω** *seelamvano*

arrivals **οι αφίξεις** *ee afeeksees*

to arrive **φτάνω** *ftano*

art **η τέχνη** *ee technee*

art gallery **η πινακοθήκη** *ee peenakotheekee*

arthritis η αρθρίτιδα ee arthreeteedha

artichoke η αγκινάρα ee angeenara

artificial τεχνητός techneetos, ψευτικός psefteekos

ashtray το τασάκι to tasakee

asleep κοιμισμένος keemeesmenos
he/she is asleep κοιμάται keemate

asparagus το σπαράγγι to sparangee

aspirin η ασπιρίνη ee aspeereenee
soluble aspirin διαλυόμενη ασπιρίνη dheealeeomenee aspeereenee

asthma το άσθμα to asthma
I have asthma έχω άσθμα ekho asthma

at σε (στο / στη / στο) se (sto / stee / sto)

atlas ο άτλαντας o atlandas

attractive (person) ελκυστικός elkeesteekos

aubergine η μελιτζάνα ee meleetzana

aunt η θεία ee theea

Australia η Αυστραλία ee afstraleea

Australian ο Αυστραλός / η Αυστραλίδα o afstralos / ee afstraleedha

automatic αυτόματος aftomatos

autoteller το ATM to ey tee em

autumn το φθινόπωρο to ftheenoporo

avalanche η χιονοστιβάδα ee kheeonos-teevadha

average ο μέσος όρος o mesos oros
on average κατά μέσο όρο kata meso oro

avocado το αβοκάντο to avokado

awake ξύπνιος kseepnios

away μακριά makreea

awful φοβερός foveros

B

baby το μωρό to moro

baby food οι βρεφικές τροφές ee vrefeekes trofes

baby milk το βρεφικό γάλα to vrefeeko ghala

baby's bottle το μπιμπερό to beebero

baby seat (in car) το παιδικό κάθισμα to pedheeko katheesma

baby-sitter η μπεϊμπισίτερ ee beibisiter

baby wipes τα υγρά μαντηλάκια για μωρά ta eeghra mandeelakya ya mora

back (of a person) η πλάτη ee platee

backpack το σακκίδιο to sakeedheeo

bad (of food) χαλασμένος khalasmenos
(of weather) κακός kakos

bag (small) η τσάντα ee tsanda
(suitcase) η βαλίτσα ee valeetsa

baggage οι αποσκευές ee aposkeves

baggage reclaim η παραλαβή αποσκευών ee paralavee aposkevon

bait (for fishing) το δόλωμα to dholoma

baker's ο φούρνος o foornos

balcony το μπαλκόνι to balkonee

bald (person, tyre) φαλακρός falakros

ball η μπάλα ee bala

banana η μπανάνα ee banana

band (musical) η ορχήστρα ee orkheestra

bandage ο επίδεσμος o epeedhesmos

bank η τράπεζα ee trapeza

bank account ο τραπεζικός λογαριασμός o trapezeekos logharyasmos

banknote το χαρτονόμισμα to khartonomeesma

bankrupt πτωχευτικός ptokhefteekos

bar το μπαρ to bar
bar of chocolate η πλάκα σοκολάτα ee plaka sokolata

barbecue η ψησταριά ee pseestarya

barber ο κουρέας o kooreas

to bark γαυγίζω ghavgheezo

barn η σιταποθήκη ee seetapotheekee

barrel το βαρέλι to varelee

basement το υπόγειο to eepoyeeo

basil ο βασιλικός o vaseeleekos

basket το καλάθι to kalathee

basketball το μπάσκετ to basket

bat η νυχτερίδα ee neekhtereedha
cricket bat το ρόπαλο του κρίκετ to ropalo too kreeket

bath *(tub)* **το μπάνιο** *to banyo*
to take a bath **κάνω μπάνιο** *kano banyo*

bathing cap **ο σκούφος του μπάνιου** *o skoofos too banyoo*

bathroom **το μπάνιο** *to banyo*

battery **η μπαταρία** *ee batareea*

bay **ο κόλπος** *o kolpos*

to be **είμαι** *eeme*

beach **η πλαζ** *ee plaz*, **η παραλία** *ee paraleea*
private beach **η ιδιωτική παραλία** *ee eedheeoteekee paraleea*
sandy beach **η αμμώδης παραλία** *ee amodhees paraleea*
nudist beach **η παραλία γυμνιστών** *ee paraleea gheemneeston*

bean *(haricot)* **το φασόλι** *to fasolee*
(broad) **το κουκί** *to kookee*
(green) **το φασολάκι** *to fasolakee*
(soya) **η σόγια** *ee soya*

beautiful **όμορφος** *omorfos*

beauty salon **το σαλόνι ομορφιάς** *to salonee omorfeeas*

bed **το κρεββάτι** *to krevatee*
double bed **διπλό κρεββάτι** *dheeplo krevatee*
single bed **μονό κρεββάτι** *mono krevatee*
twin beds **δύο μονά κρεββάτια** *dheeo mona krevatya*
sofa bed **καναπές κρεββάτι** *kanapes krevatee*

bedding **τα κλινοσκεπάσματα** *ta kleenoskepasmata*

bedroom **η κρεββατοκάμαρα** *ee krevatokamara*

beef **το βοδινό** *to vodheeno*, **το μοσχάρι** *to moskharee*

beer **η μπίρα** *ee beera*

beetroot **το παντζάρι** *to pandzaree*

before *(time)* **πριν (από)** *preen (apo)*
(place) **μπροστά από** *brosta apo*

to begin **αρχίζω** *arkheezo*

behind **πίσω από** *peeso apo*

to believe **πιστεύω** *peestevo*

bell *(electric)* **το κουδούνι** *to koodhoonee*

to belong to **ανήκω** *aneeko*

below **κάτω από** *kato apo*

belt **η ζώνη** *ee zonee*

beside **δίπλα** *dheepla*

best **ο καλύτερος** *o kaleeteros*

the best **ο καλύτερος** *o kaleeteros*

better (than) **καλύτερος (από)** *kaleeteros (apo)*

between **μεταξύ** *metaksee*

bib **η σαλιάρα** *ee salyara*

bicycle **το ποδήλατο** *to podheelato*

big **μεγάλος** *meghalos*

bigger **μεγαλύτερος** *meghaleeteros*

bike *(motorbike)* **η μοτοσυκλέτα** *ee motoseekleta*

bikini **το μπικίνι** *to beekeenee*

bill **ο λογαριασμός** *o logharyasmos*

bin **το καλάθι των αχρήστων** *to kalathee ton akhreeston*

bin liner **η σακούλα σκουπιδιών** *ee sakoola skoopeedhyon*

binoculars **τα κιάλια** *ta kyalya*

bird **το πουλί** *to poolee*

birth **η γέννηση** *ee yeneesee*

birth certificate **το πιστοποιητικό γεννήσεως** *to peestopyeetiko yeneeseos*

birthday **τα γενέθλια** *ta yenethleea*
happy birthday! **χρόνια πολλά** *khronya pola*

biscuit **το μπισκότο** *to beeskoto*

bit: *a bit (of)* **λίγο** *leegho*

bite *(insect)* **το τσίμπημα** *to tseebeema*
(snack) **η μπουκιά** *ee bookeea*

to bite *(of human, animal)* **δαγκώνω** *dhaghono*
(of insect) **τσιμπάω** *tseebao*

bitten: *I have been bitten* **με δάγκωσε** *me dhaghose*

bitter πικρός *peekros*

black μαύρος *mavros*

blackcurrant το μαύρο φραγκοστάφυλο *to mavro frangostafeelo*

blanket η κουβέρτα *ee kooverta*

bleach το λευκαντικό *to lefkandeeko*

to bleed αιμορραγώ *emoragho*

blister η φουσκάλα *ee fooskala*

block of flats η πολυκατοικία *ee poleekateekeea*

blocked *(pipe)* **βουλωμένος** *voolomenos*
(nose) **κλειστή** *kleestee*
(pipe, sink) **βουλωμένος** *voolomenos*
(road) **κλειστός** *kleestos*

blood group η ομάδα αίματος *ee omad-ha ematos*

blood pressure η πίεση αίματος *ee peeyesee ematos*

blond(e) *(male)* ξανθός *ksanthos* / *(female)* ξανθιά *ksanthya*

blouse η μπλούζα *ee blooza*

blow-dry στέγνωμα *steghnoma*

blue γαλάζιος *ghalazeeos*

boar *(wild)* το αγριογούρουνο *to aghree-oghoorono*

boarding card το δελτίο επιβιβάσεως *to dhelteeo epeeveevaseos*

boarding house η πανσιόν *ee pansyon*

boat *(small)* **η βάρκα** *ee varka*
(ship) **το πλοίο** *to pleeo*

boat trip η βαρκάδα *ee varkadha*

to boil βράζω *vrazo*

boiled βραστός *vrastos*
boiled water **βραστό νερό** *vrasto nero*

boiler το καζάνι *to kazanee*

bomb η βόμβα *ee vomva*

bone το κόκκαλο *to kokalo*
(fishbone) **το ψαροκόκαλλο** *to psarokokalo*

bonfire η φωτιά *ee foteea*

bonnet το καπό *to kapo*

book *n* το βιβλίο *to veevleeo*

to book *(room, tickets)* κλείνω *kleeno*

booking: ***to make a booking*** κλείνω θέση *kleeno thesee*

booking office *(railways, airlines, etc.)* **το εκδοτήριο** *to ekdhoteereeo*
(theatre) **το ταμείο** *to tameeo*

bookshop το βιβλιοπωλείο *to veevleeopoleeo*

boots οι μπότες *ee botes*

border *(frontier)* τα σύνορα *ta seenora*

boring βαρετός *varetos*

born γεννημένος *gheneemenos*
to be born **γεννιέμαι** *ghenyeme*

to borrow δανείζομαι *dhaneezome*

boss ο / η προϊστάμενος *o / ee proeestamenos*

both και οι δυο *ke ee dheeo*

bottle το μπουκάλι *to bookalee*
a bottle of wine **ένα μπουκάλι κρασί** *ena bookalee krasee*

bottle-opener το ανοιχτήρι *to aneekhteeree*

bowl το μπωλ *to bol*

bowtie το παπιγιόν *to papeeyon*

box *(container)* **το κιβώτιο** *to keevotyo*
(cardboard) **το κουτί** *to kootee*

box office το ταμείο *to tameeo*

boy το αγόρι *to aghoree*

boyfriend ο φίλος *o feelos*

bra το σουτιέν *to sootyen*

bracelet το βραχιόλι *to vrakheeolee*

to brake φρενάρω *frenaro*

brake fluid το υγρό των φρένων *to eeghro ton frenon*

brake light τα φώτα πεδήσεως *ta fota pedheeseos*

brake pads τα τακάκια *ta takakeea*

brakes τα φρένα *ta frena*

brandy το κονιάκ *to konyak*

brave γενναίος *(masc) gheneos*, γενναία *(fem) ghenea*

bread το ψωμί *to psomee*
(wholemeal) **ψωμί ολικής αλέσεως** *psomee oleekees aleseos*

to break σπάζω *spazo*

breakdown η βλάβη *ee vlavee*
nervous breakdown ο νευρικός κλονισμός *o nevreekos kloneesmos*

breakdown van το συνεργείο διασώσεως *to seeneryeeo dheeasoseos*

breakfast το πρόγευμα *to proyevma*

breast το στήθος *to steethos*

to breast-feed θηλάζω *theelazo*

to breathe αναπνέω *anapneo*

bride η νύφη *ee neefee*

bridegroom ο γαμπρός *o ghambros*

briefcase ο χαρτοφύλακας *o khartofeelakas*

to bring φέρνω *ferno*

Britain η Βρετανία *ee vretaneea*

British ο Βρετανός / η Βρετανίδα *o vretanos / ee vretaneedha*

brochure η μπροσούρα *ee brosoora*

broken σπασμένος *spasmenos*
broken down χαλασμένος *khalasmenos*

bronze μπρούντζινος *broondzeenos*

brooch η καρφίτσα *ee karfeetsa*

brother ο αδελφός *o adhelfos*

brown καφέ *kafe*

bruise ημολώπη *ee molopee*

brush η βούρτσα *ee voortsa*

bucket ο κουβάς *o koovas*

buffet ο μπουφές *o boofes*

buffet car το βαγόνι εστιατόριο *to vaghonee esteeatoreeo*

bulb *(light)* ο γλόμπος *o ghlobos*

bumbag το τσαντάκι μέσης *to tsantakee mesees*

buoy η σημαδούρα *ee seemadhoora*

bureau de change *(bank)* ξένο συνάλλαγμα *kseno seenalaghma*

burglar alarm ο συναγερμός *o seenaghermos*

to burn καίω *keo*

burnt καμένος *kamenos*

to burst σκάζω *skazo*

bus το λεωφορείο *to leoforeeo*

business η δουλειά *ee dhoolya*

bus pass το πάσο *to paso*

bus station ο σταθμός του λεωφορείου *o stathmos too leoforeeoo*

bus stop η στάση του λεωφορείου *ee stasee too leoforeeoo*

bus terminal το τέρμα του λεωφορείου *to terma too leoforeeoo*

bus tour η εκδρομή με λεωφορείο *ee ekdhromee me leoforeeo*

busy απασχολημένος *apaskholeemenos*

but αλλά *ala*

butcher's το κρεοπωλείο *to kreopoleeo*

butter το βούτυρο *to vooteero*

button το κουμπί *to koombee*

to buy αγοράζω *aghorazo*

by *(beside)* κοντά σε *konda se*
(time) μέχρι *mekhree*
by ship με πλοίο *me pleeo*

bypass η παρακάμψη *ee parakampsee*

C

cab το ταξί *to taksee*

cabbage το λάχανο *to lakhano*

cabin η καμπίνα *ee kabeena*

cabin crew το πλήρωμα *to pleeroma*

cable car το τελεφερίκ *to telefereek*

cable TV ηδορυφορική τηλεώραση *ee dhoreeforeekee teeleorasee*

café το καφενείο *to kafeneeo*
internet café ιντερνετ καφέ *internet cafe*

cake το γλύκισμα *to ghleekeesma*

cake shop το ζαχαροπλαστείο *to zakharoplasteeo*

calculator ο υπολογιστής *o eepoloyeestees*

calendar το ημερολόγιο *to eemeroloyo*

to call φωνάζω *fonazo*

call *n (telephone)* η κλήση *ee kleesee*
long-distance call η υπεραστική κλήση *ee eeperasteekee kleesee*

calm ήσυχος *eeseekhos*

camcorder η βιντεοκάμερα *ee veedeokamera*

camera η φωτογραφική μηχανή *ee fotoghrafeekee meekhanee*

to camp κατασκηνώνω *kataskeenono*

camping gas το γκαζάκι *to gazakee*

camping stove το πετρογκάζ *to petrogas*

campsite το κάμπινγκ *to camping*

can: ***I can*** μπορώ *boro*
I cannot δεν μπορώ *dhen boro*
can I...? μπορώ να΄... ; *boro na...*
can we...? μπορούμε να... ; *oroome na...*
you can μπορείς *borees*
he can μπορεί *boree*
we can μπορούμε *boroome*

can *(of food)* η κονσέρβα *ee konserva*
(for oil) ο τενεκές *o tenekes*

Canada ο Καναδάς *o kanadhas*

Canadian ο Καναδός / η Καναδή *o Kanadhos/ee Kanadhee*

canal το κανάλι *to kanalee*

candle το κερί *to keree*

to cancel ακυρώνω *akeerono*

canoe το κανό *to kano*

can-opener το ανοιχτήρι *to aneekhteeree*

cappuccino τοκαπουτσίνο *to kapootseeno*

car το αυτοκίνητο *to aftokeeneeto*

car alarm ο συναγερμός *o seenayermos*

car ferry το φεριμπότ *to fereebot*

car keys τα κλειδιά αυτοκινήτου *ta kleedhya aftokeeneetoo*

car park το πάρκινγκ *to parking*

car parts τα ανταλλακτικά αυτοκινήτου *ta antalakteeka aftokeeneetoo*

car radio το ραδιόφωνο αυτοκινήτου *to radhyofono aftokeeneetoo*

car seat *(for children)* το παιδικό κάθισμα αυτοκινήτου *to pedheeko katheesma aftokeeneetoo*

car wash το πλυντήριο αυτοκινήτων *to pleenteereeo aftokeeneeton*

carafe η καράφα *ee karafa*

caravan το τροχόσπιτο *to trokhospeeto*

card η κάρτα *ee karta*
(business) η επαγγελματική κάρτα *ee epaghelmateekee karta*

cardboard το χαρτόνι *to khartonee*

cardigan η ζακέτα *ee zaketa*

careful προσεκτικός *prosekteekos*
to be careful προσέχω *prosekho*

carpet το χαλί *to khalee*

carriage *(railway)* το βαγόνι *to vaghonee*

carrot το καρότο *to karoto*

to carry κουβαλώ *koovalo*

carton το χαρτόκουτο *to khartokooto*

case η υπόθεση *ee eepothesee*
(suitcase) η βαλίτσα *ee valeetsa*

to cash *(cheque)* εξαργυρώνω *eksaryeerono*

cash τα μετρητά *ta metreeta*

cash desk το ταμείο *to tameeo*

cash dispenser το ATM *to ay tee em*

cashier ο ταμίας *o tameeas*

casino το καζίνο *to kazeeno*

casserole dish της κατσαρόλας *tees katsarolas*

cassette η κασέτα *ee kaseta*

castle το κάστρο *to kastro*

casualty department τα επείγοντα περιστατικά *ta epeeghonda pereestateeka*

cat η γάτα *ee ghata*

cat food η τροφή για γάτες *ee trofee ya ghates*

catacombs οι κατακόμβες *ee katakomves*

catalogue οκατάλογος *o kataloghos*

to catch πιάνω *pyano*
(bus, train, etc.) παίρνω *perno*

Catholic καθολικός *katholikos*

cauliflower το κουνουπίδι *to koonoopeedhee*

cave η σπηλιά *ee speelya*

cavity *(in tooth)* η κουφάλα *ee koofala*

CD το CD *to tse de*

celery το σέλινο *to seleeno*

cellphone το κινητό τηλέφωνο *to keeneeto teelephono*

cemetery το νεκροταφείο *to nekrotafeeo*

centimetre ο πόντος *o pondos*

central κεντρικός *kendreekos*

central locking *(car)* η αυτόματη κλειδαριά *ee aftomatee kleedharya*

centre το κέντρο *to kendro*

century ο αιώνας *o eonas*

cereal *(for breakfast)* τα δημητριακά *ta deheemeetreeaka*

certificate το πιστοποιητικό *to peestopyeeteeko*

chain η αλυσίδα *ee aleeseedha*

chair η καρέκ λα *ee karekla*

chalet το σαλέ *to chalet*

challenge η πρόκληση *ee prokleesee*

champagne η σαμπάνια *ee sambanya*

change η αλλαγή *ee alayee*
(money) τα ρέστα *ta resta*

to change αλλάζω *alazo*

changing room *(beach, sports)* το αποδυτήριο *to apodheeteereeo*

chapel το παρεκκλήσι *to parekleesee*

charcoal το ξυλοκάρβουνο *to kseelokarvoono*

charge η τιμή *ee teemee*
please charge it to my account παρακαλώ χρεώστε το στο λογαριασμό μου *parakalo khreoste to sto logharyasmo moo*

charger *(for battery)* ο φορτιστής *o forteestees*

charter flight η ναυλωμένη πτήση *ee navlomenee pteesee*

cheap φτηνός *fteenos*

cheap rate *(for phone, etc)* η φτηνήταρίφα *ee fteenee tareefa*

cheaper φτηνότερος *fteenoteros*

to check ελέγχω *elenkho*

check in περνώ από τον έλεγχο εισιτηρίων *perno apo ton elenkho eeseeteereeon*

check-in desk ο έλεγχος εισιτηρίων *o elenkhos eeseeteereeon*

cheek το μάγουλο *to maghoolo*

cheerio! γεια *ya*

cheers! *(your health)* στην υγειά σας *steen eeya sas*

cheese το τυρί *to teeree*

chemist's το φαρμακείο *to farmakeeo*

cheque η επιταγή *ee epeetayee*

cheque card η κάρτα επιταγών *ee karta epeetaghon*

cherry το κεράσι *to kerasee*

chess το σκάκι *to skakee*

chestnut το κάστανο *to kastano*

chewing gum η τσίχλα *ee tseekhla*

chicken το κοτόπουλο *to kotopoolo*

chicken breast το στήθος κοτόπουλο *to steethos kotopoolo*

chickenpox η ανεμοβλογιά *ee anemovloya*

chickpeas τα ρεβίθια *ta reveetheea*

child το παιδί *to pedhee*

child safety seat *(car)* παιδικό κάθισμα αυτοκινήτου *pedheeko katheesma aftokeeneetoo*

children τα παιδιά *ta pedhya*

chilli το τσίλλι *to tseelee*

chilled: ***is the wine chilled?*** είναι κρύο το κρασί; *eene kreeo to krasee*

chips πατάτες τηγανητές *patates teeghaneetes*

chocolate η σοκολάτα *ee sokolata*

choice η επιλογή *ee epiloghee*

to choose επιλέγω *epeelegho*

Christian name το Χριστιανικό όνομα *to chreestyaneeko onoma*

Christmas τα Χριστούγεννα *ta khreestooyena*
merry Christmas! καλά Χριστούγεννα! *kala khreestooyena*

church η εκκλησία *ee ekleeseea*

cigar το πούρο *to pooro*

cigarette το τσιγάρο *to tseegharo*

cigarette paper το τσιγαρόχαρτο *to tseegharokharto*

cinema ο κινηματογράφος *o keeneematoghrafos*

cistern το πηγάδι *to peeghadhee*

city η πόλη *ee polee*

city centre το κέντρο της πόλης *to kendro tees polees*

clean καθαρός *katharos*

to clean καθαρίζω *kathareezo*

cleaner ο καθαριστής / η καθαρίστρια *o kathareestees / ee kathareestreea*

cleansing cream η κρέμα καθαρισμού *ee krema kathareesmoo*

client ο πελάτης / η πελάτισσα *o pelatees / ee pelateesa*

cliffs ο ιύφαλοι *ee eefalee*

climbing η ορειβασία *ee oreevaseea*

climbing boots οι μπότες ορειβασίας *ee botes oreevaseeas*

clingfilm το σελαφάν *to selofan*

cloakroom η γκαρνταρόμπα *ee gardaroba*

clock το ρολόι *to roloee*

to close κλείνω *kleeno*

close *(near)* κοντινός *kondeenos*
(weather) αποπνιχτικός *apopneekhteekos*

closed κλειστός *kleestos*

cloth το πανί *to panee*
(for floor) το σφουγγαρόπανο *to sfoongaropano*

clothes τα ρούχα *ta rookha*

clothes line το σκοινί για τα ρούχα *to skeenee ya ta rookha*

clothes peg το μανταλάκι *to mandalakee*

cloudy συννεφιασμένος *seenefyasmenos*

cloves *(spice)* το γαρίφαλο *to ghareefalo*

club η λέσχη *ee leskhee*

coach *(railway)* το βαγόνι *to vaghonee*
(bus) το πούλμαν *to poolman*
(instructor) ο προπονητής *o proponeetees*

coach station ο σταθμός λεωφορείων *o stathmos leoforeeon*

coach trip το ταξίδι με πούλμαν *to takseedhee me poolman*

coast οι ακτές *ee aktes*

coastguard η ακτοφυλακή *ee aktofeelakee*

coat το παλτό *to palto*

coat hanger η κρεμάστρα *ee kremastra*

cockroach η κατσαρίδα *ee katsareedha*

cocoa το κακάο *to kakao*

coffee ο καφές *o kafes*
black coffee σκέτος καφές *sketos kafes*
white coffee καφές με γάλα *kafes me ghala*

coin το νόμισμα *to nomeesma*

colander το σουρωτήρι *to sooroteeree*

cold κρύος *kreeos*
I have a cold είμαι κρυωμένος *eeme kreeomenos*
I'm cold κρυώνω *kreeono*
it's cold (weather) κάνει κρύο *kanee kreeo*

cold sore ο έρπητας *o erpeetas*

Coliseum το Κολοσαίο *to koloseo*

collection η συλλογή *ee seeloghee*

to collect *(someone)* παίρνω *perno*

colour το χρώμα *to khroma*

colourblind δαλτωνικός *dhaltoneekos*

colour film το έγχρωμο φιλμ *to enkhromo feelm*

comb η χτένα *ee khtena*

to come έρχομαι *erkhome*

to come back γυρίζω *yeereezo*

to come in μπαίνω *beno*

comfortable αναπαυτικός *anapafteekos*

communion *(holy)* **η θεία κοινωνία** *ee theea keenoneea*

company *(firm)* **η εταιρία** *ee etereea*

compartment το διαμέρισμα *to dheeamereesma*

compass ο μπούσουλας *o boosoolas*

to complain παραπονούμαι *paraponoome*

complete ολοκληρωμένος *olokleeromenos*

to complete ολοκληρώνω *olokleerono*

compulsory υποχρεωτικός *eepokhreoteekos*

computer ο κομπιούτερ *o kompyooter*

computer software το software *to software*

concert η συναυλία *ee seenavleea*

concert hall το μέγαρο μουσικής *to megharo mooseekees*

condensed milk το ζαχαρούχο γάλα *to zakharookho ghala*

condition η κατάσταση *ee katastasee*

condom το προφυλακτικό *to profeelakteeko*

conductor *(bus)* **ο εισπράκτορας** *o eespraktoras*
(train) **ο ελεγκτής** *o elenktees*

cone ο κώνος *o konos*

conference η διάσκεψη *ee dheeaskepsee*

to confirm επιβεβαιώνω *epeeveveono*

confused μπερδεμένος *berdhemenos*

congratulations! συγχαρητήρια *seenkhareeteereea*

connection *(trains, etc.)* **η σύνδεση** *ee seendhesee*

to be constipated έχω δυσκοιλιότητα *ekho dheeskeeleeoteeta*

consulate το προξενείο *to prokseneeo*

to consult συμβουλεύομαι *seemvoolevome*

to contact επικοινωνώ *epeekeenono*

contact lenses οι φακοί επαφής *ee fakee epafees*

contact lens cleaner το καθαριστικό διάλυμα *to kathareesteeko dheealeema*

contraceptives τα αντισυλληπτικά *ta andeeseeleepteeka*

contract το συμβόλαιο *to seemvoleo*

convulsions οι σπασμοί *oi spasmee*

to cook μαγειρεύω *mayeerevo*

cooker η κουζίνα *ee koozeena*

cookies τα κουλούρια *ta kooloorya*

cool δροσερός *dhroseros*

cool box *(for picnics)* **το ψυγειάκι** *to pseeyeeakee*

copper ο χαλκός *o khalkos*

to copy *(photocopy)* **φωτοτυπώ** *fototeepo*

copy *n* **το αντίγραφο** *to andeeghrafo*

coral το κοράλλι *to koralee*

coriander ο κόλιαντρος *o kolyantros*

corkscrew το τιρμπουσόν *to teerbooson*

corn *(sweet corn)* **το καλαμπόκι** *to kalambokee*

corner η γωνία *ee ghoneea*

cornflakes τα κορνφλέικς *ta cornfleiks*

cortisone η κορτιζόνη *ee korteezonee*

cosmetics τα καλλυντικά *ta kaleendeeka*

to cost στοιχίζω *steekheezo*

costume *(swimming)* **το μαγιό** *to mayo*

cotton το βαμβάκι *to vamvakee*

cotton buds οι μπατουέτες *ee batooetes*

cotton wool το βαμβάκι *to vamvakee*

couchette η κουκέτα *ee kooketa*

cough ο βήχας *o veekhas*

country η χώρα *ee khora*
(not town) **η εξοχή** *ee eksokhee*

couple *(two people)* **το ζευγάρι** *to zevgharee*
***a couple of...* κανά δύο...** *kana dheeo*

courgette το κολοκυθάκι *to kolokeethakee*

courier *(for tourists)* ο / η συνοδός *o / ee seenodhos*

course *(meal)* το πιάτο *to pyato*

cousin ο εξάδελφος / η εξαδέλφη *o eksadhelfos / ee eksadhelfee*

cover charge το κουβέρ *to koover*

crab το καβούρι *to kavooree*

crafts είδη χειροτεχνίας *eedhee kheerotekhneeas*

cramp η κράμπα *ee krampa*

to crash συγκρούομαι *seengkroo-ome*

crash η σύγκρουση *ee seengroosee*

crash helmet το κράνος *to kranos*

cream η κρέμα *ee krema*

credit card η πιστωτική κάρτα *ee peestoteekee karta*

crime το έγκλημα *to engkleema*

crisps τα πατατάκια *ta patatakya*

croquette η κροκέτα *ee kroketa*

cross οσταυρός *o stafros*

to cross διασχίζω *dheeaskheezo*

crossroads το σταυροδρόμι *to stavrodhromee*

crowded γεμάτος *yematos*

cruise η κρουαζιέρα *ee krooazyera*

crutches τα δεκανίκια *ta dhekaneekya*

cucumber το αγγούρι *to angooree*

cup το φλυτζάνι *to fleedzanee*

cupboard το ντουλάπι *to doolapee*

currant η σταφίδα *ee stafeedha*

current *(electric)* το ρεύμα *to revma*

cushion το μαξιλάρι *to makseelaree*

custard η κρέμα *ee krema*

customer ο πελάτης *o pelatees*

customs το τελωνείο *to teloneeo*

to cut κόβω *kovo*

cut το κόψιμο *to kopseemo*

cutlery τα μαχαιροπήρουνα *ta makheropeeroona*

to cycle ποδηλατώ *podheelato*

cycling η ποδηλασία *ee podheelaseea*

cyst η κύστις *ee keestees*

cystitis η κυστίτιδα *ee keesteeteedha*

D

daily ημερήσιος *eemereeseeos*

dairy products ταγαλακτοκομικά προϊόντα *ta ghalaktokomeeka proeeonda*

dam το φράγμα *to fraghma*

damage η ζημιά *ee zeemya*

damp υγρός *eeghros*

dance *n* ο χορός *o khoros*

to dance χορεύω *khorevo*

danger ο κίνδυνος *o keendheenos*

dangerous επικίνδυνος *epeekeend-heenos*

dark *(colour)* σκούρο *skooro*
(night) σκοτάδι *skotadhee*
it's dark είναι σκοτεινά *eene skoteena*

date η ημερομηνία *ee eemeromeeneea*
what's the date? τι ημερομηνία είναι; *tee eemeromeeneea eene*

date of birth η ημερομηνία γεννήσεως *ee eemeromeeneea yeneeseos*

daughter η κόρη *ee koree*

day η μέρα *ee mera*
all day όλη μέρα *olee mera*
every day κάθε μέρα *kathe mera*

dead νεκρός *nekros*

dear αγαπητός *aghapeetos*
(expensive) ακριβός *akreevos*

decaffeinated χωρίς καφεΐνη *khorees kafeeenee*

deck chair η ξαπλώστρα *ee ksaplostra*

to declare δηλώνω *dheelono*

deep βαθύς *vathees*

deep freeze η κατάψυξη *ee katapseek-see*

deer το ελάφι *to elafee*

to defrost ξεπαγώνω *ksepaghono*

delay η καθυστέρηση *ee katheestereesee*

delayed καθυστερισμένος *katheestereesmenos*

delicious νόστιμος *nosteemos*

demonstration η επίδειξη *ee epeedheeksee*

dentist ο / η οδοντογιατρός *o / ee odhondoyatros*

dentures η οδοντοστοιχία *ee odhondosteekheea*

deodorant το αποσμητικό *to aposmeeteeko*

to depart αναχωρώ *anakhoro*

department το τμήμα *to tmeema*

department store το πολυκατάστημα *to poleekatasteema*

departure η αναχώρηση *ee anakhoreesee*

departure lounge η αίθουσα αναχωρήσεων *ee ethoosa anakhoreeseon*

deposit *(part payment)* η προκαταβολή *ee prokatavolee*

desk το γραφείο *to ghrafeeo*

dessert το επιδόρπιο *to epeedhorpeeo*

details οι λεπτομέρειες *ee leptomereeyes*

detergent το απορρυπαντικό *to aporeepandeeko*

detour: ***to make a detour*** βγαίνω από το δρόμο *vyeno apo to dhromo*

to develop αναπτύσσω *anapteeso*

diabetic διαβητικός *dheeaveeteekos*

to dial παίρνω αριθμό *perno areethmo*

dialect η διάλεκτος *ee dheealektos*

dialling code ο τηλεφωνικός κώδικας *o teelefoneekos kodheekas*

diamond το διαμάντι *to dheeamandee*

diapers οι πάνες *ee panes*

diaphragm το διάφραγμα *to dheeafraghma*

diarrhoea η διάρροια *ee dheeareea*

diary το ημερολόγιο *to eemeroloyo*

dictionary το λεξικό *to lekseeko*

diesel το ντίζελ *to deezel*

diet η δίαιτα *ee dheeeta*
I'm on a diet κάνω δίαιτα *kano dhee-eta*
special diet ειδική δίαιτα *eedheekee dhee-eta*

different διαφορετικός *dheeaforeteekos*

difficult δύσκολος *dheeskolos*

dilute αραιώνω *areono*

dinghy η μικρή βάρκα *ee meekree varka*

dining room η τραπεζαρία *ee trapezareea*

dinner το δείπνο *to dheepno*

dinner jacket το σμόκιν *to smokeen*

direct άμεσος *amesos*

directory *(telephone)* ο τηλεφωνικός κατάλογος *o teelefoneekos kataloghos*

directory enquiries οι πληροφορίες καταλόγου *ee pleeroforeeyes kataloghoo*

dirty ακάθαρτος *akathartos*

disability η αναπηρία *ee anapeereea*

disabled ανάπηρος *anapeeros*

to disagree διαφωνώ *dheeafono*

disco η ντισκοτέκ *ee deeskotek*

discount η έκπτωση *ee ekptosee*

dish το πιάτο *to pyato*

dish towel η πετσέτα πιάτων *ee petseta pyaton*

dishwasher το πλυντήριο πιάτων *to pleenteereeo pyaton*

disinfectant το απολυμαντικό *to apoleemandeeko*

disk *(floppy)* η δισκέτα *ee dheesketa*

disposable διαθέσιμος *dheeatheseemos*

distance η απόσταση *ee apostasee*

distilled water το απεσταγμένο νερό *to apestaghmeno nero*

diving η κατάδυση *ee katadheesee*

divorced ο χωρισμένος / η χωρισμένη *o khoreesmenos / ee khoreesmenee*

dizzy ζαλισμένος *zaleesmenos*

to do: *I do* κάνω *kano*
you do κάνεις *kanees*

doctor ο / η γιατρός *o / ee yatros*

documents τα έγγραφα *ta engrafa*

dog το σκυλί *to skeelee*

dog food η τροφή για σκύλους *ee trofee ya skeeloos*

dog lead το λουρί *to looree*

doll η κούκλα *ee kookla*

dollar το δολάριο *to dholareeo*

domestic *(flight)* εσωτερικός *esotereekos*

done: *is it done?* είναι έτοιμο; *eene eteemo*
have you done it? το έκανες; *to ekanes*
I've done it το έκανα *to ekana*

donkey το γαϊδούρι *to ghaeedhooree*

donor card η κάρτα δότη *ee karta dhotee*

door η πόρτα *ee porta*

door bell το κουδούνι *to koodhoonee*

double διπλός *dheeplos*

double bed το διπλό κρεββάτι *to dheeplo krevatee*

double room το δίκλινο δωμάτιο *to dheekleeno dhomateeo*

down: *to go down* κατεβαίνω *kateveno*

downstairs κάτω *kato*

drain η αποχέτευση *ee apokhetefsee*

draught *(of air)* το ρεύμα *to revma*

draught lager ημπίρααπόβαρέλι *ee beera apo varelee*

drawer το συρτάρι *to seertaree*

drawing το σχέδιο *to skhedheeo*

dress το φόρεμα *to forema*

to dress ντύνομαι *deenome*

dressing *(for salad)* το λαδολέμονο *to ladholemono*
(for wound) ο επίδεσμος *o epeedhesmos*

dressing gown η ρόμπα *ee roba*

drill τρυπώ *treepo*

drink *n* το ποτό *to poto*
to have a drink παίρνω ένα ποτό *perno ena poto*

to drink πίνω *peeno*

drinking water το πόσιμο νερό *to poseemo nero*

to drive οδηγώ *odheegho*

driver ο οδηγός *o odheeghos*

driving licence η άδεια οδήγησης *ee adheea odheeyeesees*

to drown πνίγομαι *pneeghome*

drug *(illegal)* το ναρκωτικό *to narkoteeko*
(medicine) το φάρμακο *to farmako*

drunk μεθυσμένος *metheesmenos*

dry στεγνός *steghnos*

to dry στεγνώνω *steghnono*

dry-cleaners το καθαριστήριο *to katha-reesteereeo*

duck η πάπια *ee papya*

due: *when is the train due?* πότε θα φτάσει το τραίνο; *pote tha ftasee to treno*

dummy η πιπίλα *ee peepeela*

during κατά τη διάρκεια *kata tee dheearkeea*

dust η σκόνη *ee skonee*

dustpan and brush η σκούπα και το φαράσι *ee skoopa ke to farasee*

duty-free αδασμολόγητος *adhas-mologheetos*

duvet το πάπλωμα *to paploma*

duvet cover ηπαπλωματοθήκη *ee paplomatotheekee*

E

each κάθε *kathe*
100 euros each εκατό ευρώ ο καθένας *ekato evro o kathenas*

ear το αυτί *to aftee*

earache: *I have earache* με πονάει το αυτί μου *me ponaee to aftee moo*

earlier νωρίτερα *noreetera*

early νωρίς *norees*
I'm early είμαι νωρίς *eeme norees*

earplugs οι ωτοασπίδες *ee otoaspeedhes*

earrings τα σκουλαρίκια *ta skoolareekya*

earthquake ο σεισμός *o seesmos*

east η ανατολή *ee anatolee*

Easter το Πάσχα *to paskha*
happy Easter! Καλό Πάσχα! *kalo Paskha*

easy εύκολος *efkolos*

to eat τρώω *tro-o*

economy η οικονομία *ee eekonomeea*

eel το χέλι *to khelee*

egg το αβγό *to avgho*
fried eggs αβγά τηγανητά *avgha teeghaneeta*
boiled eggs αβγά βραστά *avgha vrasta*
poached eggs αβγά ποσέ *avgha pose*

either ... or ή ... ή *ee ...ee*, είτε ... είτε *eete ... eete*

elastic το ελαστικό *to elasteeko*

elastic band το λαστιχάκι *to lasteekhakee*

electric blanket η ηλεκτρική κουβέρτα *ee eelektreekee kooverta*

electrician ο ηλεκτρολόγος *o eelektrologhos*

electricity meter ο μετρητής ηλεκτρισμού *o metreetees eelektreesmoo*

electric razor η ξυριστική μηχανή *ee kseereesteekee meekhanee*

else: *nothing else* τίποτα άλλο *teepota alo*
anything else? κάτι άλλο; *katee alo*
what else? τι άλλο; *tee alo*

e-mail το e-mail *to e-mail*
to e-mail someone στέλνω e-mail *stelno e-mail*

e-mail address η e-mail διεύθυνση *ee e-mail dheeeftheensee*

embassy η πρεσβεία *ee presveea*

emergency: *it's an emergency* είναι επείγον περιστατικό *eene epeeghon pereestateeko*

empty άδειος *adheeos*

end το τέλος *to telos*

engaged *(to marry)* αρραβωνιασμένος / η *aravonyasmenos/ee*
(toilet) κατειλημένη *kateeleemenee*
(phone) μιλάει *meelaee*

engine η μηχανή *ee meekhanee*

England η Αγγλία *ee angleea*

English αγγλός *angleekos*

Englishman/woman ο Άγγλος / η Αγγλίδα *o anglos / ee angleedha*

to enjoy oneself διασκεδάζω *dheeaskedhazo*

enjoy your meal καλή όρεξη *kalee oreksee*

enough αρκετά *arketa*
enough bread αρκετό ψωμί *arketo psomee*

enquiry desk / office το γραφείο πληροφοριών *to ghrafeeo pleeroforeeon*

to enter μπαίνω *beno*

entertainment η ψυχαγωγία *ee pseekhaghoyeea*

entrance η είσοδος *ee eesodhos*

entrance fee η τιμή εισόδου *ee teemee eesodhoo*

envelope ο φάκελος *o fakelos*

equipment ο εξοπλισμός *o eksopleesmos*

eruption η έκρηξη *ee ekreeksee*

escalator η κυλιόμενη σκάλα *ee keelyomenee skala*

especially ειδικά *eedheeka*

essential απαραίτητος *apareteetos*

euro το ευρό *to evro*

Eurocheque η ευρωεπιταγή *ee evroepeetayee*

Europe η Ευρώπη *ee evropee*

European ο Ευρωπαίος / η Ευρωπαία *o evropeos / ee evropea*

European Union η Ευρωπαική Ένωση *ee evropa-eekee enosee*

even number ο ζυγός αριθμός *o zeeghos areethmos*

evening το βράδυ *to vradhee*
this evening απόψε *apopse*
tomorrow evening αύριο το βράδυ *avreeo to vradhee*
in the evening το βράδυ *to vradhee*

every κάθε *kathe*

everyone όλοι *olee*

everything όλα *ola*

exact ακριβής *akreevees*

examination η εξέταση *ee eksetasee*

excellent εξαιρετικός *eksereteekos*

except εκτός από *ektos apo*

excess luggage επί πλέον αποσκευές *epee pleon aposkeves*

exchange rate η τιμή του συναλλάγματος *ee teemee too seenalaghmatos*

excursion η εκδρομή *ee ekdhromee*

excuse me με συγχωρείτε *me seenkhoreete*

exhaust pipe η εξάτμιση *ee eksat-meesee*

exhibition η έκθεση *ee ekthesee*

exit η έξοδος *ee eksodhos*

expensive ακριβός *akreevos*

expert ο / η ειδικός *o / ee eedheekos*

to expire λήγω *leegho*

expired έχει λήξει *ekhee leeksee*

to explain εξηγώ *ekseegho*

express *(train)* η ταχεία *ee takheea*

express letter το κατεπείγον γράμμα *to katepeeghon ghrama*

extra: ***it costs extra*** στοιχίζει επιπλέον *steekheezee epeepleon*
extra money περισσότερα χρήματα *pereesotera khreemata*
an extra bed ένα έξτρα κρεβάτι *ena extra krevatee*

eyes τα μάτια *ta matya*

eyeshadow η σκιά για τα μάτια *ee skeea ya ta matya*

F

fabric το ύφασμα *to eefasma*

face το πρόσωπο *to prosopo*

facilities οι ευκολίες *ee efkoleeyes*

factory το εργοστάσιο *to erghostaseeo*

to fail αποτυχαίνω *apoteekheno*

to faint λιποθυμώ *leepotheemo*

fainted λιποθύμησε *leepotheemeese*

fair *adj (hair)* ξανθός *ksanthos*
(just) δίκαιος *dheekeos*

fair *n (trade fair)* η έκθεση *ee ekthesee*
(fun fair) το λουνα-πάρκ *to loonapark*

to fall πέφτω *pefto*
he / she has fallen έπεσε *epese*

family η οικογένεια *ee eekoyenya*

famous διάσημος *dheeaseemos*

fan *(electric)* ο ανεμιστήρας *o anemeesteeras*

fan belt το λουρί του ψυγείου *to looree too pseeyeeoo*

fancy dress τα αποκρηάτικα ρούχα *ta apokryateeka rookha*

far μακριά *makreeya*

fare *(bus, train)* το εισιτήριο *to eeseeteereeo*

farm το αγρόκτημα *to aghrokteema*

farmhouse η αγροικία *ee aghreekeea*

fast γρήγορα *ghreeghora*

fat *adj* χοντρός *khondros*

fat *n* το λίπος *to leepos*
saturated fats τα κεκορασμένα λιπαρά *ta kekoresmena leepara*
unsaturated fats τα ακόρεστα λιπαρά *ta akoresta leepara*

father ο πατέρας *o pateras*

father-in-law ο πεθερός *o petheros*

fault *(mistake)* το λάθος *to lathos*
it's not my fault δε φταίω εγώ *dhe fteo egho*

favour η χάρη *ee kharee*

favourite ο πιο αγαπημένος *o pyo aghapeemenos*

fax το φαξ *fax*
by fax με φαξ *me fax*

feather το φτερό *to ftero*

to feed τρέφω *trefo*
(baby) ταΐζω *taeezo*

to feel αισθάνομαι *esthanome*
I feel sick θέλω να κάνω εμετό *thelo na kano emeto*

female θηλυκός *theeleekos*

ferry το φεριμπότ *to fereebot*

festival το φεστιβάλ *to festeeval*

to fetch φέρνω *ferno*

fever ο πυρετός *o peeretos*

few: *a few* μερικοί / μερικές / μερικά *mereekee (masculine) / mereekes (feminine) / mereeka (neuter)*

fiancé(e) ο αρραβωνιαστικός / η αρραβωνιαστικιά *o aravonyasteekos / ee aravonyasteekya*

field το χωράφι *to khorafee*

to fight μαλλώνω *malono*

file *(nail)* η λίμα *ee leema*
(computer) το αρχείο *to arkheeo*
(folder) το ντοσιέ *to dhosye*

to fill γεμίζω *yemeezo*
fill it up! (car) γεμίστε το *yemeeste to*

fillet το φιλέτο *to feeleto*

filling *(in cake, etc.)* η γέμιση *ee yemeesee*
(in tooth) το σφράγισμα *to sfrayeesma*

film *(for camera)* το φιλμ *to feelm*
(in cinema) η ταινία *ee teneea*

filter το φίλτρο *to feeltro*

to find βρίσκω *vreesko*
where can I find...? πού μπορώ να βρώ; *poo boro na vro*
did you find it? το βρήκες; *to vreekes*

to finish τελειώνω *teleeono*

fire *(heater)* η θερμάστρα *ee thermastra*
fire! φωτιά! *fotya*
fire brigade η πυροσβεστική *ee peerosvesteekee*
fire extinguisher ο πυροσβεστήρας *o peerosvesteeras*

fireworks τα πυροτεχνήματα *ta peerotekhneemata*

firm *(company)* η εταιρία *ee etereea*

first πρώτος *protos*

first aid οι πρώτες βοήθειες *ee protes voeetheeyes*

first class *(seat, etc.)* η πρώτη θέση *ee protee thesee*

first floor ο πρώτος όροφος *o protos orofos*

first name το όνομα *to onoma*

fish το ψάρι *to psaree*

to fish ψαρεύω *psarevo*

fishing rod το καλάμι ψαρέματος *to kalamee psarematos*

fit *(healthy)* υγιής *eeyee-ees*

to fix επιδιορθώνω *epeedheeorthono*
(arrange) κανονίζω *kanoneezo*

fizzy *(drink)* αεριούχο *aeryookho*

flame η φλόγα *ee flogha*

flash *(on camera)* το φλας *to flas*

flask το θερμός *to thermos*

flat *(apartment)* το διαμέρισμα *to dheeamereesma*

flat tyre: *I have a flat tyre* έχω σκασμένο λάστιχο *ekho skasmeno lasteekho*

flea ο ψύλλος *o pseelos*

flesh η σάρκα *ee sarka*

flight η πτήση *ee pteesee*

flippers *(swimming)* τα βατραχοπέδιλα *ta vatrakhopedheela*

flood η πλημμύρα *ee pleemeera*

floor το πάτωμα *to patoma*
(storey) ο όροφος *o orofos*
first floor ο πρώτος όροφος *o protos orofos*
second floor ο δεύτερος όροφος *o dhefteros orofos*

flour το αλεύρι *to alevree*

flower το λουλούδι *to looloodhee*

flu η γρίππη *ee ghreepee*

to fly πετώ *peto*

fly η μύγα *ee meegha*

to follow ακολουθώ *akolootho*

food το φαγητό *to fayeeto*

food poisoning η τροφική δηλητηρίαση *ee trofeekee dheeleeteereeasee*

foot το πόδι *to podhee*

football το ποδόσφαιρο *to podhosfero*

for για *ya*

foreign ξένος *ksenos*

forest το δάσος *to dhasos*

to forget ξεχνώ *ksekhno*

fork το πηρούνι *to peeroonee*
(in road) η διακλάδωση *ee dheeaklad-hosee*

fortnight το δεκαπενθήμερο *to dhekapentheemero*

found: ***I found it*** το βρήκα *to vreeka*

fountain το σιντριβάνι *to seendreeva-nee*

fracture *(of bone)* το κάταγμα *to kataghma*

fragrance το άρωμα *to aroma*

France η Γαλλία *ee ghaleea*

free ελεύθερος *eleftheros*
(costing nothing) δωρεάν *dhorean*

to freeze *(food)* ψύχω *pseekho*

freezer ο καταψύκτης *o katapseektees*

French *(thing)* γαλλικός *ghaleekos*

Frenchman ο γαλλος *ghalos*

Frenchman η γαλλίδα *ghaleedha*

French beans τα φασολάκια *ta fasolakya*

frequent συχνός *seekhnos*

fresh φρέσκος *freskos*

fridge το ψυγείο *to pseeyeeo*

fried τηγανητός *teeghaneetos*

friend ο φίλος / η φίλη *o feelos / ee feelee*

friendly φιλικός *feeleekos*

from από *apo*

front: ***the front*** το μπροστινό (μέρος) *to brosteeno (meros)*
in front μπροστά *brosta*

frozen *(water)* παγωμένος *paghomenos*
(food) κατεψυγμένος *katepseeghmenos*

fruit τα φρούτα *ta froota*

fruit juice ο χυμός φρούτων *o kheemos frooton*

fruit salad η φρουτοσαλάτα *ee frootosalata*

frying pan το τηγάνι *to teeghanee*

fuel τα καύσιμα *ta kafseema*

fuel pump η αντλία καυσίμων *ee andleea kafseemon*

fuel tank το ντεπόζιτο βενζίνης *to depozeeto venzeenees*

full γεμάτος *yematos*

full board (η) πλήρης διατροφή *(ee) pleerees dheeatrofee*

fumes *(of car)* τα καυσαέρια *ta kaf-saereea*

funeral η κηδεία *ee keedheea*

funny αστείος *asteeos*

fur η γούνα *ee ghoona*

furniture τα έπιπλα *ta epeepla*

fuse η ασφάλεια *ee asfaleea*

fuse box οηλεκτρικόςπίνακας *o eelek-treekos peenakas*

G

gallery *(art)* η πινακοθήκη *ee peenakotheekee*

game το παιγνίδι *to peghneedhee*
(to eat) το κυνήγι *to keeneeyee*

garage *(for parking car)* το γκαράζ *to garaz*
(for petrol) το πρατήριο βενζίνης *to prateereeo venzeenees*

garden ο κήπος *o keepos*

garlic το σκόρδο *to skordho*

gas το γκάζι *to gazee*

gas cooker η γκαζιέρα *ee ghaszyera*

gas cylinder η φιάλη γκαζιού *ee feealee gazyoo*

gastritis η γαστριτιδα *ee ghastreeteed-ha*

gate *(at airport)* ηέξοδος *ee eksodhos*

gay *(person)* ομοφυλόφιλος *omofeelofeelos*

gears οι ταχύτητες *ee takheeteetes*
first gear πρώτη *protee*
second gear δεύτερη *dhefteree*
third gear τρίτη *treetee*
fourth gear τετάρτη *tetartee*
neutral νεκρή *nekree*
reverse όπισθεν *opeesthen*

gearbox το κιβώτιο ταχυτήτων *to keevotyo takheeteeton*

gently απαλά *apala*

gents *(toilet)* Ανδρών *andhron*

genuine γνήσιος *ghneeseeos*
(leather) αληθινός *aleetheenos*
(silver) καθαρός *katharos*
(antiques, pictures, etc.) γνήσιος *ghneeseeos*

germs τα μικρόβια *ta meekroveea*

German measles η ερυθρά *ee ereethra*

to get παίρνω *perno*
(fetch) φέρνω *ferno*

to get in *(car, etc.)* μπαίνω *beno*

to get off *(from bus)* κατεβαίνω από *kateveno apo*

to get on *(bus)* ανεβαίνω στο λεωφορείο *aneveno sto leoforeeo*

to get through *(on the phone)* συνδέομαι *seendheome*

gift το δώρο *to dhoro*

gift shop το κατάστημα δώρων *to katasteema dhoron*

gin το τζιν *to dzin*

ginger η πιπερόρριζα *ee peeperoreeza*

girl το κορίτσι *to koreetsee*

girlfriend η φίλη *ee feelee*

to give δίνω *dheeno*

to give back επιστρέφω *epeestrefo*

glacier ο παγετώνας *o payetonas*

glass *(to drink from)* το ποτήρι *to poteeree*
a glass of water ένα ποτήρι νερό *ena poteeree nero*
(substance) το γυαλί *to yalee*

glasses *(spectacles)* τα γυαλιά *ta yalya*

glasses case η θήκη γυαλιών *ee theekee yalyon*

gloves τα γάντια *ta ghandeea*

glucose η γλυκόζη *ee ghleekozee*

glue *n* η κόλλα *ee kola*

to glue κολλώ *kolo*

to go πηγαίνω *peeyeno*
I go / I'm going πηγαίνω *peeyeno*
you go / you're going πηγαίνεις *peeyenees*
we go / we're going πηγαίνουμε *peeyenoome*

to go back γυρίζω πίσω *yeereezo peeso*

to go down κατεβαίνω *kateveno*

to go in μπαίνω *beno*

to go out βγαίνω *vyeno*

to go up ανεβαίνω *aneveno*

goat η κατσίκα *ee katseeka*

goggles τα γυαλιά *ta yalya*

gold ο χρυσός *o khreesos*
(made of gold) χρυσός *khreesos*

golf το γκολφ *to golf*

golf course το γήπεδο του γκολφ *to yeepedho too golf*

good καλός *kalos*

good afternoon χαίρετε *kherete*

goodbye αντίο *adeeo*

good day καλημέρα *kaleemera*

good evening καλησπέρα *kaleespera*

good morning καλημέρα *kaleemera*

good night καληνύχτα *kaleeneekhta*

goose η χήνα *ee kheena*

gram το γραμμάριο *to ghramareeo*

grandchild το εγγόνι *to eghonee*

granddaughter η εγγονή *ee eghonee*

grandfather ο παππούς *o papoos*

grandmother η γιαγιά *ee yaya*

grandparents ο παππούς και η γιαγιά *o papoos ke ee yaya*

grandson ο εγγονός *o eghonos*

grapefruit το γκρέιπ-φρουτ *to greipfroot*

grapes τα σταφύλια *ta stafeelya*

grated cheese τοτυρίτριμένο *to teeree treemeno*

grater οτρίφτης *o treeftees*

greasy λιπαρός *leeparos*

great *(big)* μεγάλος *meghalos* *(wonderful)* υπέροχος *eeperokhos*

Great Britain η Μεγάλη Βρετανία *ee meghalee vretaneea*

Greece η Ελλάδα *ee eladha*

Greek *(person)* ο Έλληνας / η Ελληνίδα *o eleenas / ee eleeneedha*

Greek *adj* ελληνικός *eleeneekos*

green πράσινος *praseenos*

grey γκρίζος *greezos*

grill το γκριλ *to grill*

grilled της σχάρας *tees skharas*

grocer's το μπακάλικο *to bakaleeko* // το παντοπωλείο *to pandopoleeo*

ground *n* το έδαφος *to edhafos*

ground *adj (coffee, etc)* αλεσμένος *alesmenos*

ground floor το ισόγειο *to eesoyeeo*

groundsheet ο μουσαμάς εδάφους *o moosamas edhafoos*

group η ομάδα *ee omadha*

to grow μεγαλώνω *meghalono*

guarantee η εγγύηση *ee engeeyeesee*

guard *(on train)* ο υπεύθυνος τρένου *o eepeftheenos trenoo*

guest ο φιλοξενούμενος *o feeloksenoomenos*

guesthouse ο ξενώνας *o ksenonas*

guide ο / η ξεναγός *o / ee ksenaghos*

to guide ξεναγώ *ksenagho*

guidebook ο οδηγός *o odheeghos*

guided tour η περιήγηση με ξεναγό *ee peree-eeyeesee me ksenagho*

gym το γυμναστήριο *to gheemnasteereeo*

gym shoes τα αθλητικά παπούτσια *ta athleeteeka papootsya*

H

haemorrhoids οι αιμορροΐδες *ee emoroeedhes*

hair τα μαλλιά *ta malya*

hairbrush η βούρτσα *ee voortsa*

haircut το κούρεμα *to koorema*

hairdresser ο κομμωτής / η κομμώτρια *o komotees / ee komotreea*

hairdryer το πιστολάκι *to peestolakee*

half το μισό *to meeso*
half an hour μισή ώρα *meesee ora*

half board (η) ημιδιατροφή *(ee) eemeedheeatrofee*

half-bottle το μικρό μπουκάλι *to meekro bookalee*

half fare το μισό εισιτήριο *to meeso eeseeteereeo*

half price μισήτιμή *meesee teemee*

ham το ζαμπόν *to zambon*

hamburger το χάμπουργκερ *to khamboorger*

hammer το σφυρί *to sfeeree*

hand το χέρι *to kheree*

handbag η τσάντα *ee tsanda*

handicapped ανάπηρος *anapeeros*

handkerchief το μαντήλι *to mandeelee*

hand luggage οι χειραποσκευή *ee kheeraposkevee*

hand-made χειροποίητος *kheeropeeeetos*

hands-free phone το hands-free *to hands-free*

to hang up *(phone)* κλείνω *kleeno*

to happen συμβαίνω *seemveno*
what happened? τι συνέβη; *tee seenevee*

happy ευτυχισμένος *efteekheesmenos*

harbour το λιμάνι *to leemanee*

hard *(difficult)* δύσκολος *dheeskolos*

hard-boiled *(egg)* σφιχτό *sfeekhto*

hardware shop το σιδηροπωλείο *to seedheeropoleeo*

harvest ο θερισμός *o thereesmos*

hat το καπέλο *to kapelo*

to have έχω *ekho*

hay fever η αλλεργικη ρινίτιδα *ee aleryeekee reeneeteedha*

hazelnut το φουντούκι *to foondookee*

he αυτός *aftos*

head το κεφάλι *to kefalee*

headache: ***I have a headache*** έχω πονοκέφαλο *ekho ponokefalo*

headlights οι προβολείς του αυτοκινήτου *ee provolees too aftokeeneetoo*

headphones τα ακουστικά *ta akoosteeka*

to hear ακούω *akooo*

health η υγεία *ee eeyeea*

healthy υγιής *eeyee-ees*

hearing aid το ακουστικό βαρηκοΐας *to akoosteeko vareekoeeas*

heart η καρδιά *ee kardhya*

heart attack η καρδιακή προσβολή *ee kardheeakee prosvolee*

heartburn η καούρα *ee kaoora*

heater η θερμάστρα *ee thermastra*

heating η θέρμανση *ee thermansee*

heavy βαρύς *varees*

heel το τακούνι *to takoonee*

hello γεια σας *ya sas*

helmet οκράνος *o kranos*

to help βοηθώ *voeetho*
help! βοήθεια *voeetheea*

hepatitis η ηπατίτιδα *ee eepateeteedha*

her αυτή *aftee*, τήν *teen*
it's her! αυτή είναι! *aftee eene*
I love her τήν αγαπώ *teen aghapo*
her passport το διαβατήριό της *to dheeavateereeo tees*
her room το δωμάτιο της *to dhomateeo tees*

herb το βότανο *to votano*

herbal tea το τσάι του βουνού *to tsaee to voonoo*

here εδώ *edho*

hernia ηκήλη *ee keelee*

high ψηλός *pseelos*
(price) η υψηλή τιμή *ee eepseelee teemee*

eng-greek h

(number) ο μεγάλος αριθμός *o meghalos areethmos*
(speed) η μεγάλη ταχύτητα *ee meghalee takheeteeta*

high blood pressure η ψηλή πίεση *ee pseelee peeyesee*

high chair η ψηλή παιδική καρέκλα *ee pseelee pedheekee karekla*

hill ο λόφος *o lofos*
(slope) η πλαγειά *ee playa*

hill walking η ορειβασία *ee oreevaseea*

him αυτός *aftos*

to hire νοικιάζω *neekyazo*

hire η ενοικίαση *ee eneekeeasee*
car hire ενοικίασεις αυτοκινήτων *eneekeeasees aftokeeneeton*
bike hire ενοικιάσεις μοτοποδηλάτων *eneekeeasees motopadheelaton*
boat hire ενοικιάσεις σκαφών *eneekeeasees skafon*
ski hire ενοικιάσεις σκι *eneekeeasees ski*

hired car μισθωμένο αυτοκίνητο *meesthomeno aftokeeneeto*

his του *too*
his passport το διαβατηριό του *to dheeavateereeo too*
his room το δωμάτιό του *to dhomateeo too*

to hit χτυπώ *khteepo*

hitchhike το οτοστόπ *to otostop*

HIV positive θετικός για ΕΙΤΖ *theteekos ya eidz*

to hold κρατώ *krato*

hold-up η καθυστέρηση *ee katheestereesee*

hole η τρύπα *ee treepa*

holiday οι διακοπές *ee dheeakopes*

holiday rep ο, η συνοδός *o, ee seenodhos*

home το σπίτι *to speetee*
at home στο σπίτι *sto speetee*

honey το μέλι *to melee*

honeymoon ο μήνας του μέλιτος *o meenas too meleetos*

hook *(fishing)* τσαγκίστρι *to angkeestree*

to hope ελπίζω *elpeezo*

hors d'œuvre τα ορεκτικά *ta orekteeka*

horse το άλογο *to alogho*

horse-riding η ιππασία *ee eepaseea*

hospital το νοσοκομείο *to nosokomeeo*

hot ζεστός *zestos*
I'm hot ζεσταίνομαι *zestenome*
it's hot έχει ζέστη *ekhee zestee*
hot water το ζεστό νερό *to zesto nero*

hotel το ξενοδοχείο *to ksenodhokheeo*

hour η ώρα *ee ora*
1 hour μία ώρα *meea ora*
2 hours δύο ώρες *dheeo ores*
in an hour σε μία ώρα *se meea ora*

house το σπίτι *to speetee*

housewife η νοικοκυρά *ee neekokeera*

house wine το κρασί χύμα *to krasee kheema*

how πώς *pos*
how long? πόση ώρα; *posee ora*
how much? πόσο; *poso*
how many? πόσα; *posa*
how are you? πώς είστε; *pos eeste*

hummous η ρεβυθοσαλάτα *ee reveethosalata*

hungry: *I'm hungry* πεινώ *peeno*

to hunt κυνηγώ *keeneegho*

hunting permit η άδεια κυνηγιού *ee adheea keeneeyoo*

to hurry: *I'm in a hurry* βιάζομαι *vyazome*
hurry up! βιάσου *vyasoo*

to hurt: *that hurts* με πονά *me pona*

husband ο σύζυγος *o seezeeghos*
this is my husband απο 'δω ο συζυγός μου *apo dho o seezeeghos moo*

hydrofoil το ιπτάμενο δελφίνι *to eeptameno dhelfeenee*

hypodermic needle η υποδερμική βελόνα *ee eepodhermeekee velona*

I

I εγώ *egho*

ice ο πάγος *o paghos*
without ice χωρίς πάγο *khorees pagho*

ice cream / ice lolly το παγωτό *to paghoto*

iced *(drink)* παγωμένος *paghomenos*

iced coffee το φραπέ *to frape*

iced tea παγωμένο τσάι *paghomeno tsaee*

icon η εικόνα *ee eekona*

idea η ιδέα *ee eedhea*
I've no idea δεν έχω ιδέα *dhen ekho eedhea*

identity card η ταυτότητα *ee taftoteeta*

if αν *an*

ignition η ανάφλεξη *ee anafleksee*

ignition key το κλειδίμίζας *to kleedhee meezas*

ill άρρωστος *arostos*

illness η αρρώστια *ee arostya*

immediately αμέσως *amesos*

immigration η μετανάστευση *ee metanastefsee*

immunisation ο εμβολιασμός *o emvoleeasmos*

to import εισάγω *eesagho*

important σπουδαίος *spoodheos*

impossible αδύνατο *adheenato*
it's impossible είναι αδύνατο *eene adheenato*

to improve βελτιώνω *velteeono*

in μέσα *mesa*
(with countries, towns) σε (στο / στη / στο) *se (sto / stee / sto)*
in front of μπροστά από *brosta apo*

included συμπεριλαμβάνεται *seembereelamvanete*

inconvenient άβολος *avolos*

increase αυξάνω *afksano*
to increase volume δυναμώνω την ένταση *dheenamono teen entasee*

indicator ο δείκτης *o dheektees*
(car) το φλας *to flas*

indigestion η δυσπεψία *ee dheespepseea*

indoors εσωτερικά *esotereeka*

infection η μόλυνση *ee moleensee*

infectious μεταδοτικός *metadhoteekos*

informal άτυπος *ateepos*

information οι πληροφορίες *ee pleeroforeeyes*

information desk/office το γραφείο πληροφοριών *to ghrafeeo pleeroforeeon*

inhaler η συσκευή εισπνοής *ee seeskevee eespnoees*

injection η ένεση *ee enesee*

injured τραυματισμένος *travmateesmenos*

injury ο τραυματισμός *o travmateesmos*

ink το μελάνι *to melanee*

inner tube η σαμπρέλα *ee sambrela*

insect το έντομο *to endomo*

insect bite το τσίμπημα *to tseembeema*

insect repellent το εντομοαπωθητικό *to endomoapotheeteeko*

inside *n (interior)* το εσωτερικό *to esotereeko*
inside the car μέσα στο αυτοκίνητο *mesa sto aftokeeneeto*
it's inside είναι μέσα *eene mesa*

instant coffee στιγμιαίος καφές *steeghmyeos kafes*

instructor ο εκπαιδευτής *o ekpedheftees*

insulin η ινσουλίνη *ee eensooleenee*

insurance η ασφάλεια *ee asfaleea*

insurance certificate η βεβαίωση ασφαλίσεως *ee veveosee asfaleeseos*

insured ασφαλισμένος *asfaleesmenos*

to intend to σκοπεύω να... *skopevo na...*

interesting ενδιαφέρων *endheeaferon*

international διεθνής *dhee-ethnees*

internet το ιντερνέτ *to eenternet*

internet café το ιντερνετ καφέ *to internet kafe*

interpreter ο / η διερμηνέας *o / ee dhee-ermeeneas*

interval *(theatre)* το διάλειμμα *to dheealeema*

into σε (στο / στη / στο) *se (sto / stee / sto)*
into the centre στο κέντρο *sto kendro*

invitation η πρόσκληση *ee proskleesee*

to invite προσκαλώ *proskalo*

invoice το τιμολόγιο *to teemoloyo*

Ireland η Ιρλανδία *ee eerlandheea*

Irish *(person)* ο Ιρλανδός / η Ιρλανδή *o eerlandhos / ee eerlandhee*

iron *(for clothes)* το σίδερο *to seedhero* *(metal)* ο σίδηρος *o seedheeros*

to iron σιδερώνω *seedherono*

ironmonger's το σιδηροπωλείο *to seedheeropoleeo*

is: *he/she is* αυτός / αυτή είναι *aftos / aftee eene*

island το νησί *to neesee*

it το *to*

Italian Ιταλικός *eetaleekos*

Italy η Ιταλία *ee eetaleea*

itch η φαγούρα *ee faghoora*
it itches με τρώει *me troee*

itemised bill ο αναλυτικός λογαριασμός *o analeeteekos logharyasmos*

J

jack ο γρύλος *o ghreelos*

jacket το μπουφάν *to boofan*

jam η μαρμελάδα *ee marmeladha*

jammed στριμωγμένος *streemoghmenos*

January Ιανουάριος *eeanooareeos*

jar το βάζο *to vazo*

jaundice ο ίκτερος *o eekteros*

jeans το μπλου τζιν *to bluejean*

jelly το ζελέ *to zele*

jellyfish η τσούχτρα *ee tsookhtra*

jersey η φανέλα *ee fanela*

to jetski το jetski *to jetski*

jetty ο μώλος *o molos*

jeweller's το κοσμηματοπωλείο *to kosmeematopoleeo*

jewellery τα κοσμήματα *ta kosmeemata*

Jewish Εβραίος / Εβραία *evreos / evrea*

job η δουλειά *ee dhoolya*

to jog κάνω τζόκινγκ *kano jogging*

to join συνδέω *seendheo*

to join in συμμετέχω *seemetekho*

joint *(of body)* η άρθρωση *ee arthrosee*

joke το αστείο *to asteeo*

journey το ταξίδι *to takseedhee*

jug η κανάτα *ee kanata*

juice ο χυμός *o kheemos*

jump leads τα καλώδια μπαταρίας *ta kalodheea batareeas*

junction *(crossroads)* η διασταύρωση *ee dheeastavrosee*

just: ***just two*** μόνο δύο *mono dheeo*
I've just arrived μόλις έφτασα *molees eftasa*

K

to keep *(retain)* κρατώ *krato*
keep the change! κράτα τα ρέστα *krata ta resta*

kettle ο βραστήρας *o vrasteeras*

key το κλειδί *to kleedhee*

keyboard το πληκτρολόγιο *to pleektroloyeeo*

key-ring το μπρελόκ *to brelok*

to kick κλοτσώ *klotso*

kid *(meat)* τοκατσικάκι *to katseekakee*
(child) το παιδί *to pedhee*

kidneys τα νεφρά *ta nefra*

kilo το κιλό *to keelo*
a kilo of apples ένα κιλό μήλα *ena keelo meela*
2 kilos δύο κιλά *dheeo keela*

kilogram το χιλιόγραμμο *to kheeleeoghramo*

kilometre το χιλιόμετρο *to kheelyometro*

kind *n (sort)* το είδος *to eedhos*

kind *adj* ευγενικός *efyeneekos*

king ο βασιλιάς *o vaseelyas*

kiosk το περίπτερο *to pereeptero*

to kiss φιλώ *feelo*

kitchen η κουζίνα *ee koozeena*

kitchen paper το χαρτί κουζίνας *to khartee koozeenas*

kitten το γατάκι *to ghatakee*

kiwi fruit τοακτινίδιο *to akteeneedheeo*

knee το γόνατο *to ghonato*

knee highs οικάλτσες *ee kaltses*

knickers *(women's)* η κυλότα *ee keelota*

knife το μαχαίρι *to makheree*

to knock down *(by car)* χτυπώ με αυτοκίνητο *khteepo me aftokeeneeto*

to knock over *(vase, glass)* ρίχνω κάτω *reekhno kato*

to know ξέρω *ksero*
I don't know δεν ξέρω *dhen ksero*
do you know? ξέρεις; *kserees*

to know how to ξέρω να... *ksero na...*
I don't know how to swim δεν ξέρω να κολυμπώ *dhen ksero na koleebo*

L

label η ετικέτα *ee eteeketa*

lace η δαντέλα *ee dhandela*

laces *(of shoe)* τα κορδόνια *ta kordhoneea*

ladder η σκάλα *ee skala*

ladies *(toilet)* Γυναικών *yeenekon*

lady η κυρία *ee keereea*

lager η μπίρα *ee beera*

lake η λίμνη *ee leemnee*

lamb το αρνάκι *to arnakee*

lame κουτσός *kootsos*

lamp η λάμπα *ee lamba*

lampshade το αμπαζούρ *to abazoor*

to land *(plane)* προσγειώνω *prosyeeono*

landslide η καθίζηση *ee katheezeesee*

language η γλώσσα *ee ghlosa*

language school **η σχολή ξένων γλωσσών** *ee skholee ksenon ghloson*

laptop **το λάπτοπ** *to laptop*

large **μεγάλος** *meghalos*

last **τελευταίος** *telefteos*
last time **την τελευτάια φορά** *teen teleftea fora*
at last! **επιτέλους!** *epeeteloos*

late *(in the day)* **αργά** *argha*
I'm late **έχω αργήσει** *ekho aryeesee*

later **αργότερα** *arghotera*

latest: *at the latest* **το αργότερο** *to arghotero*

to laugh **γελώ** *ghelo*

laundrette **το πλυντήριο** *to pleendeereeo*

laundry service **η υπηρεσία πλυντηρίου** *ee eepeereseea pleendeereeoo*

lavatory **η τουαλέτα** *ee tooaleta*

lawn **το γρασίδι** *to ghraseedhee*

lawyer **ο / η δικηγόρος** *o / ee dheekeeghoros*

laxative **το καθαρτικό** *to katharteeko*

lay-by **η βοηθητική λωρίδα** *ee voeetheeteekee loreedha*

lazy **τεμπέλης** *tembelees*

lead *(electric)* **το καλώδιο** *to kalodheeo*

lead-free **αμόλυβδος** *amoleevdhos*

leader *(guide)* **ο / η ξεναγός** *o / ee ksenaghos*

leaf **το φύλλο** *to feelo*

to leak **τρέχω,** *trekho*
it's leaking **τρέχει** *trekhee*

leak **η διαρροή** *ee dheearoee*
(of gas, liquid) **η διαρροή γκαζιού** *ee dhearoee ghazyoo*
the roof is leaking **η σκεπή τρέχει** *ee skepee trekhee*

to learn **μαθαίνω** *matheno*

least: *at least* **τουλάχιστο** *toolakheesto*

leather **το δέρμα** *to dherma*

leather goods **τα δερμάτινα είδη** *ta dhermateena eedhee*

to leave *(go away)* **φεύγω** *fevgho*
leave behind **αφήνω** *afeeno*
(train, bus etc.) **αφήνω** *afeeno*

leek **το πράσσο** *to praso*

left: *(on/to the) left* **αριστερά** *areestera*

left-luggage *(office)* **η φύλαξη αποσκευών** *ee feelaksee aposkevon*

left-luggage locker **η θυρίδα φύλαξης αποσκευών** *ee theereedha feelaksees aposkevon*

leg **το πόδι** *to podhee*

leggings **οι περισκελίδες** *ee pereeskeleedhes*

lemon **το λεμόνι** *to lemonee*

lemonade **η λεμονάδα** *ee lemonadha*

lemon tea **το τσάι με λεμόνι** *to tsaee me lemonee*

to lend **δανείζω** *dhaneezo*

length **το μήκος** *to meekos*

lens *(camera)* **ο φακός** *o fakos*
contact lens **ο φακός επαφής** *o fakos epafees*

lenses **οι φακοί** *ee fakee*

lentils **οι φακές** *ee fakes*

lesbian **λεζβία** *lezveea*

less: *less milk* **λιγότερο γάλα** *leeghotero ghala*
less than **λιγότερο από** *leeghotero apo*

lesson **το μάθημα** *to matheema*

to let *(allow)* **επιτρέπω** *epeetrepo*
(hire out) **νοικιάζω** *neekyazo*

letter **το γράμμα** *to ghrama*

letterbox **το γραμματοκιβώτιο** *to ghramatokeevotyo*

lettuce **το μαρούλι** *to maroolee*

level crossing **η σιδηροδρομική διασταύρωση** *ee seedheerodhromeekee dheeastavrosee*

library **η βιβλιοθήκη** *ee veevleeotheekee*

licence **η άδεια** *ee adheea*

to lie down **ξαπλώνω** *ksaplono*

lie *(untruth)* **το ψέμα** *to psema*

to lie **λέω ψεματα** *leo psemata*

life belt **το σωσίβιο** *to soseeveeo*

lifeboat η ναυαγοσωστική λέμβος *ee navaghososteekee lemvos*

lifeguard ο ναυαγοσώστης *o navaghosostees*

life insurance η ασφάλειαζωής *ee asfaleea zoees*

life jacket το σωσίβιο *to soseeveeo*

lift *(elevator)* το ασανσερ *to asanser*
(in car) μεταφέρω *metafero*

lift pass *(skiing)* το εισιτήριο *to eesee-teereeo*

light *(illumination)* το φως *to fos*
(not heavy) ελαφρύς *elafrees*
(colour) ανοιχτό *aneekhto*
have you got a light? έχετε φωτιά; *ekhete fotya*

light bulb ο γλόμπος *o ghlobos*

lighter *(to light a cigarette)* ο αναπτήρας *o anapteeras*

lighthouse ο φάρος *o faros*

lightning ο κεραυνός *o keravnos*

to like: ***I like...*** μου αρέσει *moo aresee*
do you like it? σου αρέσει; *soo aresee*

like: ***like this*** σαν *san*
a book like this ένα βιβλίο σαν αυτό *ena veevleeo san afto*
like that έτσι *etsee*
don't talk to me like that! μην μου μιλάς έτσι! *meen moo meelas etsee*

lilo το φουσκωτό στρώμα *to fooskoto stroma*

lime *(fruit)* το γλυκολέμονο *to ghleekolemono*

line η γραμμή *ee ghramee*

lip reading η χειλοανάγνωση *ee khee-loanaghnosee*

lip salve το προστατευτικό στικ *to prostatefteeko stick*

lipstick το κραγιόν *to krayon*

liqueur το λικέρ *to leeker*

to listen ακούω *akooo*

litre το λίτρο *to leetro*
a litre of milk ένα λίτρο γάλα *ena leetro ghala*

litter τα σκουπίδια *ta skoopeedhya*

little *(small)* μικρός *meekros*
a little λίγο *leegho*

to live μένω *meno*
he lives in London μένει στο Λονδίνο *menee sto londheeno*
he lives in a flat μένει σε διαμέρισμα *menee se dyamereesma*

liver το συκώτι *to seekotee*

living room το καθιστικό *to katheesteeko*

lizard η σαύρα *ee savra*

loaf *(of bread)* το καρβέλι *to karvelee*

lobster ο αστακός *o astakos*

local τοπικός *topeekos*

lock η κλειδαριά *ee kleedharya*

to lock κλειδώνω *kleedhono*
I'm locked out κλειδώθηκα έξω *kleedhotheeka ekso*

locker *(luggage)* η θήκη *ee theekee*

locksmith ο κλειδαράς *o kleedharas*

log book η άδεια κυκλοφορίας *ee adheea keekloforeeas*

logs τα κούτσουρα *ta kootsoora*

lollipop το γλειφιτζούρι *to ghleefeed-zooree*

London το Λονδίνο *to londheeno*

long μακρύς *makrees*

to look at κοιτάζω *keetazo*

to look after φροντίζω *frondeezo*

to look for γυρεύω *yeerevo*

loose λυμένος *leemenos*
it's come loose λύθηκε *leetheeke*

lorry το φορτηγό *to forteegho*

to lose χάνω *khano*

lost χαμένος *khamenos*
I've lost my wallet έχασα το πορτοφόλι μου *ekhasa to portofolee moo*
I'm lost χάθηκα *khatheeka*
we're lost χαθήκαμε *khatheekame*

lost-property office το γραφείο απωλεσθέντων αντικειμένων *to ghrafeeo apolesthendon andeekeemenon*

lot: ***a lot (of)*** πολύς *polees*

lotion η λοσιόν *ee losyon*

loud δυνατός *dheenatos*

lounge *(at airport)* η αίθουσα *ee ethoosa*
(in hotel, house) το σαλόνι *to salonee*

to love αγαπώ *aghapo*
I love you σ'αγαπώ *sagapo*

lovely: *how lovely!* Τι ωραία! *tee orea*

low χαμηλός *khameelos*

low-alcohol beer η μπίρα χαμηλή σε αλκοόλ *ee beera khameelee se alko-ol*

lower χαμηλότερα *khameelotera*

low-fat λαϊτ *laeet*

luggage οι αποσκευές *ee aposkeves*

luggage allowance το επιτρεπόμενο βάρος αποσκευών *to epeetrepomeno varos aposkevon*

luggage rack ο χώρος αποσκευών *o khoros aposkevon*

luggage tag η ετικέτα *ee eteeketa*

luggage trolley το καροτσάκι αποσκευών *to karotsakee aposkevon*

lump ηεξόγκωση *ee eksogosee*

lunch το μεσημεριανό *to meseemereeano*

lunchbreak το μεσημεριανό διάλειμμα *to meseemeryano dheealeema*

lung ο πνεύμονας *o pnevmonas*

luxury η πολυτέλεια *ee poleeteleea*

M

machine η μηχανή *ee meekhanee*

mad *(insane)* τρελός *trelos*
(angry) θυμωμένος *theemomenos*

magazine το περιοδικό *to pereeodheeko*

magnifying glass ομεγενθυτικός φακός *o meyentheeteekos fakos*

maiden name το πατρώνυμο *to patroneemo*

main course *(of meal)* το κύριο πιάτο *to keereeo pyato*

main road ο κύριος δρόμος *o keereeos dhromos*

mains *(electric)* ο κεντρικός αγωγός *o kendreekos aghoghos*

to make *(generally)* κάνω *kano*
(meal) μαγειρεύω *megheerevo*

make-up το μακιγιάζ *to makeeyaz*

male αρσενικός *arseneekos*

mallet ξύλινο σφυρί *kseeleeno sfeeree*

man ο άντρας *o andras*

to manage διευθύνω *dhee-eftheeno*

manager ο διαχειριστής *o dheeakheereestees*

many πολλοί *polee*
many people πολλοί άνθρωποι *polee anthropee*

manual χειρωνακτικός *kheeronakteekos*

map ο χάρτης *o khartees*

marble το μάρμαρο *to marmaro*

March ο Μαρτιος *o marteeos*

margarine η μαργαρίνη *ee margharee-nee*

marina η μαρίνα *ee mareena*

mark το σημάδι *to seemadhee*

market η αγορά *ee aghora*

market day η μέρα της αγοράς *ee mera tees aghoras*

marketplace η αγορά *ee aghora*

marmalade η μαρμελάδα *ee marmelad-ha*

marriage certificate το πιστοποιητικό γάμου *to peestopyeeteeko ghamoo*

married παντρεμένος *pandremenos*

marry: *to get married* παντρεύομαι *padhrevome*

mass *(in church)* η Θεία Λειτουργία *ee theea leetooryeea*

masterpiece το αριστούργημα *to areestoorgheema*

match *(game)* ο αγώνας *o aghonas*

matches τα σπίρτα *ta speerta*

material *(cloth)* το υλικό *to eeleeko*

matter: *it doesn't matter* δεν πειράζει *dhen peerazee*
what's the matter with you? τι έχεις; *tee ekhees*

May ο Μαιος *o maeeos*

mayonnaise η μαγιονέζα *ee mayoneza*

mayor ο Δήμαρχος *o dheemarkhos*

maximum το μέγιστο *to megheesto*

me εγώ *egho* / (ε)μένα *(e)mena* / μου *moo* / μού *moo* / με *me*
it's me, John! Εγώ είμαι, ο Γιάννης! *egho eeme o Yannis*
he gave it to me το έδωσε σε μένα *to edhose se mena*
give me a book δώσε μου ένα βιβλίο *dhose moo ena veevleeo*
he told me a story μού είπε μιά ιστορία *moo eepe meea eestoreea*
he hit me με χτύπησε *me khteepeese*

meal το γεύμα *to yevma*

to mean εννοώ *eno-o*
what does this mean? τι σημαίνει αυτό; *tee seemenee afto*

measles η ιλαρά *ee eelara*

meat το κρέας *to kreas*

mechanic ο μηχανικός *o meekhaneekos*

medicine *(drug)* το φάρμακο *to farmako*

Mediterranean η Μεσόγειος *ee mesoy-eeos*

medium *(wine)* μέτριο γλυκύ *metreeo ghleekee*
(steak, size) μέτριο *metreeo*

to meet συναντώ *seenando*

meeting η συνάντηση *ee seenandeesee*

meeting point το σημείο συνάντησης *to seemeeo seenanteesees*

melon το πεπόνι *to peponee*
(watermelon) το καρπούζι *to karpoozee*

member *(of club)* το μέλος *to melos*

membership card η κάρτα μέλους *ee karta meloos*

memory η μνήμη *ee mneemee*

men οι άντρες *ee andres*

menu ο κατάλογος *o kataloghos* // το μενού *to menoo*
à la carte menu το μενου αλά καρτ *to menoo ala kart*

message το μήνυμα *to meeneema*

metal το μέταλο *to metalo*

meter ο μετρητής *o metreetees*

metre το μέτρο *to metro*

microwave *(oven)* ο φούρνος μικροκυμάτων *o foornos meekrokeematon*

midday το μεσημέρι *to meseemeree*
at midday το μεσημέρι *to meseemeree*

middle μεσαίος *meseos*

middle-aged μεσήλικας *meseeleekas*

midge η σκνίπα *ee skneepa*

midnight τα μεσάνυχτα *ta mesaneekhta*

migraine η ημικρανία *ee eemeekraneea*

mild ήπιος *eepeeos*

mile το μίλι *to meelee*

milk το γάλα *to ghala*
full-cream milk το ολόπαχο γάλα *to olopakho ghala*
without milk χωρίς γάλα *khorees ghala*
semi-skimmed milk το ημίπαχο γάλα *to eemeepakho ghala*

milkshake το μιλκσέικ *to meelkseyk*

millimetre το χιλιοστόμετρο *to kheelyostometro*

million το εκατομμύριο *to ekatomeereeo*

mince ο κιμάς *o keemas*

to mind: *do you mind if...?* σας ενοχλεί αν...; *sas enokhlee an...*

mineral water το επιτραπέζιο νερό *to epeetrapezeeo nero*
(sparkling) το αεριούχο μεταλλικό νερό *to aeryookho metaleeko nero*

minibar το μίνι μπαρ *to meenee bar*

minimum ελάχιστος *elakheestos*

minor road ο δευτερεύων δρόμος *o dhefterevon dhromos*

mint *(herb)* ο δυόσμος *o dheeosmos*

minute το λεπτό *to lepto*

mirror ο καθρέφτης *o kathreftees*

to misbehave συμπεριφέρομαι άσχημα *seebereeferome askheema*

miscarriage η αποβολή *ee apovolee*

to miss *(train, etc.)* χάνω *khano*

Miss η Δεσποινίς *ee dhespeenees*

missing χαμένος *khamenos*

mistake το λάθος *to lathos*

mistaken: ***I think you're mistaken*** νομίζω είστε λανθασμένος *nomeezo eeste lanthasmenos*

misunderstanding η παρεξήγηση *ee parekseeyeesee*

mobile phone το κινητό τηλέφωνο *to keeneeto teelefono*

moisturizer η υδατική κρέμα *ee eedhateekee krema*

monastery το μοναστήρι *to monasteeree*

money τα χρήματα *ta khreemata*, τα λεφτά *ta lefta*

money order η ταχυδρομική επιταγή *ee takheedhromeekee epeetayee*

month ο μήνας *o meenas*

monument το μνημείο *to mneemeeo*

moon το φεγγάρι *to fengaree*

more περισσότερο *pereesotero*
more bread κι άλλο ψωμί *kee alo psomee*
more wine κι άλλο κρασί *kee alo krasee*

morning το πρωί *to proee*

morning-after pill το χάπι της επομένης *to khapee tees epomenees*

mosaic το μωσαϊκό *to mosaeeko*

mosque το τζαμί *to dzamee*

mosquito το κουνούπι *to koonoopee*

mosquito bite το δάγκωμα κουνουπιού *to dhakoma koonoopeeoo*

mosquito net η κουνουπιέρα *ee koonoopyera*

mosquito repellent το εντομοαπωθητικό *to entomoapotheeteeko*

most το περισσότερο *to pereesotero*

moth η πεταλουδίτσα *ee petaloodheetsa*

mother η μητέρα *ee meetera*

mother-in-law η πεθερά *ee pethera*

motor η μηχανή *ee meekhanee*

motorbike η μοτοσικλέτα *ee motoseekleta*

motorboat η βενζινάκατος *ee venzeenakatos*

motorway ο αυτοκινητόδρομος *o aftokeeneetodhromos*

mould η μούχλα *ee mookhla*

mountain το βουνό *to voono*

mouse *(also for computer)* το ποντίκι *to pondeekee*

mousse το μους *to moos*

moustache το μουστάκι *to moostakee*

mouth το στόμα *to stoma*

to move κινούμαι *keenoome*
it isn't moving δεν κινήτε *dhen keeneete*

movie η ταινία *ee teneea*

to mow κουρεύω *koorevo*

Mr Κύριος *keereeos*

Mrs Κυρία *keereea*

much πολύς *polees*
too much πάρα πολύ *para polee*
very much πάρα πολύ *para polee*

mud η λάσπη *ee laspee*

muddy λασπωμένος *laspomenos*

mumps οι μαγουλάδες *ee maghooladhes*

muscle ο μυς *o mees*

museum το μουσείο *to mooseeo*

mushroom το μανιτάρι *to maneetaree*

music η μουσική *ee mooseekee*

mussel το μύδι *to meedhee*

must πρέπει να... *prepee na...*
I must (εγώ) πρέπει να... *(egho) prepee na...*
we must (εμείς) πρέπει να... *vprepee na...*
I mustn't (εγώ) δεν πρέπει να... *dhen prepee na...*
we mustn't (εμείς) δεν πρέπει να... *(emees) dhen prepee na...*
I must go πρέπει να πάω *prepee na pao*

you must go πρέπει να πας *prepee na pas*
he / she must go πρέπει να πάει *prepee na paee*
we must go πρέπει να πάμε *prepee na pame*

mustard η μουστάρδα *ee moostardha*

my μου *moo*
my passport το διαβατηριό μου *to dheeavateereeo moo*
my room το δωματιό μου *to dhomateeo moo*

N

nail *(metal)* το καρφί *to karfee*
(on finger, toe) το νύχι *to neekhee*

nail polish το βερνίκι νυχιών *to verneekee neekhyon*

nail polish remover το ασετόν *to aseton*

nailbrush η βούρτσα των νυχιών *ee voortsa ton neekhyon*

naked γυμνός *yeemnos*

name το όνομα *to onoma*

napkin η πετσέτα *ee petseta*

nappy η πάνα *ee pana*

narrow στενός *stenos*

nationality η υπηκοότητα *ee eepeekooteeta*

natural φυσικός *feeseekos*

nature reserve το φυσικό απόθεμα *to feeseeko apothema*

navy blue μπλε *ble*

near κοντά *konda*

necessary απαραίτητος *apareteetos*

neck ο λαιμός *o lemos*

necklace το κολιέ *to kolye*

to need: *I need...* χρειάζομαι ... *khreeazome ...*

needle η βελόνα *ee velona*
a needle and thread βελόνα και κλωστή *velona ke klostee*

negative *(photography)* αρνητικός *arneeteekos*

neighbour ο γείτονας / η γειτόνισσα *o yeetonas / ee yeetoneesa*

nephew ο ανιψιός *o aneepsyos*

never ποτέ *pote*

new καινούριος *kenooryos*

news *(TV, radio)* οι ειδήσεις *ee eedheesees*

newspaper η εφημερίδα *ee efeemereedha*

New Year: *happy New Year!* καλή χρονιά! *kalee khronya*

New Zealand η Νέα Ζηλανδία *ee nea zeelandheea*

next επόμενος *epomenos*
the next bus το επόμενο λεωφορείο *to epomeno leoforeeo*

nice *(thing)* ωραίος *oreos*
(person) καλός *kalos*

niece η ανιψιά *ee aneepsya*

night η νύχτα *ee neekhta*

nightclub το νυχτερινό κέντρο *to neekhtereeno kendro*

nightdress το νυχτικό *to neekhteeko*

night porter ο νυχτερινός θυρωρός *o neekhtereenos theeroros*

no όχι *okhee*
no thanks όχι, ευχαριστώ *okhee, efkhareesto*
no problem κανένα πρόβλημα *kanena provleema*

nobody κανένας *kanenas*

noisy θορυβώδης *thoreevodhees*

non-alcoholic μη οινοπνευματώδης *mee eenopnevmatodhees*

none κανένα *kanena*

non-smoking μη καπνίζοντες *mee kapneezondes*

non-smoker ο μή καπνιστής *o mee kapneestees*

north ο βορράς *o voras*

Nothern Ireland η Βόρεια Ιρλανδία *ee voreea eerlandheea*

nose η μύτη *ee meetee*

not μη *mee*
I'm not δεν είμαι *dhen eeme*

I do not speak Greek δεν μιλώ ελληνικά *dhen meelo eleeneeka*

note (banknote) το χαρτονόμισμα *to khartonomeesma*
(letter) το σημείωμα *to seemeeoma*

note pad το σημειωματάριο *to seemeeomatareeo*

nothing τίποτα *teepota*
nothing else τίποτα άλλο *teepota alo*

now τώρα *tora*

nowhere πουθενά *poothena*

nudist beach η παραλία γυμνιστών *ee paraleea yeemneeston*

number ο αριθμός *o areethmos*

number plate η πινακίδα κυκλοφορίας *ee peenakeedha keekloforeeas*

nurse η νοσοκόμα *ee nosokoma*

nursery το παιδικό δωμάτιο *to pedheeko dhomateeo*
day nursery ο βρεφικός σταθμός *o vrefeekos stathmos*

nursery slope πλαγιά για αρχάριους *playa ya arkhareeoos*

nut (peanut) το φιστίκι *to feesteekee*
(walnut) το καρύδι *to kareedhee*
(hazelnut) το φουντούκι *to foondookee*
(for bolt) το παξιμάδι *to pakseemadhee*

O

oar το κουπί *to koopee*

occasionally κάπου-κάπου *kapoo-kapoo*

octopus το χταπόδι *to khtapodhee*

odd number ο μονός αριθμός *o monos areethmos*

of: *of course* βέβαια *vevea*
a bottle of water ένα μπουκάλι νερό *ena bookalee nero*

off (light, machine, etc.) σβυστός *sveestos*
it's off (rotten) είναι χαλασμένο *eene khalasmeno*

to offer προσφέρω *prosfero*

office το γραφείο *to ghrafeeo*

often συχνά *seekhna*
how often? πόσο συχνά; *poso seekhna*

oil το λάδι *to ladhee*

oil filter το φίλτρο του λαδιού *to feeltro too ladhyoo*

ointment η αλοιφή *ee aleefee*

OK εντάξει *endaksee*

old (person) ηλικιωμένος *eeleeky-omenos*
(thing) παλιός *palyos*
how old are you? πόσων χρονών είστε; *poson khronon eeste*

olive oil το ελαιόλαδο *to eleoladho*

olives οι ελιές *ee elyes*

omelette η ομελέτα *ee omeleta*

on (light, radio, TV) ανοιχτός *aneekhtos*
on the table στο τραπέζι *sto trapezee*

once μία φορά *meea fora*

one ένας / μία / ένα *enas* (masculine) / *meea* (feminine) / *ena* (neuter)

one-way (street) ο μονόδρομος *o mon-odhromos*
(ticket) το απλό εισιτήριο *to aplo eeseeteereeo*

onion το κρεμμύδι *to kremeedhee*

only μόνο *mono*

to open ανοίγω *aneegho*

open *adj* ανοικτός *aneektos*

opera η όπερα *ee opera*

opera house η όπερα *ee opera*

operator (telephone) η τηλεφωνήτρια *ee teelefoneetreea*

opposite απέναντι *apenandee*
opposite the hotel απέναντι από το ξενοδοχείο *apenantee apo to ksenod-hokheeo*

or ή *ee*

orange (fruit) το πορτοκάλι *to por-tokalee*
(colour) πορτοκαλί *portokalee*

orange juice ο χυμός πορτοκαλιού *o kheemos portokalyoo*

orchard το περιβόλι *to pereevolee*

orchestra η ορχήστρα *ee orkheestra*

to order παραγγέλλω *parangelo*

organic βιολογικός *veeologheekos*
is it organic? είναι βιολογικό; *eene veeologheeko*

to organize οργανώνω *orghanono*

original αρχικός *arkheekos*

ornament το στολίδι *to stoleedhee*

Orthodox *(religion)* ορθόδοξος *orthodhoksos*

other άλλος *alos*

our μας *mas*
our car το αυτοκινητό μας *to aftokeeneeto mas*
our hotel το ξενοδοχείο μας *to ksenodhokheeo mas*

out *(light, etc.)* σβησμένος *sveesmenos*
he's out λείπει *leepee*

outdoors στην ύπαιθρο *steen eepethro*

outside έξω *ekso*

outskirts τα περίχωρα *ta pereekhora*

oven ο φούρνος *o foornos*

over πάνω από *pano apo*
over there εκεί πέρα *ekee pera*

to oversleep παρακοιμάμαι *parakeemame*

to owe: *you owe me* μου χρωστάς *moo khrostas*

owner ο ιδιοκτήτης *o eedheeokteetees*

oxygen το οξυγόνο *to okseeghono*

oyster το στρείδι *to streedhee*

P

pace το βήμα *to veema*

to pack πακετάρω *paketaro*

package το δέμα *to dhema*

package tour η οργανωμένη εκδρομή *ee orghanomenee ekdhromee*

packet το πακέτο *to paketo*

paddling pool η λιμνούλα για παιδιά *ee leemnoola ya pedhya*

padlock το λουκέτο *to looketo*

page η σελίδα *ee seleedha*

paid πληρωμένος *pleeromenos*
I've paid έχω πληρώσει *ekho pleerosee*
have you paid? έχετε πληρώσει; *ekhete pleerosee*

painful οδυνηρός *odheeneeros*

painkiller το παυσίπονο *to pafseepono*

to paint *(wall, house)* βάφω *vafo*
(picture) ζωγραφίζω *zoghrafeezo*

painting ο πίνακας *o peenakas*

pair το ζευγάρι *to zevgharee*

palace το παλάτι *to palatee*

pale χλωμός *khlomos*

pan η κατσαρόλα *ee katsarola*

pancake η κρέπα *ee krepa*

panties η κυλότα *ee keelota*

pants *(underpants)* το σώβρακο *to sovrako*

pantyliner το σερβιετάκι *to servee-etakee*

paper το χαρτί *to khartee*

paper hankies τα χαρτομάντηλα *ta khartomanteela*

paragliding το θαλάσσιο αλεξίπτωτο *to thalaseeo alekseeptoto*

paralysed παράλυτος *paraleetos*

parcel το δέμα *to dhema*

pardon παρακαλώ *parakalo*
I beg your pardon με συγχωρείτε *me seenkhoreete*

parents οι γονείς *o ghonees*

park *n* το πάρκο *to parko*

to park *(in car)* παρκάρω *parkaro*

parmesan η παρμεζάνα *ee parmezana*
grated parmesan η τριμμένη παρμεζάνα *ee treemenee parmezana*

parsley ο μαϊντανός *o maeendanos*

part το μέρος *to meros*

party *(group)* η ομάδα *ee omadha*
(celebration) το πάρτυ *to partee*

passenger ο επιβάτης *o epeevatees*

passport το διαβατήριο *to dheeavateereeo*

passport control ο έλεγχος διαβατηρίων *o elengkhos dheeavateereeon*

passport number ο αριθμός διαβατηρίου *o areethm**o**s dheeavateer**ee**oo*

pasta τα ζυμαρικά *ta zeemareek**a***

pastry η ζύμη *ee z**ee**mee* (*cake*) το γλύκισμα *to ghl**ee**keesma*

path το μονοπάτι *to monop**a**tee*

patient υπομονετικός *eepomoneteek**o**s* (*hospital*) ο ασθενής *o asthen**ee**s*

pavement το πεζοδρόμιο *to pezodhr**o**meeo*

to pay πληρώνω *pleer**o**no*

payment η πληρωμή *ee pleerom**ee***

peach το ροδάκινο *to rodh**a**keeno*

peak hour η ώρα αιχμής *ee **o**ra ekhm**ee**s*

peanut το φιστίκι *to feest**ee**kee*

peanut allergy η αλλεργία στα φυστίκια *ee alergh**ee**a sta feest**ee**keea*

pear το αχλάδι *to akhl**a**dhee*

peas οι αρακάδες *ee arak**a**des*

pebble το πετραδάκι *to petradh**a**kee*

pedal το πεντάλ *to ped**a**l*
pedal boat/pedalo το ποδήλατο θαλάσσης *to podh**ee**lato thal**a**sees*

pedestrian (*person*) ο πέζος / η πεζή *o p**e**zos / ee pez**ee***

pedestrian crossing η διασταύρωση πεζών *ee dheeast**a**vrosee pez**o**n*

to pee κατουρώ *katoor**o***

to peel ξεφλουδίζω *kefloodh**ee**zo*

peg (*for tent*) ο πάσσαλος *o p**a**salos* (*for clothes*) το μανταλάκι *to mandal**a**kee*

pen τοστύλο *to st**ee**lo*

pencil το μολύβι *to mol**ee**vee*

penicillin η πενικιλλίνη *ee peneekeel**ee**nee*

penknife ο σουγιάς *o sooy**a**s*

pension η σύνταξη *ee s**ee**dhaksee*

pensioner ο / η συνταξιούχος *o / ee seendaksy**oo**khos*

people οι άνθρωποι *ee **a**nthropee*

pepper (*spice*) το πιπέρι *to peep**e**ree* (*vegetable*) η πιπεριά *ee peeper**ya***

eng-greek p

per: ***per hour*** την ώρα *teen **o**ra*
per day ανά μέρα *an**a** m**e**ra*
per person κατά άτομο *kat**a** **a**tomo*

perfect τέλειος *t**e**leeos*

performance η παράσταση *ee par**a**stasee*

perfume το άρωμα *to **a**roma*

perhaps ίσως *ee**sos***

period (*menstruation*) η περίοδος *ee per**ee**odhos*

perm η περμανάντ *ee perman**a**nd*

permit άδεια *a**dheea***

person το πρόσωπο *to pr**o**sopo*

personal stereo το προσωπικό στερεοφωνικό *to prosopeek**o** stereofoneek**o***

pet το κατικοίδιο ζώο *to kateek**ee**dhyo z**o**-o*

pet food τροφή για ζώα *trof**ee** ya z**o**a*

petrol η βενζίνη *ee venz**ee**nee*

petrol station το βενζινάδικο *to venzeen**a**dheeko* // το πρατήριο βενζίνης *to prat**ee**reeo venz**ee**nees*

phone το τηλέφωνο *to teel**e**fono* (*see also* **telephone**)

to phone τηλεφωνώ *teelefon**o***

phonebook ο τηλεφωνικός κατάλογος *o teelefoneek**o**s kat**a**logos*
yellow pages ο χρυσός οδηγός *o khrees**o**s odheegh**o**s*

phonebox ο τηλεφωνικός θάλαμος *o teelefoneek**o**s th**a**lamos*

phonecard η τηλεκάρτα *ee teelek**a**rta*

phone number ο αριθμός τηλεφώνου *o areetm**o**s teelef**o**noo*

photocopy η φωτοτυπία *ee fototeep**ee**a*
I need a photocopy χρειάζομαι μία φωτοτυπία *khree**a**zome m**ee**a fofoteep**ee**a*

photograph η φωτογραφία *ee fotoghraf**ee**a*

phrase book το βιβλιαράκι φράσεων *to veevleear**a**kee fr**a**seon*

to pick *(fruit, flowers)* **μαζεύω** *mazevo* *(to choose)* **διαλέγω** *dheealegho*

picnic **το πικνικ** *to picnic*

picture *(painting, photo)* **η εικόνα** *ee eekona*

pie **η πίτα** *ee peeta*

piece **το κομμάτι** *to komatee*

pier **η αποβάθρα** *ee apovathra*

pig **το γουρούνι** *to ghooroonee*

pill **το χάπι** *to khapee*

pillow **το μαξιλάρι** *to makseelaree*

pillowcase **η μαξιλαροθήκη** *ee maksee-larotheekee*

pilot **ο πιλότος** *o peelotos*

pin **η καρφίτσα** *ee karfeetsa*

pine **το πεύκο** *to pefko*

pineapple **ο ανανάς** *o ananas*

pink **ροζ** *roz*

pipe **η πίπα** *ee peepa*

pistachio nut **το φυστίκι Αιγίνης** *to feesteekee eyeenees*

pity: ***what a pity!*** **τι κρίμα!** *tee kreema*

pizza **η πίτσα** *ee peetsa*

place **ο τόπος** *o topos*
place of birth **ο τόπος γεννήσεως** *o topos gheneeseos*

plain *(unflavoured)* **απλός** *aplos*

plait **η πλεξούδα** *ee pleksoodha*

plan **το σχέδιο** *to skhedheeo*

to plan **σχεδιάζω** *skhedheeazo*

plant **το φυτό** *to feeto*

plaster *(for broken limb)* **ο γύψος** *o yeepsos*

plastic **πλαστικός** *plasteekos*

plastic bag **η πλαστική σακούλα** *ee plasteekee sakoola*

plate **το πιάτο** *to pyato*

platform **η αποβάθρα** *ee apovathra*

to play **παίζω** *pezo*

play area **ο παιδοχώρος** *o pedhokhoros*

play park **η παιδική χαρά** *ee pedhee-kee khara*

playroom **το δωμάτιο των παιδιών** *to dhomateeo ton pedhyon*

please **παρακαλώ** *parakalo*

pleased **ευχαριστημένος** *efkhareesteemenos*
pleased to meet you **χάρηκα για τη γνωριμία** *khareeka ya tee ghnoreemeea*

plenty **υπεραρκετά** *eeperarketa*

pliers **η πένσα** *ee pensa*

plug *(electric)* **η πρίζα** *ee preeza*

to plug in **βάζω στην πρίζα** *vazo steen preeza*

plum **η βανίλια** *ee vaneelya*

plumber **ο υδραυλικός** *o eedhravleekos*

plumbing **τα υδραυλικά** *ta eedhravleeka*

p.m. **μετά μεσημβρίας (μ.μ.)** *meta meseemvreeas*

pocket **η τσέπη** *ee tsepee*

poisonous **δηλητηριώδης** *dheelee-teereeodhees*

police **η αστυνομία** *ee asteenomeea*

policeman **ο αστυνόμος** *o asteenomos*

police station **το αστυνομικό τμήμα** *to asteenomeeko tmeema*

polish *(for shoes)* **το βερνίκι** *to vernee-kee*

pollen **η γύρη** *ee gheeree*

polluted **μολυσμένος** *moleesmenos*

pollution **η ρύπανση** *ee reepansee*

pony **το πόνυ** *to ponee*

pony trekking **η ιππασία** *ee eepaseea*

pool *(for swimming)* **η πισίνα** *ee peeseena*

pool attendant **ο επιμελητής πισίνας** *o epeemeleetees peeseenas*

popular **δημοφιλής** *dheemofeelees* *(fashionable)* **κοσμικός** *kosmeekos*

pork **το χοιρινό** *to kheereeno*
I don't eat pork **δεν τρώω χοιρινό** *dhen troo kheereeno*

port *(harbour)* **το λιμάνι** *to leemanee*

porter **ο αχθοφόρος** *o akhthoforos*

portion η μερίδα *ee mereedha*

possible δυνατός *dheenatos*
is it possible? είναι δυνατό; *eene dheenato*

to post *(letter)* ταχυδρομώ *takheedhromo*

postbox το ταχυδρομικό κουτί *to takheedhromeeko kootee*

postcard η καρτποστάλ *ee kartpostal*

postcode ο κωδικός *o kodheekos*

poster η αφίσα *ee afeesa*

post office το ταχυδρομείο *to takheedhromeeo*

pot η κατσαρόλα *ee katsarola*

potato η πατάτα *ee patata*

pottery τα κεραμικά *to kerameeka*

pound *(money)* η λίρα *ee leera*

powdered milk το γάλα σε σκόνη *to ghala se skonee*

power η δύναμη *ee dheenamee*

power cut η διακοπή ρεύματος *ee dheeakopee revmatos*

pram το καροτσάκι *to karotsakee*

prawn η γαρίδα *ee ghareedha*

to prefer προτιμώ *proteemo*

pregnant έγγυος *engeeos*

to prepare ετοιμάζω *eteemazo*

prescription η συνταγή *ee seendayee*

present *(gift)* το δώρο *to dhoro*

preservative το συντηρητικό *to seedeereeteeko*

president ο πρόεδρος *o proedhros*

pressure η πίεση *ee pee-esee*
tyre pressure η πίεση στα λάστυχα *ee pee-esee sta lasteekha*

pretty ωραίος *oreos*

price η τιμή *ee teemee*

price list ο τιμοκατάλογος *o teemokataloghos*

priest ο παπάς *o papas*

printer ο εκτυπωτής *o ekteepotees*

prison η φυλακή *ee feelakee*

private ιδιωτικός *eedheeoteekos*

prize το βραβείο *to vraveeo*

probably πιθανώς *peethanos*

problem το πρόβλημα *to provleema*

programme το πρόγραμμα *to proghrama*

prohibited απαγορευμένος *apaghorevmenos*

promise η υπόσχεση *ee eeposkhesee*

to pronounce προφέρω *profero*
how do you pronounce this? πώς το προφέρετε; *pos to proferete*

protein η πρωτείνη *ee prote-eene*

Protestant διαμαρτυρόμενος *dheeamarteeromenos*

to provide παρέχω *parekho*

prune το δαμάσκηνο *to dhamaskeeno*

public δημόσιος *dheemoseeos*

public holiday η γιορτή *ee yortee*

to pull τραβώ *travo*

pullover το πουλόβερ *to poolover*

to pull over *(car)* τραβώ στην άκρη *travo steen akree*

puncture το τρύπημα *to treepeema*

puncture repair kit τα εργαλεία αλλαγής ελαστικού *ta erghaleea alaghees elasteekoo*

purple πορφυρός *porfeeros*

purse το τσαντάκι *to tsandakee*

to push σπρώχνω *sprokhno*

push chair το καροτσάκι (μωρού) *to karotsakee (moroo)*

to put βάζω *vazo*
to put down βάζω κάτω *vazo kato*
to put back ξαναγυρίζω *ksanagheereezo*

pyjamas οι πιζάμες *ee peezames*

Q

quality η ποιότητα *ee peeoteeta*

quay η προκυμαία *ee prokeemea*

queen η βασίλισσα *ee vaseeleesa*

query η απορία *ee aporeea*

question η ερώτηση *ee eroteesee*

queue η ουρά *ee oora*
is there a queue? έχει ουρά; *ekhee oora*

quick γρήγορος *ghreeghoros*

quickly γρήγορα *ghreeghora*

quiet ήσυχος *eeseekhos*
a quiet room ένα ήσυχο δωμάτιο *ena eeseekho dhomateeo*

quilt *(duvet)* το πάπλωμα *to paploma*

quite εντελώς *entelos*
quite the opposite εντελώς το αντίθετο *entelos to anteetheto*

quiz show το κουίζ *to quiz*

R

rabbit το κουνέλι *to koonelee*

rabies η λύσσα *ee leesa*

racket η ρακέτα *ee raketa*

radiator *(heater)* το καλοριφέρ *to kaloreefer*
(in car engine) το ψυγείο *to pseeyeeo*

radio το ραδιόφωνο *to radheeofono*

radish το ραπανάκι *to rapanakee*

railway station ο σιδηροδρομικός σταθμός *o seedheerodhromeekos stathmos*

rain η βροχή *ee vrokhee*
it's raining βρέχει *vrekhee*

raincoat το αδιάβροχο *to adheeavrokho*

raisin η σταφίδα *ee stafeedha*

raped βιασμένη *veeasmenee*
I've been raped με βίασαν *me veeasan*

rare *(uncommon)* σπάνιος *spanyos*
(steak) μισοψημένος *meesopseemenos*

rash *(skin)* το εξάνθημα *to eksantheema*

raspberries τα βατόμουρα *ta vatomoora*

rat ο αρουραίος *o arooreos*

rate ο ρυθμός *o reethmos*
rate of exchange η ισοτιμία *ee eesoteemeea*

raw ωμός *omos*

razor το ξυραφάκι *to kseerafakee*

razor blade το ξυράφι *to kseerafee*

to read διαβάζω *dheeavazo*

ready έτοιμος *eteemos*

real πραγματικός *praghmateekos*

to realize αντιλαμβάνομαι *anteelamvanome*

reason ο λόγος *o loghos*

receipt η απόδειξη *ee apodheeksee*

recently τελευταία *teleftea*

reception *(desk)* η ρεσεψιόν *ee resepsyon*

recipe η συνταγή *ee seendayee*

to recommend συνιστώ *seeneesto*

record *(disc)* ο δίσκος *o dheeskos*

to record καταγράφω *kataghrafo*

to recycle ανακυκλώνω *anakeeklono*

red κόκκινος *kokeenos*

reduction η έκπτωση *ee ekptosee*

to refer to παραπέμπω *parapebo*

refill *(for pen, lighter)* το ανταλλακτικό *to andalakteeko*

refund η επιστροφή χρημάτων *ee epeestrofee khreematon*

regarding σχετικά με... *skheteeka me...*

registered *(letter)* συστημένο *seesteemeno*

regulations οι κανονισμοί *ee kanoneesmee*

to reimburse αποζημιώνω *apozeemeeono*

relations *(family)* οι συγγενείς *ee seengenees*

relationship η σχέση *ee skhesee*

to relax ξεκουράζομαι *ksekoorazome*

reliable *(person)* αξιόπιστος *akseeopeestos*
(car, method) δοκιμασμένος *dhokeemasmenos*

to remain απομένω *apomeno*

to remember θυμάμαι *theemame*

removal firm η εταιρία μεταφορών *ee etereea metaforon*

to remove απομακρύνω *apomakreeno*

to rent νοικιάζω *neekeeazo*

rental το νοίκι *to neekee*

to repair επιδιορθώνω *epeedhee-orthono*

repair η επισκευή *ee epeeskevee*

to repeat επαναλαμβάνω *epanalamvano*

to report αναφέρω *anafero*

to request κάνω αίτηση *kano eteesee*

reservation η κράτηση *ee krateesee*

to reserve κρατώ *krato*

reserved κρατημένος *krateemenos*

rest ξεκούραση *ksekoorasee*
the rest οι υπόλοιποι *ee eepoleepee*

to rest ξεκουράζομαι *ksekoorazome*

restaurant το εστιατόριο *to esteeatoreeo*

restaurant car το βαγόνι ρεστωράν *to vaghonee restoran*

to retire βγαίνω στη σύνταξη *vyeno stee seendaksee*

retired συνταξιούχος *seendaksyookhos*
I'm retired είμαι συνταξιούχος *eeme seendhakseeookhos*

to return *(go back, give back)* επιστρέφω *epeestrefo*

return ticket το εισιτήριο με επιστροφή *to eeseeteereeo me epeestrofee*

to reverse αντιστρέφω *adheestrefo*

to reverse the charges αντιστρέφω τις χρεώσεις *andeestrefo tees khreosees*

reverse-charge call κλήση πληρωτέα από τον παραλήπτη *kleesee pleerotea apo ton paraleeptee*

rheumatism οι ρευματισμοί *ee revmateesmee*

rib πλευρό *plevro*, παίδι *paeedhee*

rice το ρύζι *to reezee*

rich *(person, food)* πλούσιος *plooseeos*

to ride *(in a car)* πηγαίνω με αυτοκίνητο *peeyeno me aftokeeneeto*

riding *(equestrian)* η ιππασία *ee eepaseea*

right *(correct, accurate)* σωστός *sostos*
(on/to the) right δεξιά *dheksya*

right of way δικαίωμα προτεραιότητας *dheekeoma protereoteetas*

to ring *(bell)* χτυπώ *khteepo*
(phone) παίρνω τηλέφωνο *perno teelefono*
it's ringing χτυπάει το τηλέφωνο *khteepaee to teelefono*

ring το δαχτυλίδι *to dhakhteeleedhee*

ripe ώριμος *oreemos*

river το ποτάμι *to potamee*

road ο δρόμος *o dhromos*

road map ο οδικός χάρτης *o odheekos khartees*

roast το ψητό *to pseeto*

to rob ληστεύω *leestevo*

roll *(of bread)* το ψωμάκι *to psomakee*

roof η στέγη *ee steyee*

roof rack η σχάρα *ee skhara*

room *(in house, etc.)* το δωμάτιο *to dhomateeo*
family room το καθιστικό *to katheesteeko*
(space) ο χώρος *o khoros*

room service η υπηρεσία δωματίου *ee eepeereseea dhomateeoo*

rope το σχοινί *to skheenee*

rose το τριαντάφυλλο *to treeandhafeelo*

rosé ροζέ *roze*

rotten *(fruit)* χαλασμένος *khalasmenos*

rough *(sea)* τρικυμισμένη *treekeemeesmenee*

round *(shape)* στρογγυλός *strongeelos*
round Greece γύρω στην Ελλάδα *yeero steen eladha*
round the corner στη γωνία *stee ghoneea*

route ο δρόμος *o dhromos*

to row *(boat)* κάνω κουπί *kano koopee*

rowing boat η βάρκα με κουπιά *ee varka me koopya*

royal βασιλικός *vaseeleekos*

rubber *(eraser)* η γομολάστιχα *ee ghomolasteekha*
(material) το λάστιχο *to lasteekho*

rubber band το λαστιχάκι *to lasteekhakee*

rubbish τα σκουπίδια *ta skoopeedhya*

rucksack το σακίδιο *to sakeedheeo*

ruins τα ερείπια *ta ereepya*

rum το ρούμι *to roomee*

to run τρέχω *trekho*

rush hour η ώρα αιχμής *ee ora ekhmees*

rusty σκουριασμένος *skooryasmenos*

S

sad λυπημένος *leepeemenos*

safe *adj (medicine)* **αβλαβής** *avlavees* *(beach)* **ακίνδυνος** *akeendheenos*

safe *n* **το χρηματοκιβώτιο** *to khreematokeevotyo*

safety pin η παραμάνα *ee paramana*

sailing η ιστιοπλοΐα *ee eesteeopleeya*

saint ο Άγιος / η Αγία *o agheeos / ee agheea*

salad η σαλάτα *ee salata*

salad dressing το λαδολέμονο *to ladholemono*

salary ο μισθός *o meesthos*

sale *(in shop)* **το ξεπούλημα** *to ksepooleema*

salmon ο σολομός *o solomos*

salt το αλάτι *to alatee*

same ίδιος *eedheeos*

sand η άμμος *ee amos*

sandals τα πέδιλα *ta pedheela*

sandwich το σάντουϊτς *to sandwich*

sanitary towel η σερβιέτα *ee servyeta*

sardine η σαρδέλα *ee sardhela*

sauce η σάλτσα *ee saltsa*

saucepan η κατσαρόλα *ee katsarola*

saucer το πιατάκι *to pyatakee*

sausage το λουκάνικο *to lookaneeko*

savoury πικάντικος *peekandeekos*

to say λέω *leo*

scarf *(long)* **το κασκόλ** *to kaskol* *(square)* **το μαντήλι** *to mandeelee*

scenery η θέα *ee thea*

school το σχολείο *to skholeeo*
primary school το δημοτικό *to dheemoteeko*
(for 12- to 15-year-olds) **το γυμνάσιο** *to yeemnaseeo*
(for 15- to 18- year-olds) **το λύκειο** *to leekeeo*

schedule το πρόγραμμα *to proghrama*

scissors το ψαλίδι *to psaleedhee*

Scot ο Σκωτσέζος *o skotsezos* / η Σκωτσέζα *ee skotseza*

Scotland η Σκωτία *ee skoteea*

Scottish σκωτικός *skotikos*

screw η βίδα *ee veedha*

screwdriver το κατσαβίδι *to katsaveedhee*

sculpture το γλυπτό *to ghleepto*

sea η θάλασσα *ee thalasa*

seafood τα θαλασσινά *ta thalaseena*

seam *(of dress)* **η ραφή** *ee rafee*

to search ψάχνω *psakhno*

seasickness η ναυτία *ee nafteea*

seaside η θάλασσα *ee thalasa* // η παραλία *ee paraleea*

season *(of year)* **η εποχή** *ee epokhee* *(holiday)* **η εποχή των διακοπών** *ee epokhee ton dheeakopon*

seat *(in theatre)* **η θέση** *ee thesee* *(in car, etc.)* **το κάθισμα** *to katheesma*

second δεύτερος *dhefteros*

second class *(ticket, etc.)* **δεύτερη θέση** *dhefteree thesee*

second-hand μεταχειρισμένος *metakheereesmenos*

sedative το ηρεμιστικό *to eeremeesteeko*

to see βλέπω *vlepo*

to seize κατάσχω *kataskho*

self-service το σελφ σέρβις *to self service*

to sell πουλώ *poolo*

sell-by date η ημερομηνία λήξης *ee eemeromeeneea leeksees*

Sellotape ® το σελοτέιπ *to seloteyp*

send στέλνω *stelno*

sensible λογικός *logheekos*

separate χωριστός *khoreestos*

serious σοβαρός *sovaros*

to serve σερβίρω *serveero*

service *(in restaurant, etc.)* η εξυπηρέτηση *ee ekseepeereteesee* *(in church)* η Θεία Λειτουργία *ee theea leetoorgheea*

service charge το ποσοστό υπηρεσίας *to pososto eepeereseeas*

service station το γκαράζ για σέρβις *to gharaz ya service*

set menu το καθορισμένο μενού *to kathoreesmeno menoo*

settee ο καναπές *o kanapes*

several διάφοροι *dheeaforee*

to sew ράβω *ravo*

sewerage η αποχέτευση *ee epokhetef-see*

sex *(gender)* το φύλο *to feelo* *(intercourse)* το σεξ *to sex*

shade η σκιά *ee skeea*
in the shade στη σκιά *stee skeea*

to shake *(bottle)* κουνώ *koono*

shallow ρηχός *reekhos*

shampoo το σαμπουάν *to sambooan*

shampoo and set λούσιμο και στέγνωμα *looseemo ke steghnoma*

to share μοιράζω *meerazo*

to shave ξυρίζομαι *kseereezome*

shaving cream η κρέμα ξυρίσματος *ee krema kseereesmatos*

she αυτή *aftee*

sheep το πρόβατο *to provato*

sheet το σεντόνι *to sendonee*

shellfish τα όστρακα *ta ostraka*

ship το πλοίο *to pleeo*

shirt το πουκάμισο *to pookameeso*

shock absorber το αμορτισέρ *to amor-teeser*

shoe το παπούτσι *to papootsee*

shoelaces τα κορδόνια *ta kordhoneea*

to shop ψωνίζω *psoneezo*

shop το μαγαζί *to maghazee*

shop assistant *(woman)* η πωλήτρια *ee poleetreea*
(man) ο πωλητής *o poleetees*

shop window η βιτρίνα *ee veetreena*

short κοντός *kondos*

short circuit το βραχυκύκλωμα *to vrakheekeekloma*

short cut ο συντομότερος δρόμος *o seen-domoteros dhromos*

shortage η έλλειψη *ee eleepsee*

shorts το σορτς *to shorts*

show *n (in theatre, etc.)* η παράσταση *ee parastasee*

to show δείχνω *dheekhno*

shower *(in bath)* το ντους *to doos*
(rain) η μπόρα *ee bora*

shower gel ο αφρός ντους *o afros doos*

shrimp η γαρίδα *ee ghareedha*

shrub ο θάμνος *o thamnos*

shut *(closed)* κλειστός *kleestos*

to shut κλείνω *kleeno*

shutters τα παντζούρια *ta pantzooreea*

shuttle service συνεχής συγκοινωνία *seenekhees seegheenoneea*

sick *(ill)* άρρωστος *arostos*
to be sick *(vomit)* κάνω εμετό *kano emeto*

side η πλευρά *ee plevra*

sightseeing: *to go sightseeing* επισκέπτομαι τα αξιοθέατα *epeeskep-tome ta akseeotheata*

sightseeing tour η ξενάγηση αξιοθεάτων *ee ksenagheesee akseeotheaton*

sign *(roadsign, notice, etc)* η πινακίδα *ee peenakeedha*

signature η υπογραφή *ee eepoghrafee*

signpost η πινακίδα *ee peenakeedha*

silk το μετάξι *to metaksee*

silver ασημένιος *aseemeneeos*

similar to παρόμοιος *paromeeos*

simple απλός *aplos*

since από *apo*

to sing τραγουδώ *traghoodho*

single *(not married)* ελεύθερος *eleftheros*
(not double) μονός *monos*
(ticket) μονό εισιτήριο *mono eesee-teereeo*

single bed το μονό κρεββάτι *to mono krevatee*

single room το μονόκλινο δωμάτιο *to monokleeno dhomateeo*

sink ο νεροχύτης *o nerokheetees*

sister η αδελφή *ee adhelfee*

sister-in-law η κουνιάδα *ee kooneeadha*

to sit *(down)* κάθομαι *kathome*
please, sit down παρακαλώ, καθήστε *parakalo katheeste*

size *(of clothes, shoes)* το μέγεθος *to meyethos*

skates *(ice)* τα παγοπέδιλα *ta paghoped-heela*

ski τα σκι *ta skee*

to ski κάνω σκι *kano skee*

ski boots οι μπότες του σκι *ee botes too ski*

ski instructor ο δάσκαλος του σκι *o dhaskalos too ski*

ski jacket το μπουφάν του σκι *to boofan too skee*

ski jump το άλμα με σκι *to alma me ski*

ski pants το παντελόνι του σκι *to pandelonee too skee*

ski pole το ραβδί του σκι *to ravdhee too skee*

ski run η διαδρομή του σκι *ee dheeadhromee too skee*

ski suit τα ρούχα του σκι *ta rookha too skee*

skimmed milk το αποβουτυρωμένο γάλα *to apovooteeromeno ghala*

skin το δέρμα *to dherma*

skin diving το υποβρύχιο κολύμπι *to eepovreekheeo koleembee*

skirt η φούστα *ee foosta*

sky ο ουρανός *o ooranos*

to sleep κοιμούμαι *keemoome*

to sleep in κοιμάμαι μέσα *keemame mesa*

sleeper το βαγκόν-λι *to vagon-lee*

sleeping bag το υπνόσακος *o eep-nosakos*

sleeping car το βαγκόν-λι *to vaghon-lee*

sleeping pill το υπνωτικό χάπι *to eep-noteeko khapee*

slice η φέτα *ee feta*

slide *(photography)* το σλάιντ *to slaeed*

slippery γλιστερός *ghleesteros*

slow σιγά *seegha*

small μικρός *meekros*

smaller (than) μικρότερος (από) *meekroteros (apo)*

smell η μυρωδιά *ee meerodhya*

smile το χαμόγελο *to khamoyelo*

to smile χαμογελώ *khamoyelo*

smoke ο καπνός *o kapnos*

to smoke καπνίζω *kapneezo*
can I smoke? μπορώ να καπνίσω; *boro na kapneeso*

smoked καπνιστός *kapneestos*

snack bar το σνακ μπαρ *to snack bar*

snake το φίδι *to feedhee*

snorkel ο αναπνευστήρας *o anapnevsteeras*

snow το χιόνι *to khyonee*

snow tyres τα λάστιχα με αντιολισθητικές αλυσίδες *ta lasteekha me anteeoleestheeteekes aleeseedhes*

snow plough το εκχιονιστηκό *to ekheeoneesteeko*

snowed up αποκλεισμένος από το χιόνι *apokleesmenos apo to khyonee*

snowing: *it's snowing* χιονίζει *khyoneezee*

so γι'αυτό *yee afto*
so much τόσο πολύ *toso polee*
so pretty τόσο ωραίος *toso oreos*
so that για να *ya na*

soap το σαπούνι *to sapoonee*

soap powder το απορρυπαντικό *to aporeepandeeko*

sober ξεμέθυστος *ksemetheestos*

sock η κάλτσα *ee kaltsa*

socket (electrical) η πρίζα *ee preeza*

soda (water) η σόδα *ee sodha*

soft μαλακός *malakos*

soft drink το αναψυκτικό *to anapseek-teeko*

some μερικοί *mereekee*

someone κάποιος *kapyos*

something κάτι *katee*

sometimes κάποτε *kapote*

son ο γιος *o yos*

song το τραγούδι *to traghoodhee*

soon σύντομα *seendoma*
as soon as possible το συντομότερο *to seendomotero*
sooner νωρίτερα *noreetera*

sore: *it's sore* πονάει *ponaee*

sorry: *I'm sorry* (apology) συγγνώμη *seeghnomee*
(regret) λυπούμαι *leepoome*

sort το είδος *to eedhos*

soup η σούπα *ee soopa*

south ο νότος *o notos*

souvenir το σουβενίρ *to sooveneer*

space (room) ο χώρος *o khoros*

spanner το κλειδί *to kleedhee*

spare room το διαθέσιμο δωμάτιο *to dheeatheseemo dhomateeo*

spare tyre η ρεζέρβα *ee rezerva*

spare wheel η ρεζέρβα *ee rezerva*

spark plug το μπουζί *to boozee*

sparkling (wine) αφρώδης *afrodhees*

to speak μιλώ *meelo*
do you speak English? μιλάτε Αγγλικά; *meelate aghleeka*

special ειδικός *eedheekos*

specialist ο ειδικός *o eedheekos*

speciality (in restaurant) η σπεσιαλιτέ *ee spesyaleete*

speech ο λόγος *o loghos*

speed η ταχύτητα *ee takheeteeta*

speed boat το ταχύπλοο *to takheeplo-o*

speed limit το όριο ταχύτητας *to oreeo takheeteetas*
to exceed the speed limit παραβιάζω το όριο ταχύτητας *paraveeazo to oreeo takheeteetas*

speeding η υπερβολική ταχύτητα *ee eepervoleekee takheeteeta*

speeding ticket το πρόστιμο για υπερβολική ταχύτητα *to prosteemo ya eepervoleekee takheeteeta*

spell γράφω *ghrafo*
how do you spell it? πώς γράφεται; *pos ghrafete*

spicy πικάντικος *peekandeekos*

spinach το σπανάκι *to spanakee*

spin-dryer το στεγνωτήριο ρούχων *to steghnoteereeo rookhon*

spirits τα οινοπνευματώδη ποτά *ta eenopnevmatodhee pota*

sponge το σφουγγάρι *to sfoongaree*

spoon το κουτάλι *to kootalee*

sport το σπορ *to spor*

sports centre το αθλητικό κέντρο *to athleeteeko kentro*

sports shop το κατάστημα αθλητικών ειδών *to katasteema athleeteekon eedhon*

spot το στίγμα *to steeghma*

sprain στραμπουλίζω *strabooleezo*

spring (season) η άνοιξη *ee aneeksee*

square (in town) η πλατεία *ee plateea*

squash (sport) το σκουός *to skooos*
orange squash η πορτοκαλάδα *ee portokaladha*
lemon squash η λεμονάδα *ee lemonadha*

squid το καλαμάρι *to kalamaree*

stadium το στάδιο *to stadheeo*

staff το προσωπικό *to prosopeeko*

stage η σκηνή *ee skeenee*

stain remover το αφαιρετικό λεκέδων *to afereteeko lekedhon*

stairs η σκάλα *ee skala*

stalls *(in theatre)* η πλατεία *ee plateea*

stamp το γραμματόσημο *to ghram-atoseemo*

to stand στέκομαι *stekome*

star *(in sky)* το άστρο *to astro*

starfish ο αστερίας *o astereeas*

to start αρχίζω *arkheezo*

starter *(in meal)* το ορεκτικό *to orekteeko*

station ο σταθμός *o stathmos*

stationer's το χαρτοπωλείο *to khartopoleeo*

statue το άγαλμα *to aghalma*

stay η διαμονή *dheeamonee*
enjoy your stay! καλή διανομή *kalee dheeanomee*

to stay μένω *meno*

steak το μπιφτέκι *to beeftekee*

to steam αχνίζω *akhneezo*

steep ανηφορικός *aneeforeekos*

step το βήμα *to veema*

stepdaughter η προγονή *ee proghonee*

stepfather ο πατρυιός *o patreeos*

stepmother η μητρυιά *ee meetreea*

stepson ο προγονός *o proghonos*

sterling η αγγλική λίρα *ee angleekee leera*

steward *(on a ship)* ο καμαρότος *o kamarotos*
(on plane) ο αεροσυνοδός *o aeroseen-odhos*

stewardess *(on plane)* η αεροσυνοδός *ee aeroseenodhos*

sticking plaster ο λευκοπλάστης *o lefkoplastees*

still *(yet)* ακόμα *akoma*
(immobile) ακίνητος *akeeneetos*
(water) μη αεριούχο *mee aeryookho*

sting το τσίμπημα *to tseembeema*

stockings οι κάλτσες *ee kaltses*

stolen κλεμμένος *klemenos*

stomach το στομάχι *to stomakhee*

stomach upset η στομαχική διαταραχή *ee stomakheekee dheeatarakhee*

to stop σταματώ *stamato*

stop sign το στοπ *to stop*

storm η καταιγίδα *ee kateyeedha*

straight: ***straight on*** ευθεία *eftheea*

strange παράξενος *paraksenos*

straw *(for drinking)* το καλαμάκι *to kala-makee*

strawberry η φράουλα *ee fraoola*

street ο δρόμος *o dhromos*

street plan ο οδικός χάρτης *o odheekos khartees*

strength η δύναμη *ee dheenamee*

string ο σπάγγος *o spangos*

striped ριγωτός *reeghotos*

stroke το χτύπημα *to khteepeema*
to have a stroke παθαίνω εγκεφαλικό *patheno eghefaleeko*

strong δυνατός *dheenatos*
strong coffee ο δυνατός καφές *o dheenatos kafes*
strong tea το δυνατό τσάι *to deenato tsaee*

stuck *(jammed)* κολλημένος *koleemenos*

student ο φοιτητής / η φοιτήτρια *o fee-teetees / ee feeteetreea*

student discount η φοιτητική έκπτωση *ee feeteeteekee ekptosee*

stung: *I've been stung by something* κάτι με τσίμπησε *katee me tseem-beese*

stupid ανόητος *anoeetos*

subway η υπόγεια διάβαση *ee eepoy-eea dheeavasee*

suddenly ξαφνικά *ksafneeka*

suede **το καστόρι** *to kastoree*

sugar **η ζάχαρη** *ee zakharee*

to suggest **προτείνω** *proteeno*

suit *(man's)* **το κοστούμι** *to kostoomee* *(woman's)* **το ταγιέρ** *to tayer*

suitcase **η βαλίτσα** *ee valeetsa*

sum **το ποσό** *to poso*

summer **το καλοκαίρι** *to kalokeree*

summit **η κορυφή** *ee koreefee*

sun **ο ήλιος** *o eeleeos*

to sunbathe **κάνω ηλιοθεραπεία** *kano eeleeotherapeea*

sun block **το αντιηλιακό** *to andee-eelyako*

sunburn *(painful)* **το κάψιμο από τον ήλιο** *to kapseemo apo ton eeleeo*

sunglasses **τα γιαλιά του ήλιου** *ta yalya too eeleeoo*

sunny *(weather)* **ηλιόλουστος** *eelyoloos-tos*

sunrise **η ανατολή** *ee anatolee*

sunset **η δύση** *ee dheesee*

sunshade **η ομπρέλα** *ee ombrela*

sunstroke **η ηλίαση** *ee eeleeasee*

suntan lotion **το λάδι για τον ήλιο** *to ladhee ya ton eeleeo*

supermarket **το σουπερμάρκετ** *to super-market*

supper **το δείπνο** *to dheepno*

supplement **το συμπλήρωμα** *to seembleeroma*

supply **η προμήθεια** *ee promeetheea*

surcharge **η επιβάρυνση** *ee epeeva-reensee*

sure: ***I'm sure*** **είμαι σίγουρος / σίγουρη** *eeme seeghooros / seeghooree*

to surf **κάνω σερφ** *kano surf*
to surf the net **κάνω σερφ στο δύκτιο** *kano surf sto dheekteeo*

surfboard **η σανίδα σέρφινγκ** *ee saneedha serfing*

surfing **το σέρφινγκ** *to serfing*

surname **το επώνυμο** *to eponeemo*
my surname is... **το επωνυμό μου είναι...** *to eponeemo moo eene...*

surrounded by **τριγυρισμένος από** *treeyeereesmenos apo*

to survive **επιζώ** *epeezo*

suspension **η ανάρτηση** *ee anarteesee*

to swear *(bad language)* **βρίζω** *vreezo*

to sweat **ιδρώνω** *eedhrono*

sweater **το πουλόβερ** *to poolover*

sweet *adj (taste)* **γλυκός** *ghleekos*

sweet course **το επιδόρπιο** *to epeed-horpeeo*

sweets **οι καραμέλες** *ee karameles*

sweetener **η ζαχαρίνη** *ee zakhareenee*

to swim **κολυμπώ** *koleembo*

swimming pool **η πισίνα** *ee peeseena*

swimsuit **το μαγιό** *to mayo*

swing *(for children)* **η κούνια** *ee koonya*

switch **ο διακόπτης** *o dheeakoptees*

to switch on **ανάβω** *anavo*

to switch off **σβήνω** *sveeno*

swollen *(ankle, etc.)* **πρησμένος** *preesmenos*

synagogue **η συναγωγή** *ee seenaghoy-ee*

T

table **το τραπέζι** *to trapezee*

tablecloth **το τραπεζομάντηλο** *to trape-zomandeelo*

tablespoon **το κουτάλι** *to kootalee*

tablet **το χάπι** *to khapee*

table tennis **το πινγκ πονγκ** *to ping pong*

table wine **το επιτραπέζιο κρασί** *to epeetrapezeeo krasee*

to take *(carry)* **παίρνω** *perno*
(to grab, seize) **αρπάζω** *arpazo*
(to take someone to) **πηγαίνω** *peegheno*

to take out **βγάζω** *vghazo*
(from bank account) **αποσύρω** *aposeero*

to talk μιλώ *meelo*

tall ψηλός *pseelos*

tame *(animal)* ήμερος *eemeros*

tampons τα ταμπόν *ta tambon*

tank *(car)* το ντεπόζιτο βενζίνης *to dhepozeeto venzeenees*
(fish) το ενυδρείο *to eneedhreeo*

tap η βρύση *ee vreesee*

tap water το νερό βρύσης *to nero vreesees*

tape recorder το μαγνητόφωνο *to maghneetofono*

taramosalata η ταραμοσαλάτα *ee taramosalata*

to taste δοκιμάζω *dhokeemazo*

taste *n* η γεύση *ee yefsee*

tax ο φόρος *o foros*

taxi το ταξί *to taksee*

taxi rank η πιάτσα *ee pyatsa*

tea το τσάι *to tsaee*
tea with milk το τσάι με γάλα *to tsaee me ghala*

teabag το φακελλάκι τσαγιού *to fakelakee tsayoo*

to teach διδάσκω *dheedhasko*

teacher ο δάσκαλος / η δασκάλα *o dhaskalos / ee dhaskala*

teapot η τσαγιέρα *ee tsayera*

tear *(in eye)* το δάκρυ *to dhakree*
(in material) το σχίσιμο *to skheeseemo*

teaspoon το κουταλάκι *to kootalakee*

teat η ρώγα *ee rogha*

teenager ο έφηβος *o efeevos*

teeth τα δόντια *ta dhondeea*

telegram το τηλεγράφημα *to teeleghrafeema*

telephone το τηλέφωνο *to teelefono*

telephone box ο τηλεφωνικός θάλαμος *o teelefoneekos thalamos*

telephone call το τηλεφώνημα *to teelefoneema*

telephone directory ο τηλεφωνικός κατάλογος *o teelefoneekos kataloghos*

television η τηλεόραση *ee teeleorasee*

telex το τέλεξ *to telex*

to tell λέγω *legho*
(story) διηγούμαι *dhee-eeghoome*

temperature η θερμοκρασία *ee thermokraseea*
to have a temperature έχω πυρετό *ekho peereto*

temple ο ναός *o naos*

temporary προσωρινός *prosoreenos*

tenant ο ενοικιαστής *o eneekeeastees*

tennis το τένις *to tenees*

tennis ball η μπάλα του τένις *ee bala too tennis*

tennis court το γήπεδο του τένις *to yeepedho too tenees*

tennis racket η ρακέτα του τένις *ee raketa too tenees*

tent η σκηνή *ee skeenee*

tent peg ο πάσσαλος της σκηνής *o pasalos tees skeenees*

terminus το τέρμα *to terma*

terrace η ταράτσα *ee taratsa*

to test δοκιμάζω *dhokeemazo*

testicles οι όρχεις *ee orkhees*

tetanus injection το εμβόλιο τετάνου *to emvoleeo tetanoo*

thank you ευχαριστώ *efkhareesto*

that εκείνος *ekeenos*
that book εκείνο το βιβλίο *ekeeno to veevleeo*
that one εκείνο *ekeeno*

the *(singular)* ο / η / το *o / ee / to*
(plural) οι / οι / τα *ee / ee / ta*

theatre το θέατρο *to theatro*

them αυτούς / τούς / τους /αυτοί *aftoss / toos / toos / aftee*
instead of them αντί γι' αυτούς *antee yaftoos*
I see them τούς βλέπω *toos vlepo*
listen to them ακουσέ τους *akoose toos*
it's them! αυτοί είναι! *aftee eene*

then τότε *tote*

there εκεί *ekee*
there is υπάρχει *eeparkhee*
there are υπάρχουν *eeparkhoon*

thermometer το θερμόμετρο *to thermometro*

these αυτοί / αυτές / αυτά *aftee* (masculine) / *aftes* (feminine) / *afta* (neuter)
these books αυτά τα βιβλία *afta ta veevleea*

they αυτοί *aftee*

thick χοντρός *khontros*

thief ο κλέφτης *o kleftees*

thin λεπτός *leptos*

thing το πράγμα *to praghma*

third τρίτος *treetos*

thirsty: *I'm thirsty* διψάω *dheepsao*

this αυτός / αυτή / αυτό *aftos* (masculine) / *aftee* (feminine) / *afto* (neuter)
this book αυτό το βιβλίο *afto to veevleeo*
this one αυτό *afto*

those εκείνοι *ekeenee*
those books εκείνα τα βιβλία *ekeena ta veevleea*

thread η κλωστή *ee klostee*

throat ο λαιμός *o lemos*

throat lozenges οι παστίλιες για το λαιμό *ee pasteelyes ya to lemo*

through διαμέσου *dheeamesoo*

to throw away πετάω *petao*

thunder η βροντή *ee vrondee*

thunderstorm η θύελλα *ee theeela*

ticket (bus, train etc.) το εισιτήριο *to eeseeteereeo*
(entry fee) εισιτήριο εισόδου *eeseeteereeo eesodhoo*

ticket collector ο ελεγκτής *o elengtees*

ticket inspector ο ελεγκτής *o elengtees*

ticket office η θυρίδα *ee theereedha*

tidy τακτοποιημένο *taktopee-eemeno*

to tidy up τακτοποιώ *taktopeeo*

tie η γραβάτα *ee ghravata*

tight σφιχτός *sfeekhtos*

tights το καλσόν *to kalson*

tile (floor) το πλακάκι *to plakakee*

till (cash) το ταμείο *to tameeo*

till (until) μέχρι *mekhree*

time (by the clock) η ώρα *ee ora*
what time is it? τι ώρα είναι; *tee ora eene*
do you have the time? έχετε ώρα; *ekhete ora*

timetable τα ωράριο *ta orareeo*

tin η κονσέρβα *ee konserva*

tinfoil το ασημόχαρτο *to aseemokharto*

tin-opener το ανοιχτήρι για κονσέρβες *to aneekhteeree ya konserves*

tip (to waiter, etc.) το πουρμπουάρ *to poorbwar*

tipped (cigarettes) με φίλτρο *me feeltro*

tired κουρασμένος *koorasmenos*

tissue το χαρτομάντηλο *to khartomandeelo*

to σε (στο / στη / στο) *se* (*sto* [masculine] /*stee* [feminine] /*sto* [neuter])
to Greece στην Ελλάδα *steen eladha*

toadstool το μανιτάρι *to maneetaree*

toast η φρυγανιά *ee freeghanya*

tobacco ο καπνός *o kapnos*

tobacconist's το καπνοπωλείο *to kapnopoleeo*

today σήμερα *seemera*

toddler το μωρό που μόλις άρχισε να περπατάει *to moro poo molees arkheese na perpataee*

together μαζί *mazee*

toilet η τουαλέτα *ee tooaleta*

toilet paper το χαρτί υγείας *to khartee eeyeeas*

toll τα διόδια *ta dheeodheea*

tomato η ντομάτα *ee domata*
tinned tomatoes οι ντομάτες κονσέρβα *ee domates konserva*

tomato juice ο χυμός ντομάτας *o kheemos domatas*

tomorrow αύριο *avreeo*

tongue η γλώσσα *ee ghl**o**sa*

tonic water το τόνικ *to t**o**neek*

tonight απόψε *ap**o**pse*

too *(also)* επίσης *ep**ee**sees*
(excessively) πολύ *pol**ee***
too big πολύ μεγάλος *pol**ee** megh**a**los*
too much πάρα πολύ *p**a**ra pol**ee***

tooth το δόντι *to dh**o**ndee*

toothache ο πονόδοντος *o pon**o**dhondos*

toothbrush η οδοντόβουρτσα *ee odhont**o**voortsa*

toothpaste η οδοντόκρεμα *ee odhond**o**krema*

toothpick η οδοντογλυφίδα *ee odhontoghleef**ee**dha*

top το πάνω μέρος *to p**a**no m**e**ros*
(of mountain) η κορυφή *ee koreef**ee***

torch ο φακός *o fak**o**s*

torn σχισμένος *skheesm**e**nos*

total το σύνολο *to s**ee**nolo*

tough *(of meat)* σκληρός *skleer**o**s*

tour η περιοδεία *ee pereeodh**ee**a*

tour operator ο τουριστικός πράκτορας *o tooreesteek**o**s pr**a**ktoras*

tourist ο τουρίστας / η τουρίστρια *o toor**ee**stas / ee toor**ee**streea*

tourist information οι πληροφορίες τουρισμού *ee pleerofor**ee**-es tooreesm**oo***

tourist office το τουριστικό γραφείο *to tooreesteek**o** ghraf**ee**o*

tourist ticket το τουριστικό εισιτήριο *to tooreesteek**o** eeseet**ee**reeo*

to tow ρυμουλκώ *reemoolk**o***

towel η πετσέτα *ee pets**e**ta*

tower ο πύργος *o p**ee**rghos*

town η πόλη *ee p**o**lee*

town centre το κέντρο της πόλης *to k**e**ndro tees p**o**lees*

town hall το δημαρχείο *to dheemarkh**ee**o*

town plan ο χάρτης της πόλης *o kh**a**rtees tees p**o**lees*

towrope το σχοινί ρυμούλκησης *to skheen**ee** reem**oo**lkeesees*

toxic τοξικός *tokseek**o**s*

toy το παιγνίδι *to peghn**ee**dhee*

traditional παραδοσιακός *paradhosyak**o**s*

traffic η κυκλοφορία *ee keeklofor**ee**a*

traffic lights τα φανάρια της τροχαίας *ta fan**a**reea tees trokh**e**as*

traffic warden ο τροχονόμος *o trokhon**o**mos*

trailer το τρέιλερ *to tr**e**iler*

train το τρένο *to tr**e**no*

training shoes τα αθλητικά παπούτσια *ta athleeteek**a** pap**oo**tsya*

tram το τραμ *to tram*

to transfer μεταφέρω *metaf**e**ro*

to translate μεταφράζω *metafr**a**zo*

translation η μετάφραση *ee met**a**frasee*

to travel ταξιδεύω *takseedh**e**vo*

travel agent ο ταξιδιωτικός πράκτορας *o takseedhyoteek**o**s pr**a**ktoras*

travel documents τα ταξιδιωτικά έγγραφα *ta takseedheeoteek**a** **e**ghrafa*

travel insurance η ταξιδιωτική ασφάλεια *ee takseedheeoteek**ee** asf**a**leea*

travellers' cheques ταταξιδιωτικά τσεκ *ta takseedhyoteek**a** tsek*

tray ο δίσκος *o dh**ee**skos*

tree το δέντρο *to dh**e**ndro*

trim *n (hair)* το κόψιμο *to k**o**pseemo*

trip η εκδρομή *ee ekdhrom**ee***

trolley bus το τρόλεϋ *to tr**o**ley*

trouble ο μπελάς *o bel**a**s*
to be in trouble έχω μπελάδες ***e**kho bel**a**dhes*

trousers το παντελόνι *to pandel**o**nee*

trout η πέστροφα *ee p**e**strofa*

true αληθινός *aleetheen**o**s*

trunk το μπαούλο *to ba**oo**lo*

trunks το μαγιό *to may**o***

to try προσπαθώ *prospatho*

to try on δοκιμάζω *dhokeemazo*

T-shirt το μπλουζάκι *to bloozakee*

tumble-dryer το στεγνωτήριο ρούχων *to steghnoteereeo rookhon*

tuna ο τόνος *o tonos*

tunnel η σήραγγα *ee seeranga*

turkey η γαλοπούλα *ee ghalopoola*

turn: *it's my turn* είναι η σειρά μου *eene ee seera moo*
it's your turn είναι η σειρά σου *eene ee seera soo*
whose turn is it? ποιανού η σειρά είναι; *peeanoo ee seera eene*

to turn γυρίζω *yeereezo*

to turn around στρέφομαι *strefome*

to turn off *(on a journey)* στρίβω *streevo*
(radio, etc) κλείνω *kleeno*
(engine, light) σβήνω *sveeno*

to turn on *(radio, etc.)* ανοίγω *aneegho*
(engine, light) ανάβω *anavo*

turnip η ρέβα *ee reva*

TV η τηλεόραση *ee teeleorasee*

tweezers το τσιμπίδι *to tseembeedhee*

twice δύο φορές *dheeo fores*

twin ο δίδυμος *o dheedheemos*

twin-bedded το δίκλινο δωμάτιο *to dheekleeno dhomateeo*

to type δακτυλογραφώ *dhakteeloghrafo*

typical τυπικός *teepeekos*

tyre το λάστιχο *to lasteekho*

tyre pressure η πίεση στα λάστιχα *ee peeyesee sta lasteekha*

U

ugly άσχημος *askheemos*

umbrella η ομπρέλα *ee ombrela*

uncle ο θείος *o theeos*

uncomfortable άβολος *avolos*

unconscious αναίσθητος *anestheetos*

under κάτω από *kato apo*

undercooked όχι καλά ψημένος *okhee kala pseemenos*

underground *(railway)* το μετρό *to metro*

underpants *(men's)* το σώβρακο *to sovrako*

underpass η υπόγεια διάβαση *ee eepoy-eea dheeavasee*

to understand καταλαβαίνω *katalaveno*

underwear τα εσώρουχα *ta esorookha*

unemployed άνεργος *anerghos*

unfasten λύνω *leeno*

United Kingdom το Ηνωμένο Βασίλειο *to eenomeno vaseeleeo*

United States οι Ηνωμένες Πολιτείες *ee eenomenes poleeteeyes*

university το πανεπιστήμιο *to panepeesteemeeo*

unleaded petrol η αμόλυβδη βενζίνη *ee amoleevdhee venzeenee*

unlikely απίθανος *apeethanos*

to unlock ξεκλειδώνω *ksekleedhono*

to unpack *(case)* αδειάζω *adheeazo*

unpleasant δυσάρεστος *dheesarestos*

to unplug βγάζω από την πρίζα *vghazo apo teen preeza*

until μέχρι *mekhree*

unusual ασυνήθης *aseeneethees*

up *(out of bed)* ξύπνιος *kseepneeos*
to go up ανεβαίνω *aneveno*

upstairs πάνω *pano*

urgently επειγόντως *epeeghondos*

urine τα ούρα *ta oora*

urn ο αμφορέας *o amforeas*

us εμάς / μάς / μας / εμείς *emas / mas / mas / emees*
he's looking at us κοιτάζει προς εμάς *keetazee pros emas*
he told us to go μάς είπε να φύγουμε *mas eepe na feeghoome*
listen to us άκουσέ μας *akoose mas*
it's us! εμείς είμαστε *emees eemaste*

to use χρησιμοποιώ *khreeseemopyo*

useful χρήσιμος *khreeseemos*

usual συνηθισμένος *seeneetheesmenos*

usually συνήθως *seeneethos*

V

vacancy *(room)* το διαθέσιμο δωμάτιο *to dheeatheseemo dhomateeo*

vacant κενός *kenos*

vacation οι διακοπές *ee dheeakopes*

vacuum cleaner η ηλεκτρική σκούπα *ee eelektreekee skoopa*

valid έγκυρος *engeeros*

valley η κοιλάδα *ee keeladha*

valuable πολύτιμος *poleeteemos*

valuables τα πολύτιμα αντικείμενα *ta poleeteema andeekeemena*

value η αξία *ee akseea*

van το φορτηγάκι *to forteeghakee*

vase το βάζο *to vazo*

VAT ο ΦΠΑ *o fee pee a*

veal το μοσχάρι *to moskharee*

vegetables τα λαχανικά *ta lakhaneeka*

vegetarian ο χορτοφάγος *o khortofaghos*
I'm vegetarian είμαι χορτοφάγος *eeme khortofaghos*

vein η φλέβα *ee fleva*

velvet το βελούδο *to veloodho*

ventilator ο εξαεριστήρας *o eksaereesteeras*

very πολύ *polee*

vest η φανέλα *ee fanela*

via μέσω *meso*

video το βίντεο *to veedeo*

video camera η βιντεοκάμερα *ee veedeokamera*

video recorder η συσκευή βίντεο *ee seeskevee veedeo*

view η θέα *ee thea*

villa η βίλλα *ee veela*

village το χωριό *to khoryo*

vine leaves τα κληματόφυλλα *ta kleematofeela*

vinegar το ξύδι *to kseedhee*

visa η βίζα *ee veesa*

to visit επισκέπτομαι *epeeskeptome*

visit η επίσκεψη *ee epeeskepsee*

vitamin η βιταμίνη *ee veetameenee*

vodka η βότκα *ee votka*

voice η φωνή *ee fonee*

volleyball το βόλεϊμπολ *to volleyball*

voltage η τάση *ee tasee*

W

wage ο μισθός *o meesthos*

waist η μέση *ee mesee*

waistcoat το γιλέκο *to gheeleko*

to wait for περιμένω *pereemeno*

waiter το γκαρσόνι *to garsonee*

waiting room η αίθουσα αναμονής *ee ethoosa anamonees*

waitress η σερβιτόρα *ee serveetora*

Wales η Ουαλία *ee ooaleea*

walk ο περίπατος *o pereepatos*

to walk περπατώ *perpato*

walking stick το μπαστούνι *to bastoonee*

Walkman® το γουοκμαν *to wokman*

wall ο τοίχος *o teekhos*

wallet το πορτοφόλι *to portofolee*

walnut το καρύδι *to kareedhee*

to want θέλω *thelo*
I want... θέλω *thelo*
we want... θέλουμε *theloome*

war ο πόλεμος *o polemos*

ward ο θάλαμος *o thalamos*

wardrobe η γκαρνταρόμπα *ee gardaroba*

warm ζεστός *zestos*

to warm up ζεστένω *zesteno*

warning triangle το τρίγωνο αυτοκινήτου *to treeghono aftokeeneetoo*

to wash *(clothes)* **πλένω** *pleno*
(oneself) **πλένομαι** *plenome*

wash and blow-dry **λούσιμο και στέγνωμα** *looseemo ke steghnoma*

washbasin **η νιπτήρας** *ee neepteeras*

washing machine **το πλυντήριο** *to pleendeereeo*

washing powder **το απορρυπαντικό** *to aporeepandeeko*

washing-up liquid **το υγρό για τα πιάτα** *to eeghro ya ta pyata*

wasp **η σφήκα** *ee sfeeka*

wasp sting **το τσίμπημα σφήκας** *to tseebeema sfeekas*

waste bin **το καλάθι των αχρήστων** *to kalathee ton akhreeston*

watch *n* **το ρολόι** *to roloee*

to watch *(TV)* **βλέπω** *vlepo*
(someone's luggage) **προσέχω** *pros-ekho*

watchstrap **το λουρί του ρολογιού** *to looree too rologhyoo*

water **το νερό** *to nero*
bottled water **το εμφιαλωμένο νερό** *to emfeealomeno nero*
fresh water **το γλυκό νερό** *to ghleeko nero*
mineral water **το μεταλικό νερό** *to metaleeko nero*
salt water **το αλμυρό νερό** *to almeero nero*

waterfall **ο καταρράκτης** *o kataraktees*

water heater **ο θερμοσίφωνας** *o ther-moseefonas*

water-skiing **το θαλάσσιο σκι** *to tha-laseeo skee*

watersports **τα θαλάσσιο σπορ** *ta tha-laseea spor*

watermelon **το καρπούζι** *to karpoozee*

waterproof **αδιάβροχος** *adheeavrokhos*

wave *(on sea)* **το κύμα** *to keema*

wax **το κερί** *to keree*

way *(method)* **ο τρόπος** *o tropos*
this way **από 'δω** *apodho*
that way **από 'κει** *apokee*
way in *(entrance)* **η είσοδος** *ee eesod-hos*
way out *(exit)* **η έξοδος** *ee eksodhos*
which way? **από ποιό δρόμο;** *apo peeo dhromo*

we **εμείς** *emees*

weak **αδύνατος** *adheenatos*

to wear **φορώ** *foro*

weather **ο καιρός** *o keros*

weather forecast **το δελτίο καιρού** *to dhelteeo keroo*

website **το website** *to website*

wedding **ο γάμος** *o ghamos*

wedding ring **η βέρα** *ee vera*

week **η εβδομάδα** *ee evdhomadha*
during the week **κατά τη διάρκεια της εβδομάδας** *kata tee dheearkeea tees evdhomadhas*

weekday **η καθημερινή** *ee katheemereenee*

weekend **το σαββατοκύριακο** *to savatokeereeako*

weekly *(rate, etc.)* **εβδομαδιαίος** *evd-homadhyeos*
weekly ticket **το εβδομαδιαίο εισιτήριο** *to evdhomadhee-eo eeseeteereeo*

weight **το βάρος** *to varos*

welcome **καλώς ήλθατε** *kalos eelthate*

well *(healthy)* **υγιής** *eeyee-ees*

well *(for water)* **το πηγάδι** *to peeghad-hee*

well done *(steak)* **καλοψημένος** *kalopseemenos*

Welsh *adj* **Ουαλικός** *ooaleekos*

Welshman **ο Ουαλός** *o ooalos*

Welshwoman **η Ουαλή** *ee ooalee*

west **η δύση** *ee dheesee*

wet *(damp)* **βρεγμένος** *vreghmenos*
(weather) **βροχερός** *vrokheros*

wetsuit **η στολή για υποβρύχιο ψάρεμα** *ee stolee ya eepovreekheeo psarema*

what **τι** *tee*
what is it? **τι είναι;** *tee eene*

wheat **το σιτάρι** *to seetaree*

wheel **ο τροχός** *o trokh**o**s*

wheelchair **η αναπηρική καρέκλα** *ee anapeereek**ee** kar**e**kla*

when? **πότε;** *p**o**te*

where? **πού;** *poo*

which? **ποιος;** *pyos*
which is it? **ποιο είναι;** *pyo **ee**ne*

while: *in a while* **σε λίγο** *se l**ee**gho*

whipped cream **η σαντιγύ** *ee sandeey**ee***

whisky **το ουίσκυ** *to wh**i**sky*

white **άσπρος** ***a**spros*

who **ποιος** *pyos*

whole **όλος** ***o**los*

wholemeal bread **ψωμί ολικήςαλέσεως** *psom**ee** oleek**ee**s al**e**seos*

whose: *whose is it?* **ποιου είναι;** *pyoo **ee**ne*

why? **γιατί;** *yat**ee***

wide **πλατύς** *plat**ee**s*

wife **η σύζυγος** *ee s**ee**zeeghos*
this is my wife **από 'δω η συζυγός μου** *ap**o** dho ee seezeegh**o**s moo*

window **το παράθυρο** *to par**a**theero*

windmill **ο ανεμόμυλος** *o anem**o**meelo*

windscreen **το παρμπρίζ** *to parbr**ee**z*

windsurfing **το γουιντσέρφινγκ** *to winds**u**rfing*

windy: *it's windy* **έχει αέρα** ***e**khee a**e**ra*

wine **το κρασί** *to kras**ee***

wine list **ο κατάλογος των κρασιών** *o kat**a**loghos ton krasy**o**n*

wine shop **η κάβα** *ee k**a**va*

wing **το φτερό** *to ftero*

winter **ο χειμώνας** *o kheem**o**nas*

wire **το καλώδιο** *to kal**o**dheeo*

with **με** *me*

without **χωρίς** *khor**ee**s*

witness **ο μάρτυρας** *o m**a**rteeras*

woman **η γυναίκα** *ee yeen**e**ka*

wonderful **υπέροχος** *eep**e**rokhos*

wood **το ξύλο** *to ks**ee**lo*

wool **το μαλλί** *to mal**ee***

word **η λέξη** *ee l**e**ksee*

to work **δουλεύω** *dhool**e**vo,* **λειτουργεί** *leetoory**ee***
it doesn't work **δε δουλεύει** *dhe dhool**e**vee*

work permit **η άδεια εργασίας** *ee **a**dheea erghas**ee**as*

work **ο εργο** *o **e**rgho*

worried **ανήσυχος** *an**ee**seekhos*

worse **χειρότερος** *kheer**o**teros*

worth: *20 euros worth of petrol* **20 ευρώ βενζίνη** ***ee**kosee evr**o** venz**ee**nee*
it's worth 20 euros **αξίζει 20 ευρώ** *aks**ee**zee **ee**kosee evr**o***

to wrap (up) **τυλίγω** *teel**ee**gho*

wrapping paper **το χαρτί περιτυλίγματος** *to khart**ee** pereeteel**ee**ghmatos*

to write **γράφω** *ghr**a**fo*

writing paper **το χαρτί αλληλογραφίας** *to khart**ee** aleeloghraf**ee**as*

wrong **λάθος** *l**a**thos*
you're wrong **κάνετε λάθος** *k**a**nete l**a**thos*

X

to x-ray **ακτινογραφώ** *akteenoghraf**o***

Y

yacht **το γιοτ** *to yacht*

year **ο χρόνος** *o khr**o**nos*

yearly **ετήσιος** *et**ee**seeos*

yellow **κίτρινος** *k**ee**treenos*

yes **ναι** *ne*

yesterday **χτες** *khtes*

yet **ακόμα** *ak**o**ma*
not yet **όχι ακόμα** ***o**khee ak**o**ma*

yoghurt **το γιαούρτι** *to ya**oo**rtee*

you *(singular/plural)* **εσύ / εσείς** *es**ee** / es**ee**s*

young **νέος** *n**e**os*

your **(δικός) σου / σας** *(dh**ee**kos) soo / sas*

your passport το διαβατηριό σου *to dheeavateereeo soo*
your passports τα δηβατηριά σας *ta dheeavateereea sas*
your room το δωματιό σου *to dhomateeo soo*
your rooms τα δωματιά σας *ta dhomateea sas*

youth hostel ο ξενώνας νεότητος *o ksenonas neoteetos*

Z

zebra crossing η διάβαση πεζών *ee dheeavasee pezon*

zero το μηδέν *to meedhen*

zip το φερμουάρ *to fermooar*

zone η ζώνη *ee zonee*

zoo ο ζωολογικός κήπος *o zooloyeekos keepos*

zoom lens το ζουμ *to zoom*

αβγό (το) egg
αβγά ημέρας newly-laid eggs

άγαλμα (το) statue

αγάπη (η) love

αγαπώ to love

αγγείο (το) vessel ; urn

αγγειοπλαστική (η) pottery *(craft)*

αγγελία (η) announcement

άγγελος (ο) angel

Αγγλία (η) England

αγγλικός/ή/ό English *(thing)*

Άγγλος/Αγγλίδα (ο/η) Englishman/-woman

αγγούρι (το) cucumber

άγιος/α/ο holy ; saint
Άγιον Όρος (το) Mount Athos

αγκινάρα (η) artichoke

άγκυρα (η) anchor

αγορά (η) agora ; market

αγοράζω to buy

αγοραστής (ο) buyer

αγόρι (το) young boy

άδεια (η) permit ; licence
άδεια οδηγήσεως driving licence

άδειος/α/ο empty

αδελφή (η) sister

αδελφός (ο) brother

αδιάβροχο (το) raincoat

αδιέξοδο (το) cul-de-sac ; no through road

αδίκημα (το) offence

αέρας (ο) wind

αερογραμμές (οι) airways
Βρετανικές Αερογραμμές British Airways
Κυπριακές Αερογραμμές Cyprus Airways

αεροδρόμιο (το) airport

αερολιμένας/αερολιμήν (ο) airport

αεροπλάνο (το) aeroplane

αεροπορία (η) air force
Ολυμπιακή Αεροπορία Olympic Airways

αεροπορικό εισιτήριο (το) air ticket

αεροπορικώς by air

αζήτητος/η/ο unclaimed

Αθήνα (η) Athens

αθλητικό κέντρο (το) sports centre

αθλητισμός (ο) sports

Αιγαίο (το) the Aegean Sea

αίθουσα (η) room
αίθουσα αναμονής waiting room
αίθουσα αναχωρήσεων departure lounge

αιμορραγώ to bleed

αίμα (το) to bleed

αίτημα (το) demand

αίτηση (η) application

ακάθαρτος/η/ο dirty

ακουστικά (τα) earphones
ακουστικά βαρυκοΐας hearing aids

ακουστικό (το) receiver *(telephone)*

ακούω to hear

άκρη (η) edge

Ακρόπολη/ις (η) the Acropolis

ακτή (η) beach ; shore

ακτινογραφία (η) X-ray

ακυρώνω to cancel

αλάτι (το) salt

αλεύρι (το) flour

αλιεία (η) fishing
είδη αλιείας fishing tackle

αλλαγή (η) change

αλλάζω to change
δεν αλλάζονται goods will not be exchanged

αλληλογραφία (η) correspondence

αλληλογραφώ to correspond

αλλοδαπός/ή foreign national
αστυνομία αλλοδαπών immigration police

αλμυρός/ή/ό salty

αλτ! stop!
αλυσίδα (η) chain
αμάξωμα (το) body *(of car)*
αμερικάνικος/η/ο American *(thing)*
Αμερικανός/Αμερικανίδα American *(man/woman)*
Αμερική (η) America
αμέσως at once ; immediately
αμήν amen
άμμος (η) sand
αμμουδιά (η) sandy beach
αμοιβή (η) reward ; fare ; salary ; payment
αμπέλι (το) vine
αμυγδαλίτιδα (η) tonsilitis
αμύγδαλο (το) almond
αμφιθέατρο (το) amphitheatre
αμφορέας (ο) jar ; amphor
αν if
αναβολή (η) delay
ανάβω to switch on
αναγγελία (η) announcement
αναζήτηση (η) search
ανάκριση (η) interrogation
ανάκτορα (τα) palace
αναμονή (η) waiting
αίθουσα αναμονής waiting room
ανανάς (ο) pineapple
ανανεώνω to renew
ανάπηρος/η/ο handicapped ; disabled
αναπληρώνω to replace
αναπτήρας (ο) cigarette lighter
ανασκαφή (η) excavation
ανατολή (η) east ; sunrise
ανατολικός/ή/ό eastern
ανατχώρηση (η) departure
ΑΝΑΧΩΡΗΣΕΙΣ DEPARTURES
αναψυκτήριο (το) refreshment
αναψυκτικό (το) soft drink
αναψυχή (η) recreation ; pleasure

άνδρας (ο) man
ΑΝΔΡΕΣ GENTS
ανδρική μόδα (η) men's fashions
ανελκυστήρας (ο) lift ; elevator
ανεμιστήρας (ο) fan
ανεμοβλογιά (η) chicken pox
άνθη (τα) flowers
ανθοπωλείο (το) florist's
άνθρωπος (ο) man
ανοίγω to open
ΑΝΟΙΚΤΟ OPEN
άνοιξη (η) spring
ανταλλαγή (η) exchange
ανταλλακτικά (τα) spare parts
ανταπόκριση (η) connection
αντιβιοτικά (τα) antibiotics
αντίγραφο (το) copy ; reproduction
αντίκες (οι) antiques
αντικλεπτικά (τα) anti-theft devices
αντίο goodbye
αντιπηκτικό (το) antifreeze
αντιπρόσωπος (ο) representative
αντλία (η) pump
αντλία βενζίνης petrol pump
αντρόγυνο (το) couple
ανώμαλος/η/ο uneven ; rough
αξεσουάρ (τα) accessories
αξεσουάρ αυτοκινήτου car accessories
αξία (η) value
αξία διαδρομής fare
αξιοθέατα (τα) the sights
απαγορεύω to forbid ; no...
απαγορεύεται η αναμονή no waiting
απαγορεύεται η διάβαση keep off
απαγορεύεται η είσοδος no entry
απαγορεύεται το κάπνισμα no

smoking
απαγορεύεται η στάθμευση no parking
απαγορεύονται τα σκυλιά no dogs
απαγορεύεται η φωτογράφηση no photography
απαγορεύεται τοκολύμπι no swimming
απαγορεύεται η κατασκήνωση no camping

απαίτηση (η) claim

απεργία (η) strike

απογείωση (η) takeoff

απόγευμα (το) afternoon

απόδειξη (η) receipt

αποθήκη (η) warehouse

αποκλειστικός/ή/ό exclusive

απόκριες (οι) carnival

αποσκευές (οι) luggage
αναζήτηση αποσκευών left-luggage *(office)*

απόχη (η) fishing/butterfly net

απόψε tonight

Απρίλιος (ο) April

αργότερα later

αρέσω to please
μου αρέσει I like
δεν μου αρέσει I don't like

αριθμός (ο) number
αριθμός διαβατηρίου passport number
αριθμός πτήσεως flight number
αριθμός τηλεφώνου telephone number

αριστερά left *(side)*

αρνί (το) lamb

αρρώστια (η) illness

άρρωστος/η/ο ill
άρρωστος/η (ο/η) patient

αρτοποιία (η) bakery

αρχαιολογικός χώρος (ο) archaeological site

αρχαίος/α/ο ancient

αρχή (η) start ; authority

αρχίζω to begin ; to start

άρωμα (το) perfume

ασανσέρ (το) lift ; elevator

ασθένεια (η) illness

ασθενής (ο/η) patient

άσθμα (το) asthma

άσκοπος/η/ο improper
άσκοπη χρήση improper use

ασπιρίνη (η) aspirin

άσπρος/η/ο white

αστακός (ο) lobster

αστικός νομισματοδέκτης (ο) coin-operated phone for local calls

αστυνομία (η) police
αστυνομία αλλοδαπών immigration police
Ελληνική αστυνομία Greek police

αστυνομική διάταξη (η) police notice

αστυνομική τμήμα (η) police station

αστυνομικός σταθμός (ο) police station

αστυνόμος (ο) policeman

αστυφύλακας (ο) town policeman

ασφάλεια (η) insurance ; fuse
ασφάλεια έναντι κλοπής theft insurance
ασφάλεια έναντι τρίτων third-party insurance
ασφάλεια ζωής life insurance

ασφάλιση (η) insurance
πλήρης ασφάλιση comprehensive insurance
ιατρική ασφάλιση medical insurance

ατμοπλοϊκό εισιτήριο (το) boat ticket

ατομικός/ή/ό personal

άτομο (το) person
άτομο τρίτης ηλικίας pensioner

ατύχημα (το) accident

αυγό (το) egg

ΑΥΓΟΥΣΤΟΣ AUGUST

αυτοκίνητο (το) car
ενοικιάσεις αυτοκινήτων car hire
συνεργείο αυτοκινήτων car repairs

αυτοκινητόδρομος (ο) motorway

αυτόματος/η/ο automatic

άφιξη (η) arrival

ΑΦΙΞΕΙΣ ARRIVALS

αφορολόγητα (τα) duty-free goods

Αφροδίτη Aphrodite ; Venus

αχθοφόρος (ο) porter

αχλάδι (το) pear

άχρηστα (τα) waste

αψίδα (η) arch

β Β

βαγιο (το) palm

η Κυριακή των Βαΐων Palm Sunday

βαγόνι (το) carriage *(train)*

βαλβίδα (η) valve

βαλίτσα (η) suitcase

βαμβακερός/ή/ό *(made of)* cotton

βαμβάκι (το) cotton wool *(pharmacy)*

βαρέλι (το) barrel
μπίρα από βαρέλι draught beer
βαρελίσιο κρασί (το) house wine

βάρκα (η) boat

βάρος (το) weight

βάση (η) base

βαφή (η) paint ; dye

βάφω to paint

βγάζω to take off

βγαίνω to go out

βελόνα (η) needle

βενζίνη (η) petrol ; gasoline

βήχας (ο) cough

βιβλίο (το) book

βιβλιοθήκη (η) bookcase ; library
Δημοτική Βιβλιοθήκη Public Library
Κεντρική Βιβλιοθήκη Central Library

βιβλιοπωλείο (το) bookshop

Βίβλος (η) the Bible

βιταμίνη (η) vitamin

βιτρίνα (η) shop window

βοδινό κρέας beef

βοήθεια (η) help
οδική βοήθεια breakdown service
πρώτες βοήθειες casualty *(hospital)*

βόμβα (η) bomb

βομβητής (ο) buzzer ; bleeper

βόρειος/α/ο northern

βορράς (ο) north

βοσκός (ο) shepherd

βότανα (τα) herbs

βουλή (η) parliament

βουνό (το) mountain

βούρτσα (η) brush

βουτήματα (τα) biscuits and cookies for dipping in hot beverages

βούτυρο (το) butter

βράδυ (το) evening

βράζω to cook

βραστός/ή/ό cooked

Βρετανία (η) Britain

βρετανικός/ή/ό British *(thing)*

Βρετανός/Βρετανίδα (ο/η) British *(man/woman)*

βροχή (η) rain

γ Γ

γάιδαρος (ο) donkey

γάλα (το) milk

γαλάζιος/α/ο blue ; light blue

γαλακτοπωλείο (το) dairy shop

Γαλλία (η) France

γαλλικός/ή/ό French *(thing)*

Γάλλος/Γαλλίδα (ο/η) French *(man/woman)*

γαλοπούλα (η) turkey

γάμος (ο) wedding ; marriage

γαμήλιαδεξίωση wedding reception

γαρίδα (η) shrimp ; prawn

γειά σας hello ; goodbye *(formal)*

γειά σου hello ; goodbye *(informal)*

γεμάτος/η/ο full

γεμιστά (τα) stuffed vegetables

γενέθλια (τα) birthday

γενικός/ή/ό general
Γενικό Νοσοκομείο General Hospital

γέννηση (η) birth

Γερμανία (η) Germany

γερμανικός/ή/ό German *(thing)*

Γερμανός/Γερμανίδα (ο/η) German *(man/woman)*

γεμιστός/ή/ό stuffed

γεύμα (το) meal

γέφυρα (η) bridge

για for

γιαγιά (η) grandmother

γιαούρτι (το) yoghurt

γιασεμί (το) jasmine

γιατί; why?

γιατρός (ο/η) doctor

γίνομαι to become
γίνονται δεκτές πιστωτικές κάρτες we accept credit cards

γιορτή (η) feast ; celebration ; name day

γιος (ο) son

γιοτ (το) yacht

γκάζι (το) accelerator *(car)* **; gas**

γκαλερί art gallery ; art sales

γκαράζ (το) garage

γκαρσόν (το)/γκαρσόνι (το) waiter

γλυκός/ιά/ό sweet
γλυκό (το)/γλυκά (τα) cakes and pastries ; desserts
γλυκό ταψιού traditional pastries with syrup
γλυκό του κουταλιού fruit preserve

γλύπτης/γλύπτρια (ο/η) sculptor

γλυπτική (η) sculpture

γλώσσα (η) tongue ; language ; sole *(fish)*

γονείς (οι) parents

γουιντσέρφινγκ (το) windsurfing

γράμμα (το) letter
γράμμα κατεπείγον express letter
γράμμα συστημένο registered letter

γραμμάριο (το) gramme

γραμματοκιβώτιο (το) letter box

γραμματόσημο (το) stamp

γραφείο (το) office ; desk
Γραφείο Τουρισμού Tourist Office

γρήγορα quickly

γρίππη (η) influenza

γυαλί (το) glass
γυαλιά (τα) glasses
γυαλιά ηλίου sunglasses

γυαλικός/ή/ό made of glass

γυναίκα (η) woman

ΓΥΝΑΙΚΩΝ LADIES

γύρω round ; about

γωνία (η) corner

δ Δ

δακτυλίδι (το) ring *(for finger)*

δακτύλιος (ο) ring ; circle

δαμάσκηνο (το) plum

δαντέλα (η) lace

δασκάλα (η) teacher *(female)*

δάσκαλος (ο) teacher *(male)*

δασμός (ο) duty ; tax

δάσος (το) forest

δείπνο (το) dinner

ΔΕΚΕΜΒΡΙΟΣ DECEMBER

δελτίο (το) card ; coupon
δελτίο αφίξεως arrival card

δελφίνι (το) dolphin
ιπτάμενο δελφίνι hydrofoil

Δελφοί (οι) Delphi

δέμα (το) parcel

Δεμέστιχα dry wine *(white or red)*

δεν not
δεν δίνει ρέστα no change given

ΔΕ ΛΕΙΤΟΥΡΓΕΙ OUT OF ORDER

δεξιά right *(side)*

δέρμα (το) skin ; leather

δεσποινίς/δεσποινίδα (η) Miss

ΔΕΥΤΕΡΑ MONDAY

δεύτερος/η/ο second

δήλωση (η) announcement
δήλωση συναλλάγματος currency declaration
είδη προς δήλωση goods to declare
ουδέν προς δήλωση nothing to declare

δημαρχείο (το) town hall

δημόσιος/α/ο public
δημόσια έργα road works
δημόσιος κήπος public gardens

δημοτικός/ή/ό public
Δημοτική Αγορά public market
Δημοτική Βιβλιοθήκη Public Library

διάβαση (η) crossing
διάβαση πεζών pedestrian crossing
υπόγεια διάβαση πεζών pedestrian subway

διαβατήριο (το) passport
αριθμός διαβατηρίου passport number
έλεγχος διαβατηρίων passport control

διαβήτης (ο) diabetes

διαδρομή (η) route

δίαιτα (η) diet

διακεκριμένος/η/ο distinguished
διακεκριμένη θέση business class

διακοπές (οι) holidays

διάλειμμα (το) interval ; break

διάλυση (η) closing down *(sale)* **; dilution**

διαμέρισμα (το) flat ; apartment

διανυχτερεύει open all-night

διάρκεια (η) duration
κατά τη διάρκεια της ημέρας during the day

διασκέδαση (η) entertainment
κέντρο διασκεδάσεως nightclub

διατηρώ to keep ; to preserve
διατηρείτε την πόλη καθαρή keep the town clean

διατροφή (η) diet

διεθνής/ής/ές international

διερμηνέας (ο/η) interpreter

διεύθυνση (η) address

διευθυντής (ο) manager

δικαστήριο (το) court

δικηγόρος (ο/η) lawyer

διπλός/ή/ό double
διπλό δωμάτιο double room
διπλό κρεββάτι double bed

δισκοθήκη (η) disco *(Cyprus)* **; music collection**

δίσκος (ο) record

δίχτυ (το) net

διψώ to be thirsty

διώρυγα canal

δολάριο (το) dollar

δόντι (το) tooth

δράμα (το) drama ; play

δραχμή (η) drachma

δρομολόγιο (το) timetable ; route
δρομολόγια εξωτερικού international routes

δρομολόγια εσωτερικού **domestic routes**

δρόμος (ο) **street ; way**

δύση (η) **west ; sunset**

δυσκοιλιότητα (η) **constipation**

δυστύχημα (το) **accident ; mishap**

δυτικός/ή/ό **western**

Δωδεκάνησα (τα) **the Dodecanese**

δωμάτιο (το) **room**

δωρεάν **free of charge**

δώρο (το) **present ; gift**

ε Ε

εβδομάδα (η) **week**

εγγραφή (η) **registration**

εγγύηση (η) **guarantee**

έγχρωμος/η/ο **coloured**
 έγχρωμες φωτογραφίες **colour photographs**

εδώ **here**

ΕΕ **EU**

εθνικός/ή/ό **national**
 Εθνικό Θέατρο **National Theatre**
 εθνικός οδός **motorway**
 Εθνικός Κήπος **National Garden** *(in Athens)*
 εθνικός ύμνος **national anthem**

έθνος (το) **nation**

ειδικός/ή/ό **special ; specialist**

είδος (το) **kind ; sort**
 είδη **goods**
 είδη προς δήλωση **goods to declare**
 είδη εξοχής **camping equipment**
 είδη καπνιστού **tobacconist**
 είδη κήπου **garden centre**

εισιτήριο (το) **ticket**
 απλό εισιτήριο **single ticket**
 εισιτήριο με επιστροφή **return ticket**
 ατμοπλοϊκό εισιτήριο **boat ticket**
 σιδηροδρομικό εισιτήριο **rail ticket**
 φοιτητικό εισιτήριο **student ticket**

ΕΙΣΟΔΟΣ ENTRANCE, ADMISSION

εισπράκτορας (ο) **conductor** *(on bus)*
 χωρίς εισπράκτορα **pay as you enter ; prepaid**

εκδόσεις εισιτηρίων **tickets**

εκδοτήρια (τα) **ticket machines**

εκεί **there**

έκθεση (η) **exhibition**

εκθεσιακό κέντρο (το) **exhibition centre**

εκκλησία (η) **church ; chapel**

έκπτωση (η) **discount**

ΕΚΠΤΩΣΕΙΣ SALE, DISCOUNT

εκτελούνται έργα (τα) **road works**

εκτός **except ; unless**
 εκτός λειτουργίας **out of order**

έλα! **come on!**

ελαιόλαδο (το) **olive oil**

ελαστικό (το) **tyre**
 σέρβις ελαστικών **tyre service**

ελαττώνω **to reduce ; to decrease**
 ελαττώσατε ταχύτητα **reduce speed**

έλεγχος (ο) **control**
 έλεγχος διαβατηρίων **passport control**
 έλεγχος εισιτηρίων **check-in**
 έλεγχος ελαστικών **tyre check**
 αγορανομικός έλεγχος **approved prices**

ΕΛΕΥΘΕΡΟ FREE, VACANT

ελιά (η) **olive ; olive tree**

έλκος (το) **ulcer**

Ελλάδα/Ελλάς (η) **Greece/Hellas**

Έλληνας/Ελληνίδα (ο/η) **Greek** *(man/woman)*

ελληνικά (τα) **Greek** *(language)*

ελληνικός/ή/ό **Greek** *(thing)*
 Ελληνικά Ταχυδρομεία **Greek Post Office (ELTA)**

Ελληνική Δημοκρατία Republic of Greece
Ελληνικής κατασκευής Made in Greece
το Ελληνικό Athens Airport
Ελληνικός Οργανισμός Τουρισμού Greek Tourist Organisation (EOT)
Ελληνικό προϊόν product of Greece

ΕΛΞΑΤΕ PULL

εμπρός forward ; in front

εμφανίζω to develop *(film)*

εμφάνιση (η) film development

εναντίον against

έναρξη (η) opening ; beginning

ένας/μία/ένα one

ένδυμα (το) article of clothing
έτοιμα ενδύματα ready-to-wear clothing

ένεση (η) injection

ενήλικος (ο) adult

εννέα/εννιά nine

ενοικιάζω to rent ; to hire
ενοικιάζεται to let

ενοικιάσεις for hire

ενοίκιο (το) rent

ενορία (η) parish

εντάξει all right ; OK

εντομοκτόνο (το) insecticide

έντυπο (το) form *(to fill in)*

έξι six

ΕΞΟΔΟΣ EXIT

εξοχή (η) countryside

εξυπηρέτηση (η) service

εξυπηρετώ to serve

έξω out ; outside

εξωλέμβιες (οι) outboard motor-boats

εξώστης (ο) circle ; balcony *(theatre)*

εξωτερικός/ή/ό external
το εξωτερικό abroad
εξωτερικού letters abroad *(on post-box)*
πτήσεις εξωτερικού international flights

ΕΟΚ EEC (EC)

ΕΟΤ Greek/Hellenic Tourist Organization

επάγγελμα (το) occupation ; profession

επείγον/επείγουσα urgent ; express
επείγοντα περιστατικά casualty department

επιβάτης/τρια (ο/η) passenger
διερχόμενοι επιβάτες passengers in transit

επιβατικά (τα) private cars

επιβεβαιώνω to confirm

επιβίβαση (η) boarding
κάρτα επιβιβάσεως boarding card

επιδόρπιο (το) dessert

επικίνδυνος/η/ο dangerous

επίσης also

επισκεπτήριο (το) visiting hours

επισκέπτης (ο) visitor

επισκευή (η) repair
επισκευές repairs

επίσκεψη (η) visit
ώρες επισκέψεων visiting hours

επιστολή (η) letter
επιστολή επείγουσα urgent or express letter
επιστολή συστημένη registered letter

επιστροφή (η) return ; return ticket
επιστροφή νομισμάτων returned coins
επιστροφές returned goods

επιταγή (η) cheque ; invoice
ταχυδρομική επιταγή postal order

επόμενος/η/ο next

εποχή (η) season

επτά/εφτά seven

Επτάνησα (τα) Ionian Islands

επώνυμο (το) surname ; last name

έργα (τα) works

έργα χειρός (τα) handcrafts

εργαλείο (το) tool

έργοκινηματογραφικό film

εργοστάσιο (το) factory

έργοτέχνης (το) artwork

ερώτηση (η) question

εστιατόριο (το) restaurant

εσώρουχα (τα) underwear ; lingerie

εσωτερικός/ή/ό internal
  εσωτερικού inland *(on post boxes)* ; domestic
  πτήσεις εσωτερικού domestic flights

εταιρ(ε)ία (η) company ; firm

έτος (το) year

έτσι so ; like this

ευθεία (η) straight line
  κατ' ευθείαν straight on

ευκαιρία (η) opportunity ; bargain

ευκολία (η) ease ; convenience
  ευκολίες πληρωμής credit terms

ευρώ (το) euro

ευρωπαϊκός/ή/ό European

Ευρωπαϊκή Ένωση (η) European Union

Ευρώπη (η) Europe

ευχαριστώ thank you

εφημερίδα (η) newspaper

ζ Ζ

ζάλη (η) dizziness

ζαμπόν (το) ham

ζάχαρη (η) sugar

ζαχαροπλαστείο (το) patisserie

ζέστη (η) heat
  κάνει ζέστη it's hot

ζημιά (η) damage
  πάσα ζημιά τιμωρείται anyone causing damage will be prosecuted

ζητώ to ask ; to seek

ζυγαριά (η) scales *(for weighing)*

ζυμαρικά (τα) pasta products

ζωγραφική (η) painting *(art)*

ζώνη (η) belt
  ζώνη ασφαλείας safety belt ; seat belt

ζώο (το) animal

ζωολογικός κήπος (ο) zoo

η Η

η the *(with feminine nouns)*

ή or

ηλεκτρικός/ή/ό electrical

ηλεκτρισμός (ο) electricity

ηλεκτρονικός/ή/ό electronic

ηλιακός/ή/ό solar

ηλίαση (η) sunstroke

ηλικία (η) age

ηλιοθεραπεία (η) sunbathing

ήλιος (ο) sun

Ήλιος a dry white wine from Rhodes

ημέρα (η) day

ημερήσιος/α/ο daily

ΗΜΕΡΟΜΗΝΙΑ DATE

ημερομηνία αναχωρήσεως date of departure
  ημερομηνία αφίξεως date of arrival
  ημερομηνία γεννήσεως date of birth
  ημερομηνία λήξεως expiry date

ημιδιατροφή (η) half board

Ηνωμένο Βασίλειο (το) United Kingdom

ΗΠΑ USA

Ηνωμένες Πολιτείες της Αμερικής United States of America

ησυχία (η) calmness ; quiet

ήσυχος/η/ο calm ; quiet

θ Θ

θάλασσα (η) sea

θαλάσσιος/α/ο of the sea
θαλάσσιο αλεξίπτωτο paragliding
θαλάσσιο σκι water-skiing

θέατρο (το) theatre

θέλω to want ; to need

Θεός (ο) God

θεός/θεά (ο/η) god ; goddess

Θεοτόκος (η) Virgin Mary

θεραπεία (η) treatment

θερινός/ή/ό summer
θερινές διακοπές summer holidays
θερινό θέρετρο summer resort

θέρμανση (η) heating

θερμίδα (η) calorie

θερμοστάτης (ο) thermostat

θέση (η) place ; seat
διακεκριμένη θέση business class
κράτηση θέσης seat reservation
οικονομική θέση economy class
πρώτη θέση first class

Θεσσαλονίκη (η) Salonica/Thessaloniki

θύελλα (η) storm

θύρα (η) gate *(airport)*

θυρίδα (η) ticket window

θυρωρείο (το) porter's lodge

ι Ι

ΙΑΗΟΥΑΡΙΟΣ JANUARY

ιατρική περίθαλψη (η) medical treatment

ιατρός (ο/η) doctor

ιδιοκτήτης/τρια (ο/η) owner

ΙΔΙΩΤΙΚΟΣ ΧΩΡΟΣ PRIVATE

ιθαγένεια (η) nationality

ιλαρά (η) measles

Ιόνιο Πέλαγος (το) Ionian sea

Ιόνιοι Νήσοι (οι) Ionian Islands

ΙΟΥΛΙΟΣ JULY

ΙΟΥΗΙΟΣ JUNE

ιππασία (η) horse riding

ιπποδρομίες (οι) horse racing

ιππόδρομος (ο) racetrack

ιππόκαμπος (ο) sea-horse

ιπτάμενο δελφίνι hydrofoil ('flying dolphin')

Ισθμός της Κορίνθου Corinth canal

ΙΣΟΓΕΙΟ GROUND FLOOR

ισοτιμία (η) exchange rate

Ισπανία (η) Spain

ισπανικός/ή/ό Spanish *(thing)*

Ισπανός/ίδα (ο/η) Spaniard *(man/woman)*

ιστιοπλοΐα (η) sailing

Ιταλία (η) Italy

ιταλικός/ή/ό Italian *(thing)*

Ιταλός/ίδα (ο/η) Italian *(man/woman)*

ΙΧ private cars *(parking)*

ιχθυοπωλείο (το) fishmonger's

κ Κ

κάβα (η) off-licence

κάβουρας (ο) crab

καζίνο (το) casino

καθαριστήριο (το) dry-cleaner's

καθαρίστρια (η) cleaner

καθαρός/ή/ό clean

κάθε every ; each

καθεδρικός ναός (ο) cathedral

καθημερινός/ή/ό daily
καθημερινά δρομολόγια daily departures

κάθισμα (το) seat

καθολικός/ή/ό Catholic ; total

καθυστέρηση (η) delay

και and

καιρός (ο) weather

κακάο (το) cocoa

κακοκαιρία (η) bad weather

καλά well ; all right

καλάθι (το) basket

καλαμαράκια (τα) small squid *(dish)*

καλαμάρι (το) squid ; calamari

καλημέρα good morning

καληνύχτα good night

καλησπέρα good evening

καλοκαίρι (το) summer

καλοριφέρ (το) central heating ; radiator

καλοψημένο well done *(meat)*

καλσόν (το) tights

κάλτσα (η) sock ; stocking

καμαριέρα (η) chambermaid

κάμερα (η) camcorder

καμπίνα (η) cabin

κανάλι (το) canal ; channel *(TV)*

κανέλα (η) cinnamon

κάνω to do

καπέλο (το) hat

καπετάνιος (ο) captain *(of ship)*

καπνίζω to smoke
μην καπνίζετε no smoking

καπνιστός/ή/ό smoked
καπνιστός σολομός smoked salmon
καπνιστό χοιρινό smoked ham
καπνιστό ψάρι smoked fish
καπνιστό τυρί smoked cheese

κάπνισμα (το) smoking
απαγορεύεται το κάπνισμα no smoking

καπνιστής (ο) smoker
είδη καπνιστού tobacconist's

καπνοπωλείο (το) tobacconist

καπνός (ο) smoke ; tobacco

κάποτε sometimes ; one time

καράβι (το) boat ; ship

καραμέλα (η) sweet(s)

κάρβουνο (το) coal
στα κάρβουνα charcoal-grilled

καρδιά (η) heart

καρναβάλι (το) carnival

καροτσάκι (το) pushchair

καρπούζι (το) watermelon

κάρτα (η) card ; postcard
κάρτα απεριόριστων διαδρομών railcard for unlimited monthly travel
κάρτα επιβιβάσεως boarding card
επαγγελματική κάρτα business card
μόνο με κάρτα cardholders only
πιστωτική κάρτα credit card
κάρτα αναλήψεως ATM card ; cash card

καρτοτηλέφωνο (το) card phone

καρτποστάλ (η) postcard

καρύδα (η) coconut

καρύδι (το) walnut

καρχαρίας (ο) shark

κασέτα (η) tape *(for recording)*

κασετόφωνο (το) tape recorder

κάστανο (το) chestnut

κάστρο (το) castle ; fortress

κατάθεση (η) deposit ; statement to police

καταιγίδα (η) storm

καταλαβαίνω to understand
καταλαβαίνεις; do you understand? *(familiar form)*
καταλαβαίνετε; do you understand? *(polite form)*

κατάλογος (ο) list ; menu ; directory
τηλεφωνικός κατάλογος telephone directory

καταπραϋντικό (το) tranquillizer

κατασκήνωση (η) camping

κατάστημα (το) shop

κατάστρωμα (το) deck

κατεπείγον/κατεπείγουσα urgent ; express

κατεψυγμένος/η/ο frozen

κατηγορία (η) class *(of hotel)*

κατσαρόλα (η) saucepan ; pot

κατσίκα (η) goat

κατσικάκι (το) kid *(young goat)*

κάτω under ; lower

καύσιμα (τα) fuel

καφέ brown

καφενείο (το) coffee house

καφές (ο) coffee *(usually Greek)*
καφές βαρύς γλυκός very sweet coffee
καφές γλυκός sweet coffee
καφές μέτριος medium sweet coffee
καφές σκέτος strong black coffee
καφές στιγμιαίος instant coffee
καφές φραπέ iced coffee *(Nescafé)*

καφετερία (η) cafeteria

καφετιέρα (η) coffee maker

κέικ (το) cake ; sponge

κεντρικός/ή/ό central

ΚΕΝΤΡΟ CENTRE

κέντρο centre
κέντρο αλλοδαπών immigration office
κέντρο διασκεδάσεως nightclub
κέντρο εκδώσεως ticket office
αθλητικό κέντρο sports centre
τηλεφωνικό κέντρο telephone exchange

κεράσι (το) cherry

Κέρκυρα (η) Corfu

κέρμα (το) coin

κερνώ to buy a drink

κεφάλι (το) head

κεφτέδες (οι) meatballs

κήπος (ο) garden
δημόσιος κήπος public garden
ζωολογικός κήπος zoo

κιβώτιο (το) large box
κιβώτιο ταχύτητων gearbox

κιλό (το) kilo

κίνδυνος (ο) danger
κίνδυνος θανάτου extreme danger

κινηματογράφος (ο) cinema

κινητήρας (ο) engine

κίτρινος/η/ο yellow

κλάξον (το) horn *(in car)*

κλειδί (το) key ; spanner

κλείνω to close

ΚΛΕΙΣΤΟ CLOSED

κλέφτης (ο) thief

κλέφτικο (το) meat dish

κλήση (η) summons

κλήσητροχαίας (η) traffic ticket

κλίμα (το) climate

κλινική (η) clinic ; hospital ; ward

κοινωνικός/ή/ό social
κοινωνικές ασφαλίσεις national insurance

κόκκινος/η/ο red

κολοκυθάκι (το) courgette

κολοκύθι (το) marrow

κόλπος (ο) gulf ; vagina

κολύμπι (το) swimming

κολυμπώ to swim

κολώνα (η) pillar ; column

κομμωτήριο (το) hairdresser's

κομμωτής/μώτρια (ο/η) hairstylist

κομπόστα (η) stewed fruit ; compote

κομωδία (η) comedy

κονιάκ (το) cognac ; brandy

κονσέρβα (η) tinned food

κονσέρτο (το) concert

κοντά near

κόρη (η) daughter

κορίτσι (το) young girl

κόρνα (η) horn *(in car)*

κόσμημα (το) jewellery

κοσμηματαπωλείο (το) jewellery shop

κοστούμι (το) man's suit

κότα (η) hen

κοτολέτα (η) chop

κοτόπουλο (το) chicken

κουβέρτα (η) blanket

κουζίνα (η) kitchen ; cuisine
ελληνική κουζίνα Greek cuisine specialities

κουνέλι (το) rabbit

κουνούπι (το) mosquito

κουνουπίδι (το) cauliflower

κουπί (το) oar

κουρείο (το) barber's shop

κουταλάκι (το) teaspoon

κουτάλι (το) tablespoon

κουτί (το) box

κραγιόν (το) lipstick

κρασί (το) wine
κρασί γλυκό sweet wine
κρασί ξηρό dry wine
κρασί κόκκινο red wine
κρασί λευκό white wine
κρασί ροζέ rosé wine

κρατήσεις (οι) bookings ; reservations
κρατήσεις ξενοδοχείων hotel bookings

κράτηση (η) reservation
κράτηση θέσης seat reservation

κρέας (το) meat
κρέας αρνίσιο lamb
κρέας βοδινό beef
κρέας χοιρινό pork

κρεββάτι (το) bed

κρεββατοκάμαρα (η) bedroom

κρέμα (η) cream

κρεμμύδι (το) onion

κρεοπωλείο (το) butcher's shop

Κρήτη (η) Crete

κρουαζιέρα (η) cruise

κρύος/α/ο cold

κτηνιατρείο (το) veterinary surgery

κυβερνήτης (ο) captain *(of aircraft)*

Κυκλάδες (οι) Cyclades *(islands)*

κυκλοφορία (η) traffic ; circulation

κυλικείο (το) canteen ; cafeteria

Κύπρος (η) Cyprus

Κύπριος/Κυπρία (ο/η) from Cyprus ; Cypriot *(man/woman)*

κυρία (η) Mrs ; lady

ΚΥΡΙΑΚΗ SUNDAY

κύριος (ο) Mr ; gentleman

κώδικας (ο) code
ταχυδρομικός κώδικας postcode
τηλεφωνικός κώδικας dialling code ; area code

λ Λ

λάδι (το) oil
λάδη ελιάς olive oil

λαϊκός/ή/ό popular ; folk
λαϊκή αγορά market
λαϊκή μουσική popular music
λαϊκή τέχνη folk art

λάστιχο (το) tyre ; rubber ; elastic

λαχανικά (τα) vegetables

λαχείο (το) lottery ticket

λεμονάδα (η) lemon squash ; lemonade

λεμόνι (το) lemon
χυμός λεμονιού lemon juice

λεξικό (το) dictionary

λεπτό (το) minute

λεπτός/ή/ό thin ; slim

λέσχη (η) club

λευκός/ή/ό white

λεφτά (τα) money

λεωφορείο (το) bus

λεωφόρος (η) avenue

λήξη (η) expiry

λιανικός/ή/ό retail
λιανική πώληση retail sale

λίγος/η/ο a few ; a little
λίγο ψημένο rare *(meat)*

λικέρ (το) liqueur

λιμάνι (το) **port ; harbour**

Λιμενικό Σώμα (το) **coastguard**

λιμήν (ο) **port**

λίμνη (η) **lake**

λίρα (η) **pound**

λίτρο (το) **litre**

λογαριασμός (ο) **bill**

λουκάνικο (το) **sausage**

λουκανόπιτα (η) **sausage pie**

λουκούμι (το) **Turkish delight**

λύσσα (η) **rabies**

μ Μ

μαγαζί (το) **shop**

μαγειρεύω **to cook**

μαγιό (το) **swimsuit**

μαγουλάδες (οι) **mumps**

μαϊντανός (ο) **parsley**

ΜΑΙΟΣ MAY

μακαρόνια (τα) **macaroni ; spaghetti dishes**

μάλιστα **yes ; of course**

μαλλί (το) **wool**

μαλλιά (τα) **hair**

μάλλινος/η/ο **woollen**

μαμά (η) **mum**

μανιτάρια (τα) **mushrooms**

μανταρίνι (το) **tangerine**

μαντήλι (το) **handkerchief**

μαξιλάρι (το) **pillow ; cushion**

μαργαρίνη (η) **margarine**

μαργαριτάρι (το) **pearl**

μάρμαρο (το) **marble**

μαρμαρινός/ή/ό **made of marble**

μαρμελάδα (η) **jam**

μαρούλι (το) **lettuce**

ΜΑΡΤΙΟΣ MARCH

μαύρος/η/ο **black**

μαχαίρι (το) **knife**

μαχαιροπήρουνα (τα) **cutlery**

με **with**

μεγάλος/η/ο **large ; big**

μέγαρο (το) **hall ; palace ; block of apartments**
  μέγαρομουσικής **concert hall**
  μέγαρο αστυνομίας **police headquarters**

μέγεθος (το) **size**

μεζεδάκια (τα) **mezes** *(selection of appetizers and salads served as a starter)*

μέλι (το) **honey**

μέλισσα (η) **bee**

μελιτζάνα (η) **aubergine ; eggplant**

μέλος (το) **member**

μενού (το) **menu**

μέρα (η) **day**

μερίδα (η) **portion**

μέσα **in ; inside**

μεσάνυχτα (τα) **midnight**

μεσημέρι (το) **midday**

Μεσόγειος (η) **Mediterranean Sea**

μέσω **via**

μετά **after**

μετάξι (το) **silk**

μεταξύ **between ; among**
  εν τω μεταξύ **meanwhile**

μεταφράζω **to translate**

μεταχειρισμένος/η/ο **used ; second-hand**

μετεωρολογικόδελτίο (το) **weather forecast**

μετρητά (τα) **cash**

μετρό (το) **underground** *(railway)*

μη... **do not...**
  μη καπνίζετε **no smoking**
  μην κόπτετε άνθη **do not pick flowers**
  μην πατάτε το πράσινο **keep off the grass**

μη ρίπτετε σκουπίδια **no dumping** *(rubbish)*
μη σταθμεύετε **no parking**

μηδέν **zero**

μήλο (το) **apple**

μηλόπιτα (η) **apple pie**

μήνας (ο) **month**
μήνας του μέλιτος **honeymoon**

μητέρα (η) **mother**

μηχανή (η) **machine ; engine**

μηχανικός (ο) **mechanic ; engineer**

μία **a(n) ; one** *(with feminine nouns)*

μικρός/ή/ό **small**

μόδα (η) **fashion**

μολύβι (το) **pencil**

μόλυνση (η) **infection ; pollution**

μοναστήρι (το) **monastery**

μονόδρομος (ο) **one-way street**

μονοπάτι (το) **path**

μόνος/η/ο **alone ; only**
μόνο είσοδος/έξοδος **entrance/exit only**

μονός/ή/ό **single ; alone**

μοσχάρι (το) **calf ; veal**

μοτοσικλέτα (η) **motorcycle**

ΜΟΥΣΕΙΟ **MUSEUM**

μουσείο (το) **museum**
Αρχαιολογικό Μουσείο **Archaeological Museum**
Μουσείο Λαϊκής Τέχνης **Folk Museum**

μουσική (η) **music**

μουστάρδα (η) **mustard**

μπακάλης (ο) **grocer**

μπαμπάς (ο) **dad**

μπανάνα (η) **banana ; bumbag**

μπάνιο (το) **bathroom ; bath**

μπαρμπούνι (το) **red mullet**

μπαταρία (η) **battery**

μπέικον (το) **bacon**

μπιζέλια (τα) **peas**

μπίρα (η) **beer**

μπισκότο (το) **biscuit**

μπλε **blue**

μπλούζα (η) **blouse**

μπουζούκι (το) **bouzouki**

μπουκάλι (το) **bottle**
μεγάλο μπουκάλι **large bottle**
μικρό μπουκάλι **half-bottle**

μπουρνούζι (το) **bathrobe**

μπριζόλα (η) **chop ; steak**

μπύρα (η) **beer**

Μυκήναι **Mycenae**

Μυκηναϊκός πολιτισμός (ο) **Mycenean civilization**

μύτη (η) **nose**

μωρό (το) **baby**
για μωρά **for babies**

μωσαϊκό (το) **mosaic**

ν Ν

ναι **yes**

ναός (ο) **temple ; church**
καθεδρικός ναός **cathedral**

ναύλο (το) **fare**

νάυλον **nylon**

ναυλωμένος/η/ο **chartered**
ναυλωμένη πτήση **charter flight**

ναυτία (η) **travel sickness**

ναυτικός όμιλος (ο) **sailing club**

ναυτιλιακά **yacht chandler**

νεκρός/ή/ό **dead**

νεκροταφείο (το) **cemetery**

νεοελληνικά (τα) **Modern Greek**

νερό (το) **water**
επιτραπέζιο νερό **still mineral water**
μεταλλικό νερό **mineral water**
πόσιμο νερό **drinking water**

νεφρός (ο) **kidney**

νεωτερισμός (ο) **improvement ; novelty**

νηπιαγωγείο (το) nursery school

νησί (το) island

νησίδα (η) traffic island

νίκη (η) victory

ΝΟΕΜΒΡΙΟΣ NOVEMBER

νοίκι (το) rent

νόμισμα (το) coin ; currency
επιστροφή νομισμάτων returned coins

νομισματοδέχτης (ο) coin-operated phone

νόμος (ο) the law

νοσοκομείο (το) hospital

νοσοκόμος/α (ο/η) nurse

νότιος/α/ο southern

νότος (ο) south

ντομάτα (η) tomato

ντουζίνα (η) dozen

ντους (το) shower *(in bath)*

νύκτα/νύχτα (η) night

νυκτερινός/ή/ό all-night *(chemists, etc)*

νύχι (το) nail

νυχοκόπτης (ο) nailclippers

ξ Ξ

ξεναγός (ο/η) guide

ξενοδοχείο (το) hotel
κρατήσεις ξενοδοχείων hotel reservations

ξένος/η/ο strange ; foreign
ξένος/η (ο/η) foreigner ; visitor

ξενώνας (ο) guesthouse

ξεχνώ to forget

ξηρός/ή/ό dry
ξηροί καρποί dried fruit and nuts

ξιφίας (ο) swordfish

ξύδι (το) vinegar

ξύλο (το) wood

ξυριστική μηχανή (η) safety razor

ο Ο

οδηγία (η) instruction
οδηγίες χρήσεως instructions for use

οδηγός (ο) driver ; guidebook

οδηγώ to drive

οδική βοήθεια (η) breakdown service

οδοντιατρείο (το) dental surgery

οδοντίατρος (ο/η) dentist

οδοντόβουρτσα (η) toothbrush

οδοντόκρεμα (η) toothpaste

οδοντοστοιχία (η) denture(s)

οδός (η) road ; street

οικογένεια (η) family

οικονομική θέση (η) economy class

οίκος (ο) house
οίκος μόδας fashion house

οινομαγειρείον (το) licensed restaurant with traditional cuisine

οινοπνευματώδη ποτά (τα) spirits

οίνος (ο) wine

οκτώ/οχτώ eight

ΟΚΤΩΒΡΙΟΣ OCTOBER

ολισθηρόν οδόστρωμα (το) slippery road surface

όλος/η/ο all of

Ολυμπία (η) Olympia

ολυμπιακός/ή/ό Olympic
Ολυμπιακή Αεροπορία Olympic Airways
Ολυμπιακό Στάδιο Olympic stadium
Ολυμπιακοί Αγώνες Olympic games

Όλυμπος (ο) Mount Olympus

ομελέτα (η) omelette

όμιλος (ο) club
ναυτικός όμιλος sailing club

ομπρέλα (η) umbrella

όνομα (το) name

ονοματεπώνυμο (το) full name

όπερα (η) opera

οπτικός οίκος (ο) optician's

οργανισμός (ο) organization
 Οργανισμός Σιδηροδρόμων Ελλάδος (ΟΣΕ) Greek Railways

οργανωμένος/η/ο organized
 οργανωμένα ταξίδια organized tours

ορεκτικό (το) starter ; appetizer

όρεξη (η) appetite
 καλή όρεξη! enjoy your meal!

ορθόδοξος/η/ο orthodox

όρος (ο) condition
 όροι ενοικιάσεως conditions of hire

όρος (το) mountain

όροφος (ο) floor ; storey

ΟΣΕ Greek Railways

ΟΤΕ Greek Telecom

ουδέν: ουδέν προς δήλωση nothing to declare

ούζο (το) ouzo

ουρά (η) tail ; queue

ούτε not even
 ούτε ... ούτε neither ... nor

όχι no

π Π

παγάκι (το) ice cube

παϊδάκι (το) lamb chop

πάγος (ο) ice

παγωμένος/η/ο frozen

παγωτό (το) ice cream

παιδικός/ή/ό for children
 παιδικά childrens wear
 παιδικός σταθμός criche

πακέτο (το) parcel ; packet

παλτό (το) coat

πάνα (η) nappy

Παναγία (η) the Virgin Mary

πανεπιστήμιο (το) university

πανσιόν (η) guesthouse

πάντα/πάντοτε always

παντελόνι (το) trousers

παντοπωλείο (το) grocer's

παπάς (ο) priest

πάπλωμα (το) duvet

παππούς (ο) grandfather

παπούτσι (το) shoe

παραγγελία (η) order

παραγγέλνω to order

παραγωγή (η) production
 Ελληνικής παραγωγής made in Greece

παράθυρο (το) window

παρακαλώ please

παρακαμπτήριος (ο) by-pass

παραλία (η) seashore ; beach

ΠΑΡΑΣΚΕΥΗ FRIDAY

παράσταση (η) performance

παρέα (η) company ; group

Παρθενών(ας) (ο) the Parthenon

πάρκο (το) park

παρμπρίζ (το) windscreen

πάστα (η) pastry ; cake

παστέλι (το) honey and sesame seed bar

Πάσχα (το) Easter

πατάτα (η) potato
 πατάτες πουρέ creamed/mashed potatoes
 πατάτες τηγανητές chips, fries
 πατάτες φούρνου roast potatoes

πατέρας (ο) father

παυσίπονο (το) painkiller

πάω to go

πέδιλα (τα) sandals

πεζοδρόμιο (το) pavement

ΠΕΖΟΔΡΟΜΟΣ PEDESTRIAN AREA

πεζός (ο) pedestrian

Πειραιάς/Πειραιεύς (ο) Piraeus

πελάτης/τρια (ο/η) customer

Πελοπόννησος (η) Peloponnese

ΠΕΜΠΤΗ THURSDAY

πένα (η) pen ; pence

πεπόνι (το) melon

περιοδικό (το) magazine

περιοχή (η) area

περίπατος (ο) walk

περίπτερο (το) kiosk

περιστέρι (το) pigeon ; dove

πέτρα (η) stone

πετρέλαιο (το) diesel fuel

πετρινός/ή/ό made of stone

πετσέτα (η) towel

πεύκο (το) pine tree

πηγαίνω to go

πιάτο (το) plate ; dish

ΠΙΕΣΑΤΕ PUSH

πίεση (η) pressure
  πίεση αίματος blood pressure

πιλότος (ο) pilot

πινακίδα (η) sign ; number plate
  πινακίδα κυκλοφορίας number plate

πινακοθήκη (η) art gallery ; collection of paintings

πίπα (η) pipe

πιπέρι (το) pepper
  πιπεριές γεμιστές stuffed peppers

πισίνα (η) swimming pool

πιστοποιητικό (το) certificate

πιστωτική κάρτα (η) credit card

πίσω behind ; back

πίτα (η) pie

πιτζάμες (οι) pyjamas

πίτσα (η) pizza

πιτσαρία (η) pizzeria

πλαζ (η) beach

πλάι next to

πλατεία (η) square

πλατίνες (οι) points *(in car)*

πλεκτά (τα) knitwear

ΠΛΗΡΟΦΟΡΙΕΣ INFORMATION
  πληροφορίες δρομολογίων travel information

πλήρωμα (το) crew
  τα μέλη του πληρώματος crew members

πληρωμή (η) payment
  ευκολίες πληρωμής credit facilities
  προς πληρωμή insert money

πληρώνω to pay

πλοίο (το) ship

πλυντήριο (το) washing machine
  πλυντήριο αυτοκινήτων car wash
  πλυντήριο πιάτων dishwasher

ποδηλάτης (ο) cyclist

ποδήλατο (το) bicycle
  ποδήλατο της θάλασσας pedalo

πόδι (το) foot ; leg

ποδόσφαιρο (το) football

ποιος/ποια/ποιο which

πόλη/ις (η) town ; city

πολυκατάστημα (το) department store

πολυκατοικία (η) block of flats

πολύς/πολλή/πολύ many ; much

πονόδοντος (ο) toothache

πονοκέφαλος (ο) headache

πονόλαιμος (ο) sore throat

πόνος (ο) pain

πόρτα (η) door

πορτοκαλάδα (η) orange squash

πορτοκάλι (το) orange
  χυμός πορτοκαλιού orange juice

πορτοφόλι (το) wallet

πόσα; how many?

πόσο; **how much?**
πόσο κάνει; **how much is it?**
πόσο κοστίζει; **how much does it cost?**

ποσοστό (το) **rate ; percentage**
ποσοστό υπηρεσίας **service charge**
συμπεριλαμβανομένου ποσοστού υπηρεσίας **service included**

ποσότητα (η) **quantity**

πότε; **when?**

ποτέ **never**

ποτήρι (το) **glass** *(for drinking)*

ποτό (το) **drink**

πού; **where?**

πουκάμισο (το) **shirt**

πούλμαν (το) **coach**

πουλώ **to sell**

πουρμπουάρ (το) **tip** *(to waiter, etc)*

πούρο (το) **cigar**

πράκτορας (ο) **agent**

πρακτορείο (το) **agency**

πράσινος/η/ο **green**

πρατήριο (το) **specialist shop**
πρατήριο βενζίνης **petrol station**
πρατήριο άρτου **baker's**

πρεσβεία (η) **embassy**

πρίζα (η) **plug ; socket**

πριν **before**

προβολέας (ο) **headlight**

πρόγευμα (το) **breakfast**

πρόγραμμα (το) **programme**

πρόεδρος (ο) **president**
προεδρικό μέγαρο **presidential palace**

προειδοποίηση (η) **warning**

προέλευση (η) **embarkation point**

προϊόν (το) **product**
Ελληνικό προϊόν **product of Greece**

προκαταβολή (η) **deposit**

προκρατήσεις (οι) **advance bookings**

προξενείο (το) **consulate**

πρόξενος (ο) **consul**

προορισμός (ο) **destination**

προπληρώνω **to pay in advance**

Προ-πο (το) **Greek football pools**

προσγείωση (η) **landing**

προσδεθείτε **fasten safety belts**

πρόσκληση (η) **invitation**

προσοχή (η) **attention**

προτεστάντης (ο) **Protestant**

πρόστιμο (το) **fine**

πρόχειρος/η/ο **handy ; impromptu**
πρόχειρο φαγητό **snack**

πρωί (το) **morning**

πρωινός/ή/ό **morning**

πρωινό (το) **breakfast**

πρωτεύουσα (η) **capital city**

πρωτομαγιά (η) **May Day**

πρώτος/η/ο **first**
πρώτες βοήθειες **casualty** *(hospital)*
πρώτη θέση **first class**

πρωτοχρονιά (η) **New Year's Day**

πτήση (η) **flight**
πτήσεις εξωτερικού **international flights**
πτήσεις εσωτερικού **domestic flights**
αριθμός πτήσης **flight number**
ναυλωμένη πτήση **charter flight**
τακτικές πτήσεις **scheduled flights**

πυρκαγιά (η) **fire**

πυροσβεστήρας (ο) **fire extinguisher**

πυροσβέστης (ο) **fireman**

πυροσβεστική (η) **fire brigade**
πυροσβεστική υπηρεσία **fire brigade**
πυροσβεστικός σταθμός **fire station**

πώληση (η) **sale**
λιανική πώληση **retail sale**
χονδρική πώληση **wholesale**

πωλητής/ήτρια(ο/η) **sales assistant**

ΠΩΛΕΙΤΑΙ **FOR SALE**

πώς; **how?**

ρ Ρ

ρεζέρβα (η) spare wheel
ρέστα (τα) change *(money)*
ρετσίνα (η) retsina
ρεύμα (το) current ; electricity
ρόδα (η) wheel
ροδάκινο (το) peach
ρόδι (το) pomegranate
Ρόδος (η) Rhodes
ρολόι (το) watch ; clock
ρούμι (το) rum
ρύζι (το) rice
ρυμουλκώ to tow away

σ ς Σ

ΣΑΒΒΑΤΟ SATURDAY

Σαββατοκύριακο (το) weekend
σακάκι (το) jacket *(men's)*
σαλάμι (το) salami
σαλάτα (η) salad
σαλιγκάρι (το) snail
σάλτσα (η) sauce
σαμπάνια (η) champagne
σαμπουάν (το) shampoo
σάντουιτς (το) sandwich
σαπούνι (το) soap
σβήνω to extinguish
  σβήσατε τα τσιγάρα σας extinguish cigarettes
σέρβις (το) service
σεφ (ο) chef
σήμα (το) sign ; signal
  σήμα κατατεθέν trademark
  σήμα κινδύνου emergency signal
σήμερα today
σιγά slowly
σιγή (η) silence
σιδηρόδρομος (ο) railway
  σιδηροδρομικός σταθμός (ο) railway station
  σιδηροδρομικώς by rail
σιεφταλιά (η) spicy meat kebab
σκάλα (η) ladder ; staircase
σκαλί (το) step
σκέτος/η/ο plain
  καφές σκέτος black coffee
σκηνή (η) tent ; stage
σκι (το) ski
  θαλάσσιο σκι water-skiing
σκοινί (το) rope
σκορδαλιά (η) garlic sauce
σκόρδο (ο) garlic
σκουπίδια (τα) rubbish ; refuse
σκυλί (το) dog
Σκωτία (η) Scotland
σκωτσέζικος/η/ο (η) Scottish *(thing)*
Σκωτσέζος/Σκωτσέζα (ο/η) Scotsman/Scotswoman
σόδα (η) soda
σοκολάτα (η) chocolate
σολομός (ο) salmon
σόμπα (η) stove ; heater
σούβλα (η) skewer
σουβλάκι (το) shish kebab *(meat cooked on skewer)*
σούπα (η) soup
σοφέρ(ο) chauffeur
σπανάκι (το) spinach
σπανακόπιτα (η) spinach pie
σπαράγγι (το) asparagus
σπεσιαλιτέ της κουζίνας (το) dish of the day
σπίρτο (το) match
σπίτι (το) house ; home
σπιτικός/ή/ο homemade
σπορ (τα) sports
Σποράδες (οι) the Sporades
στάδιο (το) stadium ; stage
σταθμεύω to park
  ανώτατος χρόνος σταθμεύσεως maximum parking time

απαγορεύεται η στάθμευση **no parking**
μη σταθμεύετε **no parking**
χώρος σταθμεύσεως **parking area**

σταθμός (ο) **station**
πυροσβεστικός σταθμός **fire station**
σιδηροδρομικός σταθμός **railway station**
σταθμός υπεραστικώνλεωφορείων **bus station** *(intercity)*

στάση/σις (η) **stop**
στάση εργασίας **strike**
στάσις ΗΛΠΑΠ **trolley bus stop**
στάση λεωφορείου **bus stop**

σταυροδρόμι (το) **crossroads**

σταφίδα (η) **raisin**

σταφύλι (το) **grape**

στεγνοκαθαριστήριο (το) **dry-cleaner's**

στιγμή (η) **moment**

στοά (η) **arcade**

στροφή (η) **turn ; bend**

στρώμα (το) **mattress**

συγγνώμη **sorry ; excuse me**

συγκοινωνία (η) **public transport**

συγχαρητήρια **congratulations**

συγχωρώ:με συγχωρείτε **excuse me**

σύζυγος (ο/η) **husband/wife**

σύκο (το) **fig**

συκώτι (το) **liver**

συμπεριλαμβάνω **to include**

συμπλέκτης (ο) **clutch** *(of car)*

συμπληρώνω **to fill in**

σύμπτωμα (το) **symptom**

συμφωνία (η) **agreement**

συμφωνώ **to agree**

συνάλλαγμα (το) **foreign exchange**
δήλωση συναλλάγματος **currency declaration**
η τιμή του συναλλάγματος **exchange rate**

συνάντηση (η) **meeting**

συναντώ **to meet**

συναυλία (η) **concert**

συνεργείο (το) **workshop ; garage for car repairs**
συνεργείο αυτοκινήτων **car repairs**

σύνθεση (η) **ingredients ; flower arrangement**

σύνολο (το) **total**

σύνορα (τα) **border ; frontier**

συνταγή (η) **prescription ; recipe**

ΣΥΡΑΤΕ **PULL**

σύστημα κλιματισμού (το) **air conditioning**

συστημένη επιστολή (η) **registered letter**

συχνά **often**

σφράγισμα (το) **filling** *(in tooth)*

σχηματίζω **to form**
σχηματίστε τον αριθμό **dial the number**

σχολείο (το) **school**

σχολή (η) **school**
σχολή οδηγών **driving school**
σχολή σκι **ski school**

σώζω **to save ; to rescue**

σώμα (το) **body**

σωσίβιο (το) **life jacket**

τ Τ

ταβέρνα (η) **tavern with traditional food and wine**

ταινία (η) **film ; strip ; tape**

ΤΑΜΕΙΟ **CASH DESK**

ταμίας (ο/η) **cashier**

ταμιευτήριο (το) **savings bank**

ταξί (το) **taxi**
αγοραίο ταξί **minicab** *(no meter)*
γραφείο ταξί **taxi office**
ραδιόταξί **radio taxi**

ταξίδι (το) **journey ; tour**
καλό ταξίδι **have a good trip**
ταξιδιωτικό γραφείο **travel agent**
οργανωμένα ταξίδια **organized tours**

ταξιθέτης/τρια (ο/η) **theatre attendant**

ταραμοσαλάτα (η) **taramosalata**

ταυτότητα (η) **identity ; identity card**

ταχεία (η) **express train**

ταχυδρομείο (το) **post office**
Ελληνικά Ταχυδρομεία (ΕΛΤΑ) **Greek Post Office**

ταχυδρομικά (τέλη) **postage**
ταχυδρομικές επιταγές **postal orders**
ταχυδρομικός κώδικας **postcode**
ταχυδρομικώς **by post**

ταχύμετρο (το) **speedometer**

ταχύτητα/ταχύτης (η) **speed**
κιβώτιο ταχύτητων **gearbox**

τελευταίος/α/ο **last**

τέλος (το) **end ; tax ; duty**
ταχυδρομικά τέλη **postage**
οδικά τέλη **road tax**
τέλος πάντων **well...** *(to start sentence)*

τελωνείο (το) **customs**

τένις (το) **tennis**

τέντα (η) **tent**

τέρμα (το) **terminus ; end of route**

ΤΕΤΑΡΤΗ **WEDNESDAY**

τέχνη (η) **art**
λαϊκή τέχνη **folk art**

τεχνητώς κεχρωσμένο **artificial colourings**

τζαμί (το) **mosque ; glass** *(of window)*

τζατζίκι (το) **tsatsiki** *(yoghurt, cucumber and garlic)*

τηγανίτα (η) **pancake**

τηλεγραφείο (το) **telegraph office**

τηλεγράφημα (το) **telegram**

τηλεκάρτα (η) **phonecard**

τηλεόραση (η) **television**

τηλεπικοινωνίες (οι) **telecommunications**

ΤΗΛΕΦΩΝΟ **TELEPHONE**

τηλέφωνο **telephone**
τηλεφώνημα (το) **telephone call**
τηλεφωνικός θάλαμος **phone box**
τηλεφωνικός κατάλογος **telephone directory**
τηλεφωνικός κώδικας **dialling code ; area code**

τι; **what?**
τι είναι; **what is it?**

τιμή (η) **price ; honour**
τιμή εισιτηρίου **price of ticket ; fare**

τιμοκατάλογος (ο) **price list**

τιμολόγιο (το) **invoice**

τιμόνι (το) **steering wheel**

τιμωρώ **to punish**

τίποτα **nothing**

τμήμα (το) **department ; police station**

το **it ; the** *(with neuter nouns)*

τοιχοκόλληση (η) **bill posting**

τόκος (ο) **interest** *(bank)*

τόνος (ο) **ton ; tuna fish**

τοστ (το) **toasted sandwich**

ΤΟΥΑΛΕΤΕΣ **TOILETS**

τουρισμός (ο) **tourism**

τουρίστας/στρια (ο/η) **tourist**

τουριστικός/ή/ό **tourist**
τουριστικά είδη **souvenirs**
τουριστική αστυνομία **Tourist Police**

Τουρκία (η) **Turkey**

τραγούδι (το) **song**

τραγωδία (η) **tragedy**

τράπεζα (η) **bank**

τραπεζαρία (η) **dining room**

τραπέζι (το) table

τρένο (το) train

ΤΡΙΤΗ TUESDAY

τρόλεϋ (το) trolley bus

τροφή (η) food

τροχαία (η) traffic police

τροχός (ο) wheel

τροχόσπιτο (το) caravan

τροχοφόρο (το) vehicle

τρώγω/τρώω to eat

τσάι (το) tea

τσάντα (η) bag

τσιγάρο (το) cigarette

τυρί (το) cheese

τυρόπιτα (η) cheese pie

τυφλός/ή/ό blind

υ Υ

υγεία (η) health
  στην υγειά σας your health ; cheers

υγειονομικός έλεγχος (ο) health inspection

Ύδρα (η) Hydra (island)

Υμηττός (ο) Mount Hymettos

υπεραγορά (η) supermarket

υπεραστικό λεωφορείο (το) long-distance coach

υπερωκεάνειο (το) liner

υπήκοος (ο/η) citizen

υπηκοότης/υπηκοότητα (η) nationality

υπηρεσία (η) service
  ποσοστό υπηρεσίας service charge

υπηρέτης (ο) servant

υπηρέτρια (η) maid

υπόγειος/α/ο underground
  υπόγεια διάβαση πεζών pedestrian subway

υπόγειος σιδηρόδρομος underground *(railway)*

υποδοχή (η) reception
  χώρος υποδοχής reception area

υπολογιστής (ο) computer

υποκατάστημα (το) branch office

υπουργείο (το) ministry

υψηλός/ή/ό high
  υψηλή τάση high voltage

ύφασμα (το) fabric ; cloth
  υφάσματα textiles
  υφάσματα επιπλώσεων upholstery fabrics

ύψος (το) height
  ύψος περιορισμένο height limit

φ Φ

φαγητό (το) food ; meal

φαΐ (το) food

φακός (ο) lens ; torch
  φακοί επαφής contact lenses

φανάρι (το) traffic light ; lantern

φαξ (το) fax

φαρμακείο (το) chemist's

φαρμάκι (το) poison

φάρμακο (το) medicine

φάρος (ο) lighthouse

φασολάκι (το) green bean

φασόλι (το) haricot bean

φάω to eat

ΦΕΒΡΟΥΑΡΙΟΣ FEBRUARY

φεριμπότ (το) ferry

φέτα (η) feta cheese ; slice

φιλενάδα (η) girlfriend

φιλέτο (το) fillet of meat

φιλμ (το) film
  εμφανίσεις φιλμ film developing

φιλοδώρημα (το) tip ; service charge

φίλος/η (ο/η) friend

φίλτρο (το) filter
  φίλτρο αέρος air filter

φίλτρο λαδιού **oil filter**
καφέςφίλτρου **filter coffee**

φλας (το) **flash** *(camera)*

φοιτητής/φοιτήτρια (ο/η) **student**

φοιτητικό εισιτήριο (το) **student fare**

φόρεμα (το) **dress**

φορολογημένα είδη **duty-paid goods**

φόρος (ο) **tax**
συμπεριλαμβανομένων φόρων **including taxes**

φουντούκι (το) **hazelnut**

φούρνος (ο) **oven ; bakery**

φουσκωτά σκάφη (τα) **inflatable boats**

ΦΠΑ (ο) **VAT**

φράουλα (η) **strawberry**

φρένο (το) **brake**

φρέσκος/ια/ο **fresh**

φρούτο (το) **fruit**

φρουτοσαλάτα (η) **fruit salad**

φύλακας (ο) **guard**

φύλαξη αποσκευών (η) **left-luggage office**

φυστίκι (το) **peanut**
φυστίκια Αιγίνης **pistachio nuts**

φυτό (το) **plant**

φως (το) **light**

φωτιά (η) **fire**

φωτογραφία (η) **photograph**
έγχρωμες φωτογραφίες **colour photographs**

φωτογραφίζω **to take photographs**
μη φωτογραφίζετε **no photographs**

φωτογραφική μηχανή (η) **camera**

φωτοτυπία (η) **photocopy**

χ Χ

χαίρετε **hello** *(polite)*

χάπι (το) **pill**

χάρτης (ο) **map**
οδικός χάρτης **road map**

χαρτί (το) **paper**
χαρτί κουζίνας **kitchen paper**

χαρτικά (τα) **stationery**

χαρτονόμισμα (το) **banknote**

χαρτοπωλείο (το) **stationer's shop**

χασάπικο (το) **butcher's shop**

χειροποίητος/η/ο **handmade**

χειρούργος (ο) **surgeon**

χειρόφρενο (το) **handbrake**

χέρι (το) **hand**

χιλιόμετρο (το) **kilometre**

χιόνι (το) **snow**

χοιρινό (το) **pork**

χορός (ο) **dance**

χορτοφάγος (ο/η) **vegetarian**

χορωδία (η) **choir**

χουρμάς (ο) **date** *(fruit)*

χρειάζομαι **to need**

χρήματα (τα) **money**

χρηματοκιβώτιο (το) **safe** *(for valuables)*

χρήση (η) **use**
οδηγίες χρήσεως **instructions for use**

χρήσιμος/η/ο **useful**

χρητιμοποιώ **to use**

χριστιανός/ή **Christian**

Χριστούγεννα (τα) **Christmas**
Καλά Χριστούγεννα **Merry Christmas**

χρόνος (ο) **time ; year**

χρυσαφικά (τα) **jewellery**

χρυσός/ή/ό **(made of) gold**
Χρυσός Οδηγός **Yellow Pages**

χταπόδι (το) **octopus**

χτένα (η) **comb**

χτες **yesterday**

χυμός (ο) **juice**
χυμός λεμονιού **lemon juice**
χυμός πορτοκαλιού **orange juice**

χώρα (η) **country**

χωριάτικο ψωμί (το) **bread** *(round, flat loaf)*

χωριό (το) **village**

χωρίς **without**
 χωρίς εισπράκτορα **exact fare ; pre-paid ticket**

χώρος (ο) **area ; site**
 αρχαιολογικός χώρος **archaeological site**
 ιδιωτικός χώρος **private**
 χώρος σταθμεύσεως **parking area**

ψ Ψ

ψάρεμα (το) **fishing**

ψαρεύω **to fish**

ψάρι (το) **fish**

ψαρόβαρκα (η) **fishing boat**

ψαροταβέρνα (η) **fish tavern**

ψημένος/η/ο **cooked ; roasted ; grilled**

ψητός/ή/ό **roast ; grilled**

ψυγείο (το) **fridge**

ψυχώ **to cool**

ψωμάς (ο) **baker**

ψωμί (το) **bread**

ω Ω

ΩΘΗΣΑΤΕ **PUSH**

ωτοστόπ (το) **hitchhiking**

ώρα (η) **time ; hour**
 ώρες επισκέψεως **visiting hours**
 ώρες λειτουργίας **opening hours**
 ώρες συναλλαγής **banking hours**
 της ώρας **freshly cooked** *(food)*

ωραίος/α/ο **beautiful**

ωράριο (το) **timetable**

ως **as**

ωστόσο **however**

ωφέλιμος/η/ο **useful**

ωφελώ **to be useful**